Beyond Black

Beyond Black

Celebrity and race in Obama's America

Ellis Cashmore

BLOOMSBURY ACADEMIC

First published in 2012 by

Bloomsbury Academic
An imprint of Bloomsbury Publishing Plc
50 Bedford Square, London WC1B 3DP, UK
and
175 Fifth Avenue, New York, NY 10010, USA

CIP records for this book are available from the British Library
and the Library of Congress

ISBN 978-1-78093-149-4 (paperback)
ISBN 978-1-78093-147-0 (ebook)

This book is produced using paper that is made from wood grown in managed, sustainable forests. It is natural, renewable and recyclable. The logging and manufacturing processes conform to the environmental regulations of the country of origin.

Printed and bound in Great Britain by the MPG Books Group, Bodmin, Cornwall

Cover image: © Startraks Photo/Rex features

www.bloomsburyacademic.com

Contents

1

Introduction – "I sell entertainment"

'However unwittingly, black celebrities have sold the idea that America is no longer manacled to its history. It is a history pockmarked by racism, segregation and victimization.'

For his 2011 concert tour, Snoop Dogg appeared on stage against a backdrop of dollar signs, as if to confirm the meaning, purpose and sole ambition of the appearance. His mic was adorned with a gold knuckle-duster, reaffirming his links with a past rooted in internecine violence, imploding ghettos and gang executions. And security guards added a tart, if theatrical, touch, frisking all concertgoers for weapons. The status of ballpoint pens was uncertain: recall how Joe Pesci used one such pen in *Casino*.

Snoop's first album *Doggystyle* was released in 1993. Before then he had hung with the Los Angeles Crips, and done time for possession. He had murder charges hanging over him until 1996, when he was cleared. Calvin Broadus aka Snoop Doggy Dogg swept to fame with the rise of gangsta rap, a music that was at once dangerous yet fascinating. It was black music enthusiastically embraced by whites. Few musicians ever got rich purveying the authentically gloomy, grueling nature of life in the inner city. Snoop probably realized this early on in his musical career.

By the time of *Doggumentary*, his eleventh studio album, Snoop had shamelessly adopted the same approach as his peers and sometime gangstas, such as 50 Cent and Jay-Z – an approach perhaps best summed-up by P. Diddy. "I sell entertainment," he told Guy Adams, of the *Independent* newspaper (p. 19).

All black celebrities sell entertainment of one kind or other. It's fundamental. If someone fails to engage consumers in a way the consumers find agreeable and gratifying, then they are destined never to be a celebrity. They also sell a seemingly endless range of commodities connected in some way to entertainment. And they sell ideas. All celebrities, regardless of ethnic background, offer a conception of the good life; a narrow conception perhaps, but an influential one just the same. It is a good life in which endless novelty, change and excitement are taken for granted and in which all known stimulants are available. Ambitions are structured around the possibility of possessing things, the newer the better. Celebrities personify this good life.

But black celebrities secrete additional ideas: about racism, the colorblind life and the arrival of the postracial society. Occasionally, they'll speak explicitly about these matters. Very occasionally: for the most part, they remain silent, as if subdued by the overpowering demands of behaving with good grace so as not to incite controversy or resentment. Even a once-provocative figure like Snoop (2011 earnings: $8.55 million/£5.5 million) is careful to make his ghetto posturing transparently that – behavior intended to impress or mislead.

Most of us enjoy being entertained by musicians, actors, and sports stars. We might begrudge them the often staggering amounts of money they earn, but this doesn't stop us buying downloads, going to the movies or paying our tv subscriptions. Watching Denzel Washington in a film doesn't prompt us to think about how, today, there are many, many more African American movie stars in lead roles than there were twenty years ago. And it certainly doesn't make us wonder whether Washington is representative of a new generation of high-achieving African Americans.

In 1998, before Beyoncé had gone solo, when Michael Jackson was still alive and the same year writer Toni Morrison hailed Bill Clinton as "our first black president," historian Jacqueline Jones wrote: "We find nothing incongruous in appreciating the talents of African-American entertainers and professional athletes (male and female), who are paid millions of dollars each year, while accepting the apparent fact that millions of black men, women, and children are doomed to languish in impoverished communities, without the educational credentials and work opportunities that provide access to the blessings of a high-tech society" (p. 234).

Jones was right: we don't find incongruity. There is none: being entertained by black celebrities is perfectly in harmony with accepting what Jones called the "apparent fact" that the overwhelming majority of African Americans fail to make progress or achieve success of any substantial kind. The fact is actual rather than apparent, and it remains, as I will show in chapter 12. However unwittingly, black celebrities have sold the idea that America is no longer manacled to its history. It is a history pockmarked by racism, segregation and victimization. Undeniable progress since civil rights has promoted the ideal of what many call the postracial society, a place where racism and other forms of bigotry have no purchase. The election of Barack Obama, himself a political celebrity (as I will soon argue in detail), seemed to validate if not the arrival, then the imminence of the postracial society.

Black celebrities are definitely creating an impression. But in what sense are we using "impression"? An effect, an imitation, an idea, feeling or opinion formed without conscious thought or with little evidence? This is one of the questions we might ask about black celebrities and, as the reader might already be anticipating, it leads logically to several related questions, all of which I'll address in the eleven chapters that follow. Before moving to them, I'll offer an outline.

—

Chapter 2: Prominent African Americans now populate politics, as well as entertainment and sports – the two spheres where they have traditionally excelled. In practically every area of today's society, there are black people who are not just successful, but visibly, sometimes ostentatiously successful. Earl Ofari Hutchinson discerned that Tiger Woods' success in particular had been interpreted as "final proof that America is a colorblind society, and discrimination mostly a figment of the warped imaginations of many African-Americans." Obama's political success presumably added to the weight of evidence. It's a powerful argument and one deserving closer attention.

In this second chapter, I namecheck many of the figures I will discuss in detail in subsequent chapters. Clearly Obama's impact has been considerable, as has that of the woman who endorsed, blessed and all but canonized him. Oprah Winfrey and Obama are among the many African Americans who have publicly reflected on their own prodigiously successful careers and, at times, on how they managed to navigate their ways to the top. They share with other conspicuous African Americans awareness of racism, but as an inconvenience rather than insurmountable obstacle. "It is like rain. You know you're going to get wet so grab your umbrella and get up and go out to work." Robert L. Johnson's attitude is widely shared.

I use this chapter to establish themes that recur in one way or another throughout the book. Celebrities thrive in consumer culture; in fact, their existence is predicated on the desire to buy and possess products. Beyoncé, more than any other celebrity, epitomizes this. She can, it seems, sell anything to anybody.

Chapter 3: It sounds disparaging to describe Barack Obama as a brand. His critics have done just this and intended it as an insult. Is it? A brand is typically a type of product designed, manufactured and distributed to consumers. But it also resonates among a population: it evokes images and emotions, usually of high quality. Can any politician today afford to dispense with the kind of brand-building processes associated with showbusiness entertainers?

Obama's election as president in 2008 "uncorked a virulent racism," as Julianne Malveaux put it. She means that there was widespread displeasure that a black man could actually lead the nation. Widespread, perhaps; but far from unanimous. The attitudes, sentiments and beliefs that carried Obama to power were approving of a black politician who adamantly refused either to disguise his own background or broach racial issues on the campaign. Obama's election happened at a particular node where America's pathways intersected. Hurricane Katrina, Oprah and what the writer Shelby Steele sees as America's attempt to purify itself of racism, sexism and militarism were all influences.

Chapter 4: When Oprah Winfrey tells a population, "I am here to tell you to think," they do apparently think. She really did say this and her audience duly thought about who was the best person to occupy the presidency of the United States. Oprah was – perhaps remains – one of the most influential people in the world and the source of her influence is in the unique status she has acquired since 1986, when her history-making show first appeared on national television.

Oprah used her own life as a preacher uses a parable – to illustrate a moral, perhaps even spiritual, lesson. She told it many times, never as a neutral chronicle, always as an instruction. So Oprah would readily engage with racial issues, as she would any other controversial topic, but always finishing with a simple reminder that the solutions lie inside. People should follow Oprah's example and help themselves. If they carped and complained about the world, they would get nowhere.

Oprah's critics rounded on her, accusing her of naivety in encouraging individual over social change. But her psychobabble about self-actualization made great tv and helped establish her as "an Horatio Alger for our times," as one writer put it. Oprah's philosophy of individualism chimed well with the changing times; a kind of voyeurism seemed to change America's soul, turning its denizens into peeping toms and guiltless eavesdroppers on others' private conversations. As with all the figures who feature in this book, Oprah has to be understood in context.

Chapter 5: Bill Cosby brought to life what couldn't readily be seen in actuality: black people living like whites. I should probably stress *readily*. There were many well-heeled, aspirational bourgeois African Americans; they just didn't appear much on television. Cosby was an iconoclast, in the sense that he attacked beliefs and images that had been cherished for generations and perpetuated through the media in shows that featured African Americans in only a very narrow range of roles. Cosby's innovation was in creating a fictional family that had none of the usual characteristics associated with blacks. The Huxtable family, as they were called, was headed by a doctor, with a lawyer as his wife and children who were aiming to be successful in an orthodox way rather than as a successful pimp or drug dealer.

In the 1980s, it looked as if Cosby had been granted license to do and say as he wished: his mold-breaking show was the most popular on television and he pontificated, occasionally dogmatically, particularly on the condition of African Americans. In the 2000s, he seemed in danger of having that license revoked. Still popular, but fading in the collective memory, he roared back into the headlines with a series of speeches and talks, the theme of which was condensed into a single phrase: "blame the poor." It was an undeserved abridgement of what was actually a more formal and substantial extension of what many other prominent black people had been arguing for years. Since the days of W.E.B. Du Bois (1868-1963), in fact.

Like Oprah, Cosby preached individualism: the principle of being independent and self-reliant and favoring freedom of action for individuals over state control. At the core of Cosby's philosophy was "personal responsibility." Blaming racism, whites or more abstract forces for the persistent inequalities in American society had become an easy option, as far as Cosby was concerned. He struck a chord with many, but jarred with many others.

Cosby's impact is undeniable, but the nature of his influence or effect and on whom or what is not certain. As a way of assessing this, I set Cosby's seminal show in its historical context, tracing back the presence of black people in American television. This is the only way we can reliably understand Cosby's cultural significance.

Chapter 6: In the church of celebrity, Michael Jackson occupied a status comparable with the Pope or the Dalai Lama. Even after death, he remains the spiritual leader of a worldwide movement and commands the devotion of legions. In the 1960s, when Jackson first emerged as a precocious, gifted child, Cosby was playing Robert Culp's sidekick in a tv show called *I Spy*, civil rights legislation had only just been passed and MTV was two decades from its launch. The tv channel, which is now global, was instrumental in Jackson's ascent, and, indeed, the ascent of celebrity culture.

Imagine Jackson as a figure in a Jean-Michel Basquiat artwork: the figure itself is interesting enough, but what *makes* it interesting is all the stuff that's going on around it. Jackson is both a product of a particular period in history and a character who helped make that period. It's hard to imagine that television channels avoided black artists as recently as 1983 – the year before the launch of Cosby's show. Jackson's record company had to campaign for his music to be featured on the influential MTV playlists.

Looking back to the 1980s, Jackson's rise is astonishing. After his surge to fame as a child, a likely career arc would have been a return to obscurity, followed by traumatized teens and a struggle against dependency of some sort. Not many child stars (and no black child stars) continue to rise as they mature. Jackson's specialness derived from his music and presentation, of course. But only partly: much of the fascination with Jackson had its source in his idiosyncrasies. He was a black man, who seemed to want to remain in an artificial state of childhood, surround himself with the kinds of things children like, and collect objects that grown men would usually not find interesting (the bones of the Elephant Man, for example).

Even in death, Jackson's appeal is perplexing. In this chapter, I make sense of it. I argue that Jackson's admittance to the celebrity pantheon was conditional. His oddities served to keep him in consumers' minds, but they also distinguished him in a way that turned him into visible reminder: a figure who was distinct and different, and caused people to remember what they were not. What some writers call the Other. Love him, hate him, admire or disparage him, Jackson was one of the most reclusive yet revealing characters on the postwar American landscape.

Chapter 7: Some considered Jackson weird and wonderful; others, just weird. Shortly after his death in 2009, countless commentators asked, "How will Michael Jackson be remembered?" For his music? Dancing? Videos? Or his bizarre predilections? People were justifiably curious about Jackson. He was a most singular figure. Then again, whites have been curious about black people for a long time. The curiosity dates back to slave days when white audiences would clamor to watch clumsy re-enactments of life on the plantations put to music. The same desire to know or learn about black life manifested in subsequent generations, often in popular entertainment.

Entertainment is never *just* the provision of amusement or enjoyment and, in this chapter, I explore how black entertainers have both profited and suffered as a result of their popularity with whites. Often dehumanized, occasionally fêted, black performers and exhibits – yes, exhibits – have captivated white audiences since the early nineteenth century and perhaps before. Entertainment has long been one of the two areas in which African Americans have been permitted to excel. Sports is the other area. In both, blacks have performed for the delectation of whites. They have frequently become rich and famous in the process; but they have been at the service of whites, behaving in a way that provides pleasure and an agreeable diversion. Of course, all showbusiness performers do the same. Many black performers sensed the dangers of popular entertainment: they were serious artists who refused to submit themselves to degrading "buffoonery," as the historian Thomas Boskin calls it. One such artist was Paul Robeson and I spend time examining the career of this performer extraordinaire. A commanding bass-baritone, Shakespearean actor and film star, Robeson was eventually humbled.

Robeson's life was, in many ways, cautionary: he used his popularity to launch a surprise on an unwary population. Robeson strayed far from his stage, into the world of politics, labor and civil affairs. He was considered persona non grata and, for a while, became the subject of an FBI investigation. His fortunes issued a lesson: the activities of black entertainers were monitored and circumscribed. They were supposed to entertain. Nothing more. Success for black entertainers and, for that matter, athletes was strictly conditional.

It may have seemed like progress when black entertainers began appearing on Broadway, in Hollywood movies and on tv screens. But it was a kind of chimerical progress, something hoped-for but, in fact, illusory. Female artists, in particular, were squeezed into recognizable roles that bore traces of traditional racist stereotypes. If they resisted, as Lena Horne frequently did, they were left to waste. In this chapter, I describe a second American dilemma, one facing black artists with an eye on popular success: pander to whites' appetite for buffoonery and song, or risk withering. It is a dilemma that still hasn't satisfactorily been resolved.

Chapter 8: The entertainer's job was once to offer diversion, amusement and enjoyment to audiences. Now, the brief has expanded: they have to sell. Not just tickets, but all manner of products and services, many of which have no realistic connection to the entertainer's expertise. In fact, that expertise may *itself* be selling. Consumer culture intersects with practically every theme in this book. Celebrities themselves are living advertisements, not just for the commodities they peddle, but for the life they portray – and to which consumers aspire.

Black consumers aspire differently from most: according to research, they buy membership into mainstream society. "Consuming rebuts racism," Michèle Lamont and Virág Molnár discovered during their 2001 study "How blacks use consumption to shape their collective identity" (p. 41). It's a perplexing conclusion, but one that will make sense in the context of this book.

It also helps us make sense of the rise of Tyra Banks, a one-time model who migrated into television as one of the many possible successors to Oprah. Banks' efforts to occupy a place on a catwalk dominated by white models in the 1990s offers a real-life allegory about the narrow gaps available to blacks in a business that is essentially a humongous advertisement for high-end clothes and everything that wearing them signifies.

Naomi Campbell must have heard Banks' froufrou behind her: in 1987 the London-born model became the first black subject to appear on the cover of the French edition of *Vogue*. According to Banks' own reading of the situation, Campbell was less than thrilled by the prospect of having another black supermodel join her. Banks grew weary and later revealed to Campbell, "I was tired of having to deal with you." Their rivalry – though Campbell wouldn't call it that – supplied the raw material for gossip columns, and that is no bad thing for celebrities; in fact, it's a valuable resource. But it also illustrated how the number of places available for black celebrities in any given sphere is limited.

Banks stepped out of modeling and into television. She was still selling, but this time different kinds of commodities and services. Her specialty item was transformation: anyone can change, seemed to be her communiqué. For aspirational African Americans, this had reverb: in the 1960s and 1970s, black people massed on the streets protesting against racism; in the 1980s and 1990s, they assembled, though usually over specific issues, like the Rodney King riots of 1992, or the Million Man March of 1995. In the 2000s, another option emerged: buy stuff. The kind of good life personified by celebrities might not have been within grasp but it didn't stop consumers reaching for it. Reaching, in this instance, involves consuming the kinds of good visibly displayed by celebrities. It is also in line with the kind of individualist ethos pronounced by Oprah, Cosby and practically every other black celebrity who has risen to the A-list. When, in 2001, Lamont and Molnár titled their study "How blacks use consumption to shape their collective identity," they suggested the special powers shopping had for blacks. This chapter uses Banks as a kind of lens through which to scrutinize the importance of commodities for African Americans and the role of black celebrities in promoting and maintaining avid consumption. In a way, consumption has offered an alternative to challenge.

Chapter 9: Has there ever been a music that elevates, exalts, extols and makes manifest the glory of money? Rap's acceptance of consumption as a way to happiness has complemented the clustering of aspirations around acquiring money and material things. Leading exponents, including the figure mentioned at the start of this chapter, have made no secret of their ambitions. "I see money as a facilitator," 50 Cent told Kaleem Aftab. Facilitator for what? Saving the planet? Ending war? Finding the cure for untreatable diseases? No: "If airlines don't have a plane that goes to where you want to go, a private jet will."

Hip-hop culture brought forth a music that found the pulse of black American life. That was in the 1980s when thoughts were on police oppression rather than private jets ("Try to never backpedal from the power some go to get a nigger shot," Public Enemy, 1990). Rap became reassuringly domesticated. Reassuring, that is, for those who had seen it as threatening malefaction rather than bracing critique.

Hip-hop's transition occupies the first part of this chapter, which is concerned with the evolution of what has become popularly known as "black music." The term itself is questionable: it suggests some pure form of music originated and purveyed by African Americans. The blues, jazz, R&B, soul and some other kinds of music have been regarded as such. Artists specializing in one or more of these have been respectfully acknowledged, though none has ever received the kind of global recognition of more recent hip-hop artists. Hip-hop became the dominant black music of the late 1990s and 2000s. Its success reflected the enduring fascination whites have with black culture. Was it a wholesome fascination or something rather less edifying?

Chapter 10: Music has been one of two fields of endeavor where black people have been allowed to excel, sports being the other. I could emphasize *allowed*: whites have assented to African Americans' entry into these areas, while forbidding them access to more orthodox areas of society. But there are hidden conditions that I uncover in this chapter.

The chapter's title, "The ghetto inside", is taken from the words of one of Michael Vick's neighbors, who reflected on the football player's entanglement in dogfighting. "They moved out of the ghetto," said the neighbor of Vick and his friends. "But the ghetto is still in them." Maybe the sentiment isn't widely shared. Maybe it is. Either way, it hasn't hurt the marketability of African American sports stars: since the late 1990s, the spirit of Nike has gently guided sports into the entertainment business and turned athletes into fully formed celebrities. Nike was assisted by many helpers, the most influential being media corporations that hastened the implacable advance of celebrity culture. Sports, it seems, have been on an audiovisual loop for at least 20 years. Repetitious to some, spellbinding to most, competition has become a staple of entertainment in the 21st century. And Nike's footprints are all over.

In Michael Jordan, Nike constructed a perfect emblem: a black man endowed with extraordinary physical prowess who could enchant consumers, but never induced them to think of much beyond basketball or burgers. Helán E. Page uses the phrase "embraceable male blackness" to capture the kind of quality Jordan and any number of other black athletes embodied. Not including Mike Tyson: he engendered a similar kind of response as Vick; an African American man who used his sporting gift to earn millions then regressed. So where does that leave Tiger Woods on the embraceability scale? Or Kobe Bryant? Once lauded, then despised, then, at least in Bryant's case, lauded again, both manifested signs of regression.

For decades, even centuries, people have rhapsodized over black athletes, as they have black singers. Glancing back, we understand the difference between appreciation and respect: audiences were grateful for the opportunity to witness black athletes' outstanding physical feats and acknowledge what many suspected were natural gifts; but they did not have due regard for their feelings, beliefs, wishes, rights or ambitions.

Chapter 11: All black celebrities are political figures. At least, in the way Armond White uses political figures, celebrities who "reflect the way we think about race, masculinity, humor, violence and fantasy." White is referring specifically to Will Smith, an interesting character who indulged his flair for hip-hop and sitcom before becoming one of Hollywood's leading male actors. I open this chapter by contrasting Smith with Wesley Snipes, another leading man, though one with an altogether different political presence. Every black public figure invites us, perhaps compels us, to think about beliefs and principles, about status and authority. They do not always intend to: who they are, what they do, the roles they play and the images they convey all influence our thinking. When they actually say something, we take notice.

Earlier in the book in chapter 7, I recognize the nineteenth-century minstrel shows as the *fons et origo* of whites' interest in theatrical depictions of black life. In this chapter, I reveal how changing depictions of black life have political dimensions. Up to recently, black entertainers have been restricted to themes, characters and plotlines that convey the raw material for popular thinking. When African Americans appear on the screen, on the playing field or onstage, they are affecting how others think not just about them, but about a range of issues. I risk taxing the reader's patience, but it's worth reminding ourselves once more: entertainment is never *just* the provision of amusement or enjoyment.

Every so often, a black celebrity speaks out for or against something or other. Cosby occasioned outrage, as did Kanye West. So, when Halle Berry decided to invoke the "one-drop rule" some sort of political quarrel was bound to ensue. Berry's remarks, which conjured up memories of slavery and miscegenation, were widely reported and, at first blush, sounded a crude and retrograde blurt. On closer inspection, her words were a considered and intelligent political comment on what being black means in the twenty-first century.

Chapter 12: Is whiteness normal? No one would dare say so, but for nearly four centuries that's been a popular, if unspoken assumption. Starting the final chapter of a book entitled *Beyond Black* with a discussion of whiteness sounds perverse, but it's actually essential. Without an examination of how whiteness was invented – yes, *invented* – the rest of the book would be meaningless. My logic is simple: there are no racial groups, no blacks, whites or any other kind of grouping that we have not created ourselves. Human beings do not fall naturally into pre-established categories: we have framed those categories, filled them and, over the years, loaded them with meanings. Unless there was a population of people we call white, there would be no black. So no black sportsmen, black actors, or black celebrities. And yet, as the reader will see, there were once no black people at all; nor whites.

The concluding chapter doesn't try to bring everything together in some specious homogeneity: this book is about a subject that defies glib conclusions. The narrative thread that ties everything together is, of course, the black celebrity, but this is a social-cultural chronicle that should leave the readers pondering more questions, one of which might be: "Do we live in a postracial society?"

The very phrase signals a time when race has disappeared, left behind in the vapor trail of history. The election of Barack Obama in 2008 indicated that, even if the postracial society had not materialized, there was at least evidence that it may do so over the next several years. But, if the postracial society is approaching, why is so much of America structured in a way that makes it deeply racially divided? In this chapter, I present a portrait of America's racial divisions; they are divisions that torture flagbearers for the postracial future. Race and the racism it fosters have been organizing principles of American society and, while the most obvious instances of them have gone, there remains evidence that they maintain a surreptitious presence.

Black celebrities are, by definition, successful: they have managed, in their own ways, to overcome the kind of barriers that countless other black people fail to surmount. In this sense, they serve notice that America, though once hostile to blacks, is a more welcoming place. To extend Johnson's metaphor, black celebrities have put on their raincoats, taken a precautionary umbrella and decided to brave the elements.

The chapters are interconnected rather than organized around a theory or proposition. Readers won't find chronological progression or genre-specific chapters: this is not a history of black entertainers. Even the chapters focusing on particular figures, such as Oprah, Bill Cosby and Michael Jackson, are as much about their times as lives. The book time-shuttles from the nineteenth century to the present day, and all points in between. It makes incongruous bedfellows of diverse characters, gathering movie stars and politicians in the same chapters with tv figures and jazz singers. And it ends shamelessly with a conclusion that is indefinite and lacking in assurance. It is a deficiency for which the reader will, I suspect, find justification in the preceding eleven chapters.

2

Sideshows and carnival barkers

'Look around you: not only can we boast a black president, we have
Jay-Z, the world's foremost rapper, Oscar winner Halle Berry,
Jamie Foxx, Beyoncé, Kobe Bryant ... we could go on.'

"My general point is this: we are living in a very serious time, and America has huge potential and opportunity to seize the twenty-first century. We're only gonna get there though if we have a serious conversation about the things that matter to people: jobs and gas prices and how we bring down the deficit, how do we deal with the changes going on in the world. We can't be distracted by sideshows and, as I said at my press conference, carnival barkers, who are going around trying to get attention."

Barack Obama was responding to a question from Oprah Winfrey, who, in May 2011, wondered why he had chosen to produce his detailed birth certificate from Hawaii and distribute it to the media. Persistent claims about the legitimacy of his citizenship had been circulating for over two years. "Silliness," Obama called it. Oprah seemed to agree, inviting him to widen his argument: "Do you think that there's a disconnection in general in terms of sideshows and carnival barkers?" she asked, extending his analogy for the gossip media. A carnival barker is someone who stood at the entrance of the traveling entertainment shows that were popular in the nineteenth century, loudly announcing the offerings to the crowds.

Is America living in the real world? Not to judge by its President. Obama, his admirers used to say, was careful, deliberative and admirably reluctant to rush to conclusions, but, in this instance, he was fast and definite: "The line between entertainment and politics has blurred and so reality tv is seeping into how we think about our politics."

It was meant as a criticism, or at least a sardonic reflection. Yet the President of the United States was speaking not at a press briefing or in the context of a presidential address, but on *Oprah*, the highest-rated television talk show in history; a show that, at its peak, pulled in 42 million viewers and even in its final stages drew six million. It was syndicated to over 140 countries around the world. Obama may have understood the irony of his pronouncement, but it didn't seem that way. All the same, it was a breathtakingly impudent remark to make on one of the world's foremost citadels of mass entertainment. The line between entertainment and politics has blurred.

Perhaps it was a sly acknowledgment of the unenviable trade-offs of contemporary politics: any prospective politician who isn't prepared to engage with the entertainment industry is condemned to remain exactly that – a prospective politician and not an actual one. Obama demonstrably was prepared to engage, as his presence on Oprah's show bore testimony. He even brought along his wife, Michelle, who contributed almost as much as he did to the conversation. He was, after all, making a statement and simultaneously proving the truth of that statement.

In one apparently throwaway remark, Barack Obama, elected President of the United States in 2008, gifted us an argument that, twenty years before, would have been preposterous and unbelievable. Why preposterous and unbelievable? Even in the early 1990s, there was nothing contrary to reason or commonsense in declaring that politics was edging closer to entertainment. A glance on YouTube at a Ray-Banned Bill Clinton playing "Heartbreak Hotel" on tenor sax on the Arsenio Hall Show in 1992 will remind anyone of that.

No, the unbelievable part lay not in the content of the remark, but in the person who made it and the company in which he made it. Even in the run-up to the historic 2008 election, many believed the USA would never cross a kind of political threshold and elect an African American president. Despite decades of post-civil-rights progress in politics and the rise to prominence of people like Jesse Jackson, who himself ran presidential campaigns in 1984 and 1988, the idea of a black president seemed remote.

Even more magically, Obama was not interviewed by a man, but by a woman. Not even a white woman; an African American woman who could lay every legitimate claim to being the most influential female, perhaps person, on the planet. And to make this interview more compellingly entertaining and showbusinesslike, the president brought his wife. Three black people, sitting on a couch. A president, and a black president at that, appearing with his wife, another black woman, at the time rated by *Forbes* as the most powerful woman in the world, on the world's most-watched and best-known talk show, hosted by the world's most famous and wealthiest woman, a black woman, and explaining why he needed to prove his American nativeness by reference to the lack of distinctness between politics and entertainment.

Collectively, they contrived a new and, in many ways, unexpected image of a cultural landscape where the time-honored tribulation of race no longer mattered; what some call a postracial society. Remember: less than 50 years before, Medgar Evers, a black civil rights activist from Decatur, Mississippi, was shot dead by racists while involved in trying to change the segregationist policy of the University of Mississippi.

"For African-Americans the Obama presidency is the fulfillment of what once was thought to be the impossible dream," wrote Wayne A. Jones and Douglas J. Fiore in their 2009 article, "We're confusing the black kids and scaring the white kids." "No longer do African-American children have to grow up with the perception that obtaining the highest elective office in the land is totally elusive" (p.13).

From the outset, Obama was freighted with the burdens of history. "It seems reasonable for one to view Obama's election as the beginning of a post-racial America," wrote Anthony L. Brown and Keffrelyn D. Brown in the academic journal *Race, Gender and Class*, in 2010. But only "reasonable" if you accept that "racism is solely located in the actions of individual, aberrant people rather than actions situated in and supported by historical, discursive and institutional practises" (p.124).

Both points are, of course, crucial, as is the reference to an America where race and, we presume, racism have become irrelevant. It does seem reasonable to visualize Obama as the man who broke the dam of oppression, discrimination, exploitation and, often, naked brutality that had been leaking for years, but needed one final, thunderous onslaught before it finally disintegrated. But it seems less reasonable to charge one individual with the responsibility for changing a set of social and cultural institutions that have been given specific shape and substance for over four hundred years, and which, according to some, continue to make ogres or victims of everyone.

A third point could be that Obama is but one character in a drama that had been playing for a number of years before his election victory. Maybe the others didn't have the social authority that comes with political office, but consider the impact of the person asking the questions in the sideshows and carnival barkers interview. Oprah proved that, while blackness was and may still be an impediment to advancement, it's not an immovable obstruction, or, if it is, there are ways around it.

——

In the 25 years ending with her last show on May 25, 2011, Oprah had humanized a fantasy, that fantasy being that a black woman could create a global industry, become one of the richest people in the world and even inspire new entries in our dictionaries: Oprahification; The O-Factor. More than any other contemporary figure, Oprah Winfrey cut through America's racial divides. When she emerged on her own tv show on September 8, 1986, she was an improbable emblem for a new society: a slightly podgy black woman in raspberry-colored outfit, her hair coiffed into one of those big eighties do's. Over 4,000 episodes later, Oprah, at 57, quit the daily grind of the talk show, with billions in the bank and an annual income estimated by *Forbes* at $300m.

When *The Oprah Winfrey Show* started there were plenty of high-profile black figures, though most fitted historical types. The kind of disempowered characters described by the title of Donald Bogle's book *Toms, Coons, Mulattoes, Mammies, and Bucks*, first published in 1973, were still abundant in films. And musically, African Americans were locked into specific genres. But fresh options were appearing. None were fresher than the role of a well-heeled gynecologist with an equally well-heeled wife, also a professional, with a high-spirited, quarrelsome but recognizably normal home life.

The sting of *The Bill Cosby Show* was its authenticity: it suggested there were black people whose lives were not stricken by the maladies and multiple pathologies typically associated with African Americans. Cosby had been on tv since the 1960s when he featured in *I Spy*, but his *The Bill Cosby Show*, which started in 1984, offered a tableau of black characters that was, in its way, iconoclastic; it was also compulsively watchable, running until 1992 and, for four years, topping the viewer ratings. In the 1980s, Cosby was a singular entertainer: he grandstanded shamelessly, making himself likeable to audiences and, by implication, to advertisers, who used his gift to sell their wares.

Cosby proved many things, not least of which was that audiences are prepared to work for their enlightenment. He offered an unusual image of a conservative family man, normal in all respects but one – he was black. Being white is what Howard Winant calls the "default racial status"; it is the norm in America, as I will argue later. But bear with me. In several respects, Cosby was just like one of those standard issue black comedians: an unapologetically happy jester whose main purpose in life seemed to be to amuse whites. But in other respects, he issued a challenge. His character seemed to say: I'm affluent, live in a smart home, have a well-ordered family and live in comfort, not unlike some whites, in fact; so now what have you got to laugh at? And then he made audiences laugh.

So, by the time of Oprah's arrival, American consumers had at least glimpsed a black male entertainer who didn't conform to popular expectations. But outside Cosby there was familiarity. Prodigiously gifted black musical and sports stars had been around for the whole of the twentieth century. In the 1980s, Michael Jackson was the most conspicuous and, for some, the most gifted. In 1983, Jackson had become the first ever African American artist to feature on MTV, then a 24-hour music channel. Jackson cast a spell that endured after his death.

In sport, Mike Tyson was wielding his own kind of influence on audiences. His brand of primitivism in the ring was a reminder of blacks' extraordinarily destructive prowess. Michael Jordan alternated near-miraculous basketball with completely miraculous salesmanship. In many ways the alkali to Tyson's acid, Jordan induced consumers not just to spend money on products that he endorsed, but convince them that it was empowering to do so.

More mold-breakers were to come. Denzel Washington was a relatively obscure black actor – his breakthrough role as Steve Biko in *Cry Freedom* came in 1987. Rappers were beginning to emerge: Run-DMC's version of Aerosmith's "Walk this way" became an international success in 1986, making audiences stand back with respectful awe and take notice of an interesting and relatively new genre known then simply as hip-hop.

The range of images of black people broadened with the arrival of Colin Powell, a New York-born son of Jamaican migrants, who served in the military and was promoted to the rank of General and selected as Chairman of the

Joint Chiefs of Staff, the highest military position, in 1989. Praised as the leader of Operation Desert Storm in the first Gulf War, 1991, Powell was a handsome and stellar performer on tv. He later declared himself a Republican and even contemplated a presidential campaign before taking up the position of Secretary of State, a position later occupied by Condoleezza Rice.

By the time Oprah decided to leave her leather sofa for good, black people had ascended in practically every part of American society. Traditionally restricted to success in sports and entertainment, African Americans excelled in politics, commerce, industry, the military and everywhere else. So it's easy to see how the impression of the postracial society gained credence: it's not just that your MP3 player is full of tracks by black artists, or that every movie you see has black lead actors, or even that all your favorite sports are dominated by black players; it's that your boss is black, your state governor is black, your accountant is black and your local bank has a black manager.

If this sounds like an exaggerated and distorted characterization, consider the conclusions of Stanford University scholars, Gary M. Segura and Ali A. Valenzuela in their 2010 article for *Presidential Studies Quarterly*: "The decline of old-fashioned racism – belief in the inferiority of blacks – and a corresponding rise in racial egalitarianism have been amply demonstrated in the literature of American public attitudes" (p. 502).

Even if this doesn't equate exactly to the vision of the postracial society, it comes close: the principle that all people are equally deserving of rights and opportunities – what Segura and Valenzuela call racial egalitarianism – has risen in popularity as archaic forms of bigotry have receded into America's past. The deep-seamed racism that made the country hell-on-earth for black people and split the nation in myriad ways, socially, geographically, even psychologically, was, it seems, disappearing. A country once as starkly and formally divided as a chessboard is now much more like a Eugene J. Martin collage or Jackson Pollock abstract.

———

"Americans view race through a prism of culture." So claims John Hartigan Jr. in his 2009 article, "What are you laughing at?" He doesn't deny that there are countless occasions when what he calls "the racial dimension of daily life" are glaringly transparent. But race has become less and less visible. So much so that Hartigan solemnly reports, "The worst thing that you can be labeled these days is a racist" (p.15).

Hartigan reckons his first point about "the prism of culture" hardly needs stating, but perhaps it's not quite as obvious as he thinks. He presumably means that we look at the world from our own particular viewpoints, each a product of our background and present position. We have perspectives, in other words. Hartigan's slightly troubling point is that most of us see a distorted image of society. Nowadays, it's difficult to show "Americans how widely and deeply race continues to matter" (p.15).

Why? Hartigan doesn't offer an answer. Let me try. In 1998, shortly after Tiger Woods had won his first Masters and instantly became a global celebrity, Earl Ofari Hutchinson wrote perceptively in the *New Pittsburgh Courier*: "While many whites sincerely cheered Tiger for his triumphs, many others twisted his success into final proof that America is a colorblind society, and discrimination mostly a figment of the warped imaginations of many African-Americans" (p. A7).

The years since haven't dulled Hutchinson's argument; if anything, they've sharpened it. Woods is now just one of an entire generation of conspicuously successful black American celebrities; they are abundant, superabundant you might say. They are parts of an elite group of African Americans whose wealth, glamor, flamboyance and even moral authority has positioned them, whether they like it or not, as "proof of the colorblind society," to repeat Hutchinson.

Obama and Oprah are just two of the many African Americans who have been forcefully demonstrative: they've served as persuasive evidence. "Since Obama won the presidency, this national hunger for racial optimism is overflowing with self-congratulation," writes Thomas F. Pettigrew in his 2011 commentary, "Post-racism?" (p. 279).

The self-congratulation goes beyond allowing oneself a few bouquets for being enlightened enough to elect a black president: it's an almost audible cry of "Bravo! We did it. We finally laid racism to rest. Need proof? Look around you: not only can we boast a black president, we have Jay-Z, the world's foremost rapper, Oscar winner Halle Berry, Jamie Foxx, Beyoncé, Kobe Bryant ... we could go on." Each of them earns more in a year than the gross turnover of a medium-sized petrochemical company. Their talent and the opulent lifestyle it brings them are the envy of everyone.

There's logic to this kind of reasoning. And it guides a further proposition: if these and other successful African Americans have faced the obstacles strewn across their paths by discrimination and prejudice and still managed to come out on top, why can't others? Oprah is exemplary: born to poor parents, abused as a child, lacking any kind of obvious talent – by which I mean proficiency in sports, or entertainment – or strikingly good looks, she scaled the heights with a combination of perseverance and a refusal to be thwarted by anyone or anything.

Although she didn't say it, there's little doubt Oprah would agree with the founder of BET (Black Entertainment Television) and fellow billionaire Robert L. Johnson, who, in a 2004 interview, grasped the importance of racism like this: "You know you are going to get hit with it, but you don't let it stop you from trying to be the best you can be at what you do. I never give up because I am going to run into racism" (p. 116). Depending on your perspective, his metaphor is either banal or brilliant: "It is like rain. You know you're going to get wet so grab your umbrella and get up and go out to work" (p.116).

Johnson and the other black celebrities are emblems of self-help. They're not naïve: racism hasn't evaporated in a matter of a few years. But, for them, it is like rain; unpleasant and unwelcome (except by farmers), but not debilitating. Once there were floods, then there were storms, but now there are just showers, perhaps drizzle. And it isn't only the fabulously rich African Americans who believe this, as research by Helen A. Neville et al. in 2005 confirms. One of the several important points made by Neville and her colleagues is that the "set of beliefs that serves to minimize, ignore, and/or distort the existence of race and racism" and that "racism is a thing of the past and that race and racism do not play an important role in current social and economic realities" is by no means the preserve of whites (p. 29). Many African Americans also subscribe.

Even skeptical scholars, such as Ben Pitcher, warn, "It is a mistake to view the sea change in American culture that permitted the election of a black president as an anomalous event, or as motivated solely by a weakly held abeyance to a momentarily fashionable social liberalism" (p. 356). In his 2010 article "White no longer," Pitcher contends the result of the 2008 election contained "an important statement of collective intent."

Pitcher believes an "ontological transformation in US culture" is in process, by which I infer a dramatic change in the whole nature of American society. A change to what some call the postracial society. So Hartigan's argument about the difficulty in reminding America how "widely and deeply race continues to matter" makes sense. There are too many models of black success to dismiss them as tokens or aberrant individuals. They constitute a body of evidence.

———

After Obama had finished explaining to Oprah how entertainment values had seeped into politics, she referred to the epic PBS documentary series *Eyes on the Prize*, which recounted the struggle of the civil rights movement to end decades of discrimination and segregation. "Do you sense people have lost a sense of what the prize is?" she asked.

It was an interesting question from someone who, while always engaged in good causes, has rarely explicitly aligned herself with antiracism movements or social programs that target racism. It was also a legitimate question, though one that didn't get an adequate answer. The prize is a society in which racism no longer exists and all people, regardless of ethnic background or identity, can advance as far as their abilities and resolve will take them and in any direction they choose.

Nothing stays still for long in America. Even so, race has been a constant source of conflict. From the seventeenth century till the thirteenth amendment of 1865, racism rationalized, complemented and, to use Patrick Wolfe's phrase, provided "an alibi" for slavery. Legal segregation, civil rights protests and black power resistance followed, but without obliterating race from the American cultural landscape. A glance at history can mislead us into assuming that race is a permanent, unmovable feature. But, if race is an invention rather than a force of nature – and I will argue that it is – then the dividing lines between the so-called races are changeable. They are, as Jennifer Lee and Frank D. Bean put it, "not fixed but continue to change through expression and validation" (p. 224).

Purposive efforts to eradicate race through affirmative action, equal opportunity and other policy initiatives lessened the negative impact of race from the late 1960s. But the torment continued and the racial order remained. The order is much like a wedding cake; a tiered construction on which white icing sits on top and covers everything else.

The supposition that the traditional racial hierarchy could be eased out of existence instead of destroyed was raised memorably in E. Franklin Frazier's *Black Bourgeoisie*, first published in 1955 (as *Bourgeoisie Noire*). Franklin Frazier discerned aspirational black people, not prone to spending energy on fighting racism, but by pursuing individual ambitions.

More recently in 2010, Timothy B. Neary has reflected: "Still crowded in segregated urban ghettos and denied the vote in recalcitrant southern cities, postwar African Americans, nevertheless began to identify themselves as 'consumer citizens'" (p. 120).

Terrene expectations gave way to other aspirations, according to Neary: "The extensive range of modern media exposed them [African Americans] to a world of middle-class material abundance, a dream for sale that appeared within reach" (p. 120).

The research of Clint Wilson and Félix Gutiérrez into the portrayal of ethnic groups by the media complemented this: in 1985, they examined the market's response to aspirational blacks: "Advertisers promote consumption of their products as a shortcut to the good life, a quick fix for low-income consumers" (p. 128).

The particular conception of the "good life" they have in mind is imagined as a cornucopia of material goods. "You may not be able to live in the best neighborhoods, wear the best clothes, or have the best job, but you can drink the same liquor, smoke the same cigarettes, and drive the same car as those who do," is how Wilson and Gutiérrez summarized the advertisers' message to black consumers.

Wilson and Gutiérrez's analysis is sober in its conclusions. While advertisers were wooing African Americans into consumer culture, "a system of inequality that keeps them below national norms in education, housing, income, health and other indicators" remained (p. 130).

Celebrity culture has perpetrated a falsehood, according to Christopher E. Bell; what he calls "an ideological fallacy" (p. 49). The cultural democracy supposedly introduced by celebrity culture is now a constituent part of a more equal society in which class has receded in importance. The impression that the racial hierarchy has disappeared is also fallacious and, in this book, I'll provide evidence to support this. But let me stay with Bell's observation, which prompts a further question: discomfort with persistent inequalities is arguably less than it was ten years ago. Why?

More than two decades after Wilson and Gutiérrez's reminder, there were many successful African Americans who enjoyed opulent lifestyles, elevated status and the kind of wealth that would have been unimaginable for most of the 1980s. And many, many more prepared to enter into a bargain that was less *Faust*, more *The Price Is Right*.

Pause for a moment to think of Beyoncé. All celebrities exhibit themselves in a way that makes them resemble merchandise – articles of trade that can be bought and sold in the marketplace. Yet, even in this company, Beyoncé is a rare bird. Since 2003, when she split from Destiny's Child, she has surpassed even Michael Jordan as a sales phenomenon. She's turned herself into a one-woman "Entertainment Empire," as Lacey Rose calls it, selling, among many other things, movie tickets, DVDs, CDs, tvs, ringtones, cosmetics and colognes (but not video games – more of which shortly).

According to *Forbes.com* Beyoncé makes $21 million per year from album sales alone. Gail Mitchell, of *Billboard*, reports that Beyoncé, as solo artist and with Destiny's Child, has sold over 100 million units, including albums, physical and digital singles and music DVDs. Writing and sometimes producing her own music offers another income stream amounting to $8 million per year.

With her mother, Beyoncé has launched two designer labels, House of Deréon, which specializes in upmarket clothes, and Deréon, which includes handbags, sportswear and jewelry. The two lines bring in $15 million per year.

Beyoncé is in a class of her own when it comes to endorsements: her portfolio is worth $20 million per year. Is there another celebrity in history to have lent his or her name to so many products? Armani, Pepsi, L'Oreal, and Hilfiger are among the global brands that have paid Beyoncé to link her name to their products. They all believe that featuring Beyoncé's name or perhaps just her image will help them sell products. The exact value of Beyoncé's name+image is practically impossible to calculate, although when she pulled out of a deal with Gate Five, a video company that was about to launch a game called *Starpower: Beyoncé* (in which players could perform with Beyoncé), the company sued for £100 million in lost sales.

Some measure of the businesslike ruthlessness with which Beyoncé rules her empire can be taken from her decision to fire her father Mathew as manager in 2011. He had guided her career since 1995, when Destiny's Child was formed.

While Beyoncé is currently the *ne plus ultra*, all celebrities are engaged in selling commodites. They also embody exchange values. By this I mean, they are living commodities themselves: their very presence, whether at a première or at the gym, has value, if for no other reason than we consumers are interested enough to pay for it (how many celebrity magazines feature pictures of stars driving, shopping or just doing nothing in particular?). They are also human signposts for what Wilson and Gutiérrez called "a short cut to the good life".

They allude to the prospect of a culture of extravagant consumption where an endless cycle of voracious desire maintains the demand for commodities. Where shopping is close to being the most fundamental human experience.

The consumer culture in which celebrities command attention, occasionally, adulation, and, routinely, emulation is predicated on the principle that anything – *anything* – is tradeable. In other words, it can be bought and sold in a market. Could this include the end of racism? More specifically, an end to manifold effects of racism on any consumer with means enough to buy what the likes of Beyoncé, Oprah and others glamorize and commend.

Celebrities have a lot to answer for. They are been blamed for corroding our sensibilities, for inciting people to strive for fame at any cost, and for turning heads towards meretricious commodities, things that have no relevance or any consequence of lasting importance on our lives. They're also accused of distracting us in a way that diverts our attention, energies and ambition away from attainable goals and toward fanciful dreams.

———

This book is about the effects of celebrities, but the effects of black celebrities in particular. "Blacks enter the mainstream wearing different masks," detects Shelby Steele in a 2008 interview with Ibram Rogers (p. 16). One of those masks is that of the "bargainer," whose sales pitch is, says Steele, "I will not rub the history of racism in your face if you will not hold my race against me." Then there is the "challenger," who presumes all whites are racists until they prove otherwise and so makes whites feel uncomfortable, embarrassed and guilty.

Today's generation of African Americans is not as ingratiating as bargainers, but they're certainly not challengers either. Historically, challengers have been either canonized as seers and freedom fighters, or, more usually, consigned to oblivion. If there is a bargain on offer, it's a different one from that imagined by Steele and is probably something like: "You're not going to hold anything against me because, by applauding me and acknowledging my talents, you are showing how you and, indeed, the whole of America has moved beyond race and put all the bigotry, hatred and segregation that has disfigured the nation behind us. So I might make the occasional jibe against whites and I might even venture toward social criticism every so often. But that's what you expect from a black person, right? In return, I promise not to demand anything radical and I'll direct whatever criticism I have at black people themselves more than anybody else."

However inadvertently, black celebrities have brokered a deal that pacifies Middle America and distracts at least a portion of the black population from the quest for what was once called "the prize." That prize has been replaced by commodities, products that have been vested with value far beyond their actual worth. Think about hip-hop, a culture that became an industry.

In the 1980s, fables of the hopelessness, wretchedness and defeatism that filled the ghettos were carried by DJs and MCs. Helpless but unafraid, woebegone but resourceful, often funny, usually inventive, and always sharply aware of social affairs, hip-hop artists pioneered a fresh genre. Today's hip-hop has traded the commentaries for commodities: artists with no aspiration greater than getting rich are either corporate spokesmen (occasionally, women) or, in a few cases, corporate heads. The most creative act that rap accentuates is buying products that are often beyond the means of ordinary consumers. The word left ringing in the brain is "exploit," but in which sense? To make use of and derive benefit, or to use situations or people in an unfair and selfish way?

Isn't that what celebrity culture does, we might ask? More people encouraging us to part with our hard-earned money might seem the last thing we need. But we want them, all the same: we find them entertaining or, at least, agreeably distracting. And here is the *quid pro quo*: celebrities, in return, pressurize us to spend money. Not by twisting our arms up our backs, but by gentle, perhaps hidden persuasion. It's impossible to get through a waking day without confronting an image (usually several) of a well-known figure imploring consumers to buy a product or service. Even if they don't do it openly, their clothes, jewelry, cars, homes, favored drinks, preferred films, their very presence promotes things we can either buy or dream of buying.

On the other side of the bargain, there are consumers, paying customers prepared to spend money on the "shortcut to the good life," but with an expectation that something else will emerge from the trade. "Consumption is uniquely important for blacks in gaining social membership," conclude researchers Michèle Lamont and Virág Molnár. "Consuming rebuts racism" (p. 41). There's a serpentine logic that winds back to the 1960s, when David Caplovitz's study of low-income African Americans and Puerto Ricans in New York revealed what the author called "compensatory consumption." I will uncoil this logic in the chapters to come; for the moment, let me just state that consumption has a particular significance for black people, as do the figures who promote consumption.

There are, to be sure, a multiplying number of black celebrities who are enjoying the fruits of success – and enjoying them publicly. Yet, as we will document in more detail as the book progresses, the majority of African Americans continue to underachieve in education and overachieve in graduating to prisons. Most remain at the opposite end of the social spectrum to Oprah and the others, and continue to face what Farah Jasmine Griffin, in her 2009 article "Children of Omar," calls "the instability, insecurity, and disruption that … have been a persistent part of the black experience" (p. 657).

3

Obama believes in *Obama*

'Obama was selling a new configuration, an arrangement of
familiar elements in an unfamiliar form: a black politician
who defied the usual color-coding.'

Racism has a ghost: an apparition of something that died, but becomes
manifest to the living, typically in the form of a menace. Barack Obama
was used to ghosts. So when the so-called "birthers" raised questions about the
president's origins and religion, it must have seemed like just another spooky
visitation.

Donald Trump, real estate tycoon, host of *Celebrity Apprentice,* and, at one
stage, potential Republican presidential candidate, was a flagbearer for the
birthers – a group questioning the President's origins – and publicly announced
he wasn't convinced that Obama was born in the United States. If he were
not, Obama would not have been constitutionally eligible to occupy the White
House. Even the original birth certificate, produced by an exasperated Obama
in April 2011, didn't silence his detractors; a *USA Today* poll revealed that only
38 percent of Americans believed Obama definitely was born in the US.

No sooner had the controversy simmered down, than another came to the
boil. Obama's father, Barack Obama Sr., was a serial womanizer and polygamist
whom government and university officials were trying to force out of the
country, it was claimed. Obama Sr. married Stanley Ann Dunham, a white
student from Kansas, not only when he was said to have already been married
to a woman in Kenya, but at a time, in 1961, when interracial marriages were
still illegal in many parts of the US. Obama's approval rating (which gauges
public support for presidents during tenure) slumped to an unimpressive
46 per cent (this was only temporary: his approval rating jumped 11 points in
the wake of the military mission, which he authorized and which resulted in
the death of Osama bin Laden).

Obama, for his part, expressed puzzlement about the fixation on his origins
and the willingness of many to keep asking questions unrelated to his political
behavior. Perhaps he shouldn't have been surprised. From the moment he was
elected president there had been a persistent questioning of his citizenship
and other credentials. As Julianne Malveaux wrote for *The Scanner*, in 2010:
"The election of Barack Obama in 2008 seems to have uncorked a virulent
racism among folks who are hatefully resentful of the fact that an African
American man now leads our nation" (p. 5).

In contrast, the election campaign was almost devoid of racial issues. None of Obama's rivals in the primary or general elections was prepared to risk introducing race into the discourse. Risk? Yes, any politician contemplating raising an issue that either was or could have been treated by the media as having a racial element would have been taking a chance. The race issue is, as I'll show in the chapters that follow, unpredictable.

Obama's ascent to the presidency effectively started in August 2005, when a weather system that had formed over the Bahamas moved west and then north, picking up intensity to become a category 3 hurricane as it entered the Gulf of Mexico. Katrina, as it was called, struck the Gulf Coast with devastating force at daybreak on August 29, 2005, pounding a region that included the city of New Orleans and damaging neighboring Mississippi. In all, more than 1,700 people were killed and hundreds of thousands displaced. More than a million people in three states were left without power and with submerged roads even hundreds of miles from Katrina's center. The hurricane's storm surge — the water pushed towards the shore by the force of the winds swirling around the storm — was, at 29 feet, the highest ever measured in the US. Crucially, levees failed in New Orleans, resulting in political and social upheavals that continued for years.

New Orleans is an especially poor city: 27.4 percent of its inhabitants lived below the poverty line at the time of Katrina. The hurricane wreaked destruction disproportionately on African Americans, who constituted about two-thirds of the city's population: black people represented 45.8 percent of the population of the damaged areas, compared to only 26.4 percent of the populations of areas left untouched. De facto segregation meant that the city's black population lived in distinct areas. The exodus out of the city left behind a predominantly black group of survivors. The images relayed from helicopters by journalists were raw. "What a shocked world saw exposed in New Orleans last week wasn't just a broken levee," wrote the *New York Times'* Jason DeParle on September 4, 2005. "It was a cleavage of race and class, at once familiar and startlingly new, laid bare in a setting where they suddenly amounted to matters of life and death."

On the day Katrina hit New Orleans, President George W. Bush was nearing the end of a month-long break at his ranch in Crawford Texas. After being told of the hurricane, Bush decided to inspect the devastation personally. Two days after the hurricane had hit, on August 31, Bush flew over New Orleans in Air Force One to inspect the wreckage. Much of the city was under water. It was a reconnaissance he later regretted, particularly as photographers captured the flight. "The photo of my hovering over the damage suggested I was detached from the suffering on the ground," wrote Bush in his 2010 memoir, *Decision Points.*

For some, it suggested more than that. Kanye West, in a bitter verbal attack, memorably declared, "George Bush doesn't care about black people." The context of the assertion is often erased: West was talking without autocue to NBC cameras, making an appeal to raise money for the victims in

New Orleans. He singled out the media for his initial broadside. "I hate the way they portray us in the media. If we see a black family, it says they're looting. See a white family, it says they're looking for food."

In the immediate aftermath of the hurricane, a survey (reported by Howard Kurtz in the *Washington Post*, September 9, 2005), found that 71 percent of African Americans believed the disaster showed that racial inequality remained a major problem in the USA, while 56 percent of whites felt this was not a particularly important lesson of the disaster. This was not the only perceptual discrepancy: 66 percent of blacks maintained the government's response to the crisis would have been faster if most of the storm's victims had been white, while 77 percent of whites disagreed.

Katrina left 60,000 people homeless, though the Federal Emergency Management Agency (FEMA) refused to pay for their temporary accommodation. Most public schools were closed. "Low- and moderate-income African-American students are most affected by these school closings," reported Julianne Malveaux in her article "Is the Department of Justice at war with diversity?"

In her 2010 article "Rebuilding the Park," Farah D. Gifford, of Xavier University of Louisiana, reflected: "Almost 3 years after the storm, Black victims were more likely to be still living in trailers" (p. 386).

———

Ten months before Katrina struck, Obama had won a seat on the US Senate: he'd defeated the last-minute Republican candidate Alan Keyes, taking 70 percent of the vote. The winner of the Republican primary had resigned after accusations that he took his wife to a sex club against her wishes.

Obama was only the fifth African American in history to win a seat in the US's highest legislative body. Biographical details began to filter through: son of a Kenyan politician, his mother a white American anthropologist, Obama had studied at Columbia University and Harvard Law School. He had been the first African American to be president of the *Harvard Law Review*.

In a praiseful article for the *Journal of Blacks in Higher Education*, Kenneth W. Mack, himself from Harvard, coined the term "the Obama phenomenon," and predicted he could turn into "an African-American politician who changes the nature of black politics, and American politics as well" (p. 101).

Within a week of Katrina and with the relief effort creaking into life, Obama made a speech, in which he addressed allegations that the laggardly response of FEMA was attributable to the concentration of stranded African Americans. "There's been much attention in the press about the fact that those who were left behind in New Orleans were disproportionately poor and African American," Obama remarked, adding a sentence that encapsulated ideals that would guide him to the presidency: "I do not subscribe to the notion that the painfully slow response of FEMA and the Department of Homeland Security was racially-based. The ineptitude was colorblind."

And thus Obama began to break with the shibboleths of black politicians, at the same time assuaging whites' remorse, as Eduardo Bonilla-Silva and David Dietrich explain in their 2011 article "The sweet enchantment of color-blind racism in Obamerica": "Unlike black leaders such as Jesse Jackson and Al Sharpton, he did not make them feel guilty about the state of racial affairs in the country" (p. 199).

Obama evacuated the potentially explosive race issue without defusing his own rhetoric on the necessity for change. But why did the "monumental change" have to involve putting a black man "in charge"? Unlike Bonilla-Silva and Dietrich, Shelby Steele believes whites already felt guilty and would have continued to feel this way with or without Obama. What's more, whites' persistent guilt was – and continued to be – a valuable resource. "Whites needed responsibility for our problems in order to gain their own moral authority and legitimacy," wrote Steele in his 2006 book *White Guilt* (p. 69).

Steele's argument runs as follows: over the decades, whites have been so obsessed with the virtues of owning up to the sins of history, they have actually become used to, even comfortable living with their own guilt and have learned to use it to their own advantage. Since when precisely? On Steele's account, the pangs started in the middle of the twentieth century.

On December 1, 1955, Rosa Parks refused to give up her bus seat to a white man in Montgomery, Alabama – an act that inspired the civil rights movement. Martin Luther King (1929-68) organized boycotts and led the opposition to discrimination against blacks. After nearly a decade of boycott and protests, the 1964 Civil Rights Act made racial discrimination in public places, such as theaters, restaurants and hotels, illegal. Among its other provisions was a requirement that employers provide equal employment opportunities. Steele lived through this. "I didn't understand at the time that it was precisely the fact that King had won America's acknowledgment of racism's evil that, in turn, made racism so valuable to blacks" (p. 35).

The ideological focus and direction of the post-civil rights era were unmistakable. The discriminatory laws that denied African Americans their rights as citizens were repealed after a torrid fight: those who fought for more enlightened legislation marched, rallied, sat down in protest, while police officers clubbed them with batons and let loose their dogs. After the tumult, white Americans' attempts to dissociate themselves from the racist past of their homeland took many forms, many of them tangible. Affirmative action, racial quotas and contract compliance were among the policy initiatives designed to give African Americans assistance. The post-civil rights respect for individual rights and freedoms was abandoned as white society endeavored to detach itself from a past pitted with slavery, segregation and all manner of subjugation – as well as an ill-judged war in Vietnam, which ended in 1973 and left 58,200 US soldiers and up to 250,000 South Vietnamese dead or missing in action. Steele writes of the quest for a "'dissociated man,' someone so conspicuously cleansed of racism, sexism and militarism that he would be a carrier of moral authority and legitimacy" (p. 150).

By the end of the century, the racist laws had gone and black people had progressed to all levels of society. Inequalities in employment, education, and housing indicated the persistence of racism, but remedies were nowhere near as obvious as they once were. The guilt shared by whites for the inhumanity and injustice of the past ensnared them in an obligation not to philosophical principles, but to black people – as a collectivity. Steele argues that whites' protracted attempt to dissociate themselves from America's shameful history has conferred on them a sense of moral authority.

There are profound implications for blacks. For Steele, African Americans, or at least some African Americans, became complicit in this enterprise, unwittingly aiding whites by accepting a role of intractable inferiority and trading with white guilt. While he doesn't include black celebrities in his arraignment, a case could be made. In one startling passage, Steele writes of how "even the most gifted and affluent blacks ... must pull on the Sambo mask and reinvent themselves as the sort of inferiors that will trade well with white guilt" (p. 134). In other words, whites license the liberties of black artists and entertainers, but only on strict conditions. This is a hefty proposition and I'll return to it. For now, I want to view the post-Katrina period through the lens of *White Guilt*, which was published a year after the hurricane but which makes no mention of the disaster.

Katrina issued an unwelcome reminder that, far from dissociating itself from the past, America – specifically, white America – was tormented by it. The hurricane, or more accurately the response to its calamitous effect, forced race back to the forefront of the popular imagination, though not in a straightforward way. "Mainstream America too often demonizes the Other because, well, we've been conditioned to do so," wrote Lynne Duke and Teresa Wiltz for the *Washington Post*, in 2005 (September 4). The Other, in this instance, refers to something that is distinct from or opposite to oneself. "And because it's easier to put people in a box and then shove it in the corner, away from view. Then it becomes *their* problem, not ours. To talk about race, for those who are weary of it, is to invite glazed-over eyes and stifled yawns – or even hostility. But Katrina blew open the box."

Linda Chavez, then president of the Center for Equal Opportunity and former head of the US Civil Rights Commission, came close to castigating the victims when she said: "This is a natural disaster that is exacerbated by the problems of the underclass. The chief cause of poverty today among blacks is no longer racism." Her reasoning was not unlike Steele's: "People who don't have jobs, are not used to getting up and organizing themselves and getting things done."

Sharing this perspective was African American actor Terrence Howard, who suggested that Katrina victims were accustomed to waiting for help rather than helping themselves (quoted by Yvonne Bynoe, in her 2005 article, "After Katrina – Is there justice or just us?").

By contrast, many agreed with Kanye West's crisp denunciation. Accusations of wantonness and indifference came from, among others, Radhika Parameswaran, who, in a scholarly article for the *Journal of Communication Inquiry*, argued that the catastrophe showed how "Dr Martin Luther King Jr.'s dream of economic and social justice for those living in the peripheries of American prosperity" had been "perverted" (p. 202).

Whatever absolution America earned, or thought it had earned, since the 1960s was thrown into doubt in the trail of Katrina. The race issue was renewed. In the 1960s, King's incomparable disquisitions on civil rights provided both analysis and program, and a Democratic administration (1917–63) led by a sympathetic John F. Kennedy was responsive. But, in the 2005, four decades after civil rights legislation, with a Republican government led by George W. Bush in power, there was no public figure with the visibility or gravitas to make credible pronouncements.

—

"Obama isn't black." A puzzling assessment, but one buttressed by Debra J. Dickerson in her 2007 article "Colorblind": "'Black,' in our political and social reality, means those descended from West African slaves. Voluntary immigrants of African descent (even those descended from West Indian slaves) are just that, voluntary immigrants of African descent with markedly different outlooks on the role of race in their lives and in politics."

Obama never claimed to be black; maybe his experience in the spring of 2000 taught him not to. Obama lost the Democratic nomination for a seat in United States House to incumbent Bobby L. Rush. It was a political miscalculation and perhaps a personal misjudgment. Obama's allies cautioned him about taking on incumbent congressman Rush, who had a stronghold on the South Side of Chicago, an area that was 65 percent black, overwhelmingly Democratic and solidly working class. Commenting on the election in winter 2000, the *Journal of Blacks in Higher Education* recorded the bare facts: "The district has been represented by a black congressman since 1928. Rush received the support of President Clinton and defeated Obama by a large margin" (p. 25).

Rush was born in Georgia, but had grown up in Chicago, enlisted in the Army, joined the Student Nonviolent Coordinating Committee and helped found the Illinois faction of the Black Panthers (originally, the Black Panther Party for Self-Defense) in 1968. The Black Panthers were established in Oakland, California in 1966, their aim being to patrol black ghettoes and protect residents from police brutality. Its creators, Huey P. Newton and Bobby Seales, urged members to arm themselves. In many senses, the Panthers were the yang to Martin Luther King's yin: they spurned the nonviolent disobedience favored by King. "We were reacting to police brutality, to the historical relationship between African-Americans and recalcitrant racist whites," Rush reflected. "We needed to arm ourselves."

Rush coordinated a medical clinic that pioneered mass screening for sickle cell anemia, which disproportionately affects blacks. In 1992, as an alderman, he had ousted Charles A. Hayes, a veteran of the civil rights and labor movements who was something of a political legend in Chicago. Yet Obama shrugged off Rush, claiming he represented "a politics that is rooted in the past, a reactive politics."

Obama, at 38, was 15 years younger than Rush, and had been in Chicago since his twenties after growing up in Hawaii and Indonesia. He worked as a community organizer on the South Side for three years, and then returned to the city after graduating from Harvard. He ran a voter registration drive, joined a law firm, taught constitutional law and had been elected to the state Senate from Hyde Park in 1996. The stinging defeat by Rush was the first reverse in a hitherto lustrous career. But a valuable reverse. Presumably, Obama was frustrated with his state Senate job and wanted to flex his muscles in the real political world. But, as Melissa Harris-Lacewell and Jane Junn wrote in their 2007 study "Old friends and new alliances": "Obama had faced serious racial credibility problems. In 2000, compared with Rush, he looked woefully 'inauthentic' racially" (p. 38).

Obama grew less concerned with "racial credibility" or "authenticity," and more concerned with broadening his appeal to all ethnic groups and across the class range. Harris-Lacewell and Junn call this "deracializing." It's possible that Obama could not find a grammar with which to communicate with black voters. Rush was well versed in this respect. In the aftermath of the election, Jenny Scott, of the *New York Times*, recorded Rush's perception of his rival. "Obama has never suffered from a lack of believing that he can accomplish whatever it is he decides to try," said Rush, stirring in a sardonic, "Obama believes in Obama" (September 9, 2000).

Scott also quoted Eric Edelstein, a media consultant who worked on the Rush campaign: "Certain Democrats in Chicago say it's the best thing that ever happened to him, not winning that race – that he couldn't have been positioned to run for the US Senate from that district ... you get pigeonholed pretty quickly as 'an African-American congressman,' not as a more transcendent congressman."

By this, Edelstein meant Obama intended to rise above, or cut across, ethnic groups. To win Chicago South Side, Obama would have had to work on expanding his support among blacks, including the older, church-going, Rush loyalists who vote disproportionately in primaries. Obama was struggling to find a place on a wider horizon and either couldn't or just didn't want to overdo his appeal to black voters in his bid for transcendence.

Five years later, just before Katrina arrived, it would have been possible to argue that racism had lost its convulsive potential. No one would seriously contend it was not still a fault line, a fracture across the surface of America.

But, after the Rodney King riots of 1992, there had been no major upheavals to occasion screaming headlines around the nation and, indeed, the world. Plus, there had been new arrivals at the top: Secretary of State Colin Powell and National Security Adviser Condoleezza Rice were key figures in the Republican cabinet. Black people had never had such a central role in policy-making and strategic political thinking.

Paradoxically, the attacks of September 11, 2001 had unleashed centripetal forces that thrust Americans of all backgrounds towards a common center. "Like an overwhelming majority of Americans, blacks reacted to the heinous crime of September 11 with outrage and demands for revenge against those behind it," wrote Mali Micah, of *Green Left Weekly* (February 20, 2002). "They backed Bush's new 'war on terrorism' and joined in flag-waving and other outward signs of patriotism that have become common place across the country."

A *New York Times*/CBS News poll in three months after 9/11 found three-quarters of African Americans supported the war on terrorism. Blacks became more self-consciously American: much-quoted immediately after the attack was the "I've never felt so American" proclamation of African Americans. Reports of the Stars and Stripes flying in the hood were commonplace. Coinciding with this was a change in the accent of racial profiling – Muslims, or persons who appeared to be Muslim, becoming targets.

Evidence of a nascent consciousness lay in the silence: there were few, if any incidents to compare with the litany of racial episodes leading up to the King riots: the beating of King himself in 1991, the Central Park jogger case of 1989, and the Tawana Brawley hoax of 1987, to name but three. Steele wrote of whites: "They struggle, above all, to dissociate themselves from the past sins they are stigmatized with" (appendix, p. 6). But this seemed less of a struggle, more a painless separation.

Then came Hurricane Katrina. It issued a reminder that America's race issue had been obscured and, to repeat Jason DeParle, laid bare the racial and class divide of contemporary America. Obama, by then a Democratic senator, was beginning to emerge as a possible candidate for the presidency. He had rebounded from his defeat by Rush and, far from narrowing his appeal, had remained vigilantly free of any trace of factionalism. This made him unique, as Charlton D. McIlwain recognized in his 2007 article "Perceptions of leadership and the challenge of Obama's blackness": "Obama has been distinguished from previous Black candidates such as Jesse Jackson and Shirley Chisholm, and others because of his firm support among African Americans and his broad appeal to White Americans, and his message and approach, which, different from the others, is not premised on the pursuit of racial group interests" (p. 64).

———

Theodore Cross, the editor of the *Journal of Blacks in Higher Education*, cast his publication's vote for presidency in an article "Barack Obama is the superior choice for African-American voters" and, in one evocative passage, suggested: "After the long nightmare years of slavery, lynchings, Jim Crow, and enduring race discrimination, one would expect that, in the upcoming presidential primary contest, Illinois Senator Barack Obama would be the overwhelming choice of black American voters" (p. 68).

Despite Cross's expectation, "the first broad discussion of the 'race issue' was not whether white Americans would accept Obama as an African-American president but if blacks would," as Michael C. Moynihan pointed out in his review "A transformation on race."

In summer 2007, Hillary Rodham Clinton and Obama were neck-and-neck in the contest for the Democratic presidential nomination and there was a genuine possibility that a black man or indeed a woman could become president. But Hillary was holding her own among African Americans. Her husband Bill Clinton, who served as 42nd president (1993–2001), had wooed black voters and was memorably described by Toni Morrison in 1998 as "our first black president. Blacker than any actual black person who could ever be elected in our children's lifetime."

Hillary had earned the endorsement of Morrison, along with that of other influential black figures, including Quincy Jones, Robert L. Johnson, and Maya Angelou. So, when the opportunity to introduce race into the political discourse presented itself, Hillary accepted the invitation. "There are no qualms about playing the race card," judged Cross at the time (p. 68).

During a debate on health care at Howard University, Washington DC, in June 2007, Hillary contended: "If HIV/AIDS were the leading cause of death of white women between the ages of 25 and 34, there would be an outraged outcry in this country." (At the time, the rate of new HIV infection for black women was nearly 15 times as high as that of white women and HIV/Aids was a leading cause of death of African-American women. It remains so.)

"The powerful political impact of her statement was not diminished by the circumstance that her facts were incorrect," Cross soberly reported, pointing out that, a year before, "Clinton was the only one of 20 senators of the Senate Health, Education, and Labor Committee to vote to gut a plan that would have redirected more AIDS funds to mostly black communities in the South" (pp. 68-69).

Obama didn't rise to what some might have considered bait, and Hillary's credibility among blacks strengthened. Obama's studious refusal to allow ethnically specific issues to affect his broad-brush approach won him applause from whites. But, as a black candidate, it was inevitable that he would, at some point, face a typically unpredictable issue over race. This was delivered courtesy of Obama's one-time pastor, Rev. Jeremiah A. Wright Jr., who, following the 9/11 in attacks in 2001, had paraphrased Malcolm X: "America's chickens are coming home to roost." His words insinuated retributive justice for the evils practiced on blacks by whites. In a later sermon, he referred to the USA's complicity in a genocidal program targeting African Americans with the Aids virus, and finished with: "*God damn America*, as long as she tries to act like she is God, and she is supreme. The United States government has failed the vast majority of her citizens of African descent."

Wright, a charismatic church leader from the fire and brimstone school, was an incendiary and unapologetic critic of American values and practices, especially in regard to blacks who had been treated as "less than human." In Wright's worldview, the US was treacherous, venal and endemically racist. His church was in Chicago's South Side (where Obama had met his first political setback, remember). Obama had been a church member and spiritual mentee of Wright for 20 years. When American news organizations explored the relationship between Wright and Obama, they discovered an uncomfortable closeness between the man Obama likened to an uncle and who had performed the Obamas' marriage ceremony and the prospective president.

Initial attempts to put distance between Obama's own political beliefs and Wright's seemed ineffective and Obama faced Hillary's shot: "You don't choose your family, but you choose what church you want to attend." For a while it must have seemed like Obama's own chickens were coming home. His otherwise surefooted avoidance – or transcendence – of the race issue could have had woeful consequences. In the event, the Wright contretemps was alchemized into precious metal.

Under pressure, Obama, on March 18, 2008, delivered arguably his most powerful address to date. He opened with words extracted from the Preamble to the United States Constitution, "We the people, in order to make a more perfect union," and went on to chronicle his own interconnected ethnic heritage: "I am the son of a black man from Kenya and a white woman from Kansas." Then he moved to his personal progress: "I've gone to some of the best schools in America and lived in one of the world's poorest nations." In an inspired and redolent passage, with a sure nod to his African American doubters, Obama reminded his audience: "I am married to a black American who carries within her the blood of slaves and slaveowners – an inheritance we pass on to our two precious daughters."

The repudiation was as unexpected and as startling as a thunderclap: "Reverend Wright's comments were not only wrong but divisive, divisive at a time when we need unity; racially charged at a time when we need to come together to solve a set of monumental problems." Followed by a proviso: "I can no more disown him than I can disown the black community." An intellectual curvet: "It's a racial stalemate we've been stuck in for years ... working together we can move beyond some of our old racial wounds." And a gentle swipe at older blacks, whose primary allegiances were forged in the 1960s: "We have no choice if we are to continue on the path of a more perfect union. For the African American community, that path means embracing the burdens of our past without becoming victims of our past" (full text at: http://on.msnbc.com/-MorePerfectUnion).

The speech was a tour de force. Of that there is no doubt. But was Obama baring his soul, as the *New York Times* editorial of March 19, 2008, conjectured? Or was he orchestrating a favorable response from the media and, indeed, the voters? The stage-management, the movement, position and tone could not have been better. It was a speech calculated to assuage the fears of blacks and palliate the nervousness of whites.

———

David Bradley, in a 2010 review "Misreading Obama," reflected on the multiplex impact of Obama's ascent. "To some, it was the realization of Martin Luther King Jr.'s not-by-the-color-of-their-skin-but-by-the-content-of-their-character Dream," Bradley began. "To others, it was the actualization of J. Edgar Hoover's creeping-philosophical-communist nightmare." And: "To some, it was an international relations marketing coup 'redefining the American "brand"'" (p. 91). Or maybe the Obama brand. Recall Bobby Rush's verdict from a decade before: "Obama believes in Obama."

What did Rush mean exactly? If he had added "… for Obama," an inference could be drawn, though it would be harsh – and, in 2000, premature – to sneer at an ambitious politician's self-serving streak. He could have been referring to Obama's self-confidence, which was abundant even at the start of the millennium. Or perhaps his comment was a sly exposition, the meaning of which becomes clear if we punctuate it thus: Obama believes in "Obama."

All politicians sell wares, by which I mean goods, articles, services, commodities, even if they are designed and packaged as ideas, policies, programs and the other staples with which they trade. Often, their most valuable wares are their personae, those aspects of their character that are presented and perceived by others. Obama was selling a new configuration, an arrangement of familiar elements in an unfamiliar form: a black politician who defied the usual color-coding. Who had interests in housing, education, crime, transportation and the economy as they affect everybody. Who refused to address the African American population as a homogeneous entity with unchanging interests. Who hadn't risen from the pulpit, earned his stripes in the struggles of the 1960s and purported to speak for all black people. Did this make him a brand?

Certainly some critics believed so. Of them, Christopher Hedges was one of the most scathing. Writing not so much a critique as a dismissal in the Jewish magazine *Tikkun*, Hedges proclaimed: "Brand Obama is about being happy consumers. We are entertained. We feel hopeful" (p. 33).

A brand is, of course, a type of product, manufactured for a market under a specific name. "Like all branded products spun out from the manipulative world of corporate advertising," writes Hedges, "this product is duping us into doing and supporting a lot of things that are not in our interest." Leaving aside for the moment what Hedges assumes is in "our" (by which I presume he means either all his readers, or, more probably, everyone) interest, there is a rational argument underlying the bluster. It is: "Brand Obama offers us an image that appears radically individualistic and new. It inoculates us from seeing that the old engines of corporate power and the vast military-industrial complex continue to plunder the country" (p. 33).

True, Obama rhapsodized over values which emphasized the agency, or potency of the individual in controlling destiny; he also championed initiative, self-reliance and responsibility – exactly the qualities that would encourage blacks to stop thinking of themselves as passive victims, or as vindictive nuisances, or as self-righteous gatekeepers of history. They were values adopted and embraced by the black bourgeoisie. Obama was no doubt mindful that almost 37 percent of black families fell into one of the three top income quintiles (i.e. the five equal groups into which a population can be divided) at the time of his political endeavors, compared with 23 percent in 1971 – the year, incidentally, in which Jesse Jackson established his People United to Save Humanity (later changed from "Save" to "Serve"), or PUSH, an organization "dedicated to improving the economic conditions of black communities across the United States."

Obama never actually said: "I never felt entitled to anything because I was black," but it was implicit in his brand, if we continue with Bradley's and Hedge's simile. That was certainly part of the brand image. He may have been a beneficiary of affirmative action, a key policy that involves preferential selection based on ethnicity and gender; but, on page 246 of his 2007 book *The Audacity of Hope: Thoughts on reclaiming the American Dream,* he damns the policy with faint praise: "A useful if limited tool to expand the opportunity to underrepresented minorities." (I'd add that, if Obama gained admission to Harvard courtesy of such a program, he surely offers living evidence of its effectiveness.)

The position on affirmative action was part of the new configuration and, in effect, part of the new product brand Obama offered for sale. It infuriated the likes of Jackson, who extended his well-documented catalog of gaffes by accusing Obama of "talking down to black people" and expressing a desire to separate him from his manhood. Ironically, criticism like this burnished Obama's appeal. "For a lot of younger African-Americans, the resistance of the civil rights generation to Obama's candidacy signified the failure of their parents to come to terms, at the dusk of their lives, with the success of their own struggle," discerned Matt Bail, in his "Is Obama the end of black politics?" The new struggle is "to embrace the idea that black politics might now be disappearing into American politics."

Bail expands his point: "For black Americans born in the 20th century, the chasms of experience that separate one generation from the next – those who came of age before the movement, those who lived it, those who came along after – have always been hard to traverse." It's an arresting metaphor: a chasm, or gulf, with veterans of the civil rights era standing on one side gawping incredulously at young celebrity aficionados and hip-hop fans sneering with affected arrogance and glorying in black signifiers – like jewelry, guns and canerows – that get procured by whites.

Remember: Obama's surge to power came in the post-Katrina period, a period of history marked by notable events and turning-points. As Michael Ralph understates in his *Public Culture* article in 2009: "Katrina inspired renewed discussion about what it meant to be African American" (p. 355). Even allowing for Steele's understanding of whites' "contrition and deference" and the historical power of white guilt, there is a sense in which absolution-of-sorts was in sight. Racism looked like old news: black, white and other ethnic groups seemed to have brokered a cultural rapprochement. Racial lines had softened. Katrina delivered a discomfiting dig in the ribs. The racism that progress was thought to have left behind was still lurking. Even if it appeared a flicker of a once-fearsome historical force, it warranted attention.

Obama's rise illustrates a major confluence of history and personality, a phrase I adapt from C. Wright Mills' "intersection of history and biography" to suggest how individual lives are shaped by historical circumstances and history is changed by individuals (p. 7). Obama was a very much product of his own time and, in turn, he affected that time. His public emergence at a time in history when America had been forcibly reminded that traces of the racism of yore remained was, in its way, serendipitous. The white guilt described by Steele as "one of the greatest social, cultural, and political forces in all of American history," and which had been dissipating, became dense after Katrina. Obama was cut from a different cloth from the older-generation black leaders. But he was black and he was a leader. And he did have something to sell.

Obama may not have been the man to purge America of its last vestiges of racism. But, brand Obama was a symbol of purification.

4

If Oprah can make it, what does it say about me?

'Oprah's incessant stress on individual aspiration and self-reliance has endeared her to vast audiences. It's as if she has prodded black people and asked them: "Why wait for society to help you when you can help yourself?" '

Most celebrity endorsements go in one ear and out of the other without pausing at synapses. Would anyone rush out to buy Rich Prosecu, a canned champagne-like drink, because Paris Hilton gave it her seal of approval (even if she was naked when giving her assent)? David Beckham, probably this century's most formidable pitchman, can move razors and sports gear off shelves, but could he change our spending habits when it comes to felt tip marker pens? There are limits. Well, for most people, there are. Only one can incite the Oprah Effect.

"Oprah Winfrey can get people to read Tolstoy, sell millions of magazines and turn a mail-order canvas bag into a hot item just by naming it one of her favorite things," observed Martha T. Moore, of *USA Today* (October 22, 2007). She's also helped sales of certain brands of popcorn, soap, reading tablets and dozens of other consumer items – not by appearing in advertisements, but just by mentioning them as among her favorite things. Jordan McAuley and Susan Harrow have even written a marketing guide with the prescriptive title *How to Get Booked on Oprah, in O Magazine, and on Oprah's Favorite Things.*

But could Oprah sell a president? Oprah, who for years had been a close friend of the emerging Illinois senator, reaffirmed her support for Obama's presidential candidacy during an interview on CNN's *Larry King Live* in March 2007. It was the first time that Oprah had endorsed – not to mention thrown her brand behind – a political candidate. By fall 2007, she had helped raise $3 million for the campaign. Obama was chipping away at the lead of Hillary Clinton in the polls for the Democratic nomination. Endorsements didn't guarantee votes, of course: at the time, *USA Today* reported: "More than six in 10 adults say endorsements aren't that important in deciding whom they'll support for president" (October 22, 2007).

Even so, there is this cliché they use in business circles about the power of synergy. You don't have to believe that the interaction of two or more agents produces a combined effect greater than the sum of their separate effects to realize that Oprah+Obama made a convincing, synergistic unit. Oprah's segue into politics – and I mean segue, i.e. an uninterrupted transition – happened over a period of time, though her "We *need* Barack Obama" speech at Des Moines, Iowa on December 8, 2007 was pivotal.

"I am not here to tell you how to think," she told the 10,000-strong crowd. "I am here to tell you *to* think." Distancing herself from partisan politics, she reminded the audience that she had voted Republican as many times as she had Democrat and that her conviction was personal. "I feel compelled to stand up and speak out for the man who I believe has a new vision for America." Oprah scattered references to "American Idol" and "Dancing with the Stars," and even jokingly reflected on whether she would have the same effect on politics as her book selections and "favorite things." But any hint of trivialization was removed by a closing reference to Ernest J. Gainer's 1971 novel *The Autobiography of Miss Jane Pittman,* which tells the life-story of a woman born in slavery at the end of the civil war. The book recounts how each time a new baby was born, its mother would take it to Jane Pittman, who would hold the baby John the Baptist-like and wonder aloud whether the child would be the deliverer of black people: "Is you the one?" Oprah polished the grammar, changed the context and answered affirmatively that Obama was indeed The One.

Oprah's forceful endorsement was less like one person's approving another; more like Apple admiring and applauding Rolex – a brand recommending another brand. If she was as uncertain of the true power of her endorsement as she said, she would have seen tangible evidence over the months that followed: Obama was elected president in November 2008. The Oprah Effect seemed every bit as puissant as the Midas Touch.

What exactly did Oprah add to the Obama brand? In fact, what does any celebrity with no political experience add to the campaigns of aspiring politicians? Rajan Nataraajan and Sushi Chawla's 1997 study was about "fitness" – not, in this instance, the condition of being physically healthy, but the suitability to fulfill a particular role, or task. Although the research was about the suitability of celebrities to endorse commercial products, their conclusion is relevant: source credibility sits at the top of a hierarchy of properties that affect whether consumers will take notice of the endorser. Credibility is, according to the researchers, a "multidimensional variable," the main dimensions being "expertise, trustworthiness, and attractiveness" (p. 120).

Michael Basil's earlier research in 1996 uncovered another factor: "Identification occurs when an individual adopts an attitude or behavior from another person when that attitude or behavior is associated with a satisfying self-defining relationship with that person" (p. 479). In other words, buying something (or presumably voting for someone) "being advocated by that celebrity can be seen as a way of 'hitching your wagon to the star.'"

Hillary sought credibility when she recruited former senator George McGovern, who ran for president on an anti-war platform in 1972. McGovern was, she speculated, trusted. Hillary was trying to convince voters she would end the Iraq war. Republican John McCain, a former Vietnam prisoner of war, who was basing his appeal to voters on his military and national security credentials, was supported by four former secretaries of state including Henry Kissinger, as well as several retired generals in Iowa. Expertise was the valuable resource.

Oprah couldn't legitimately boast experience or, for that matter, credibility – at least not political credibility. She did, however, have other properties. For instance, she was attractive: not in the sense of being overtly sexually alluring, but she had beneficial qualities or features that induced her followers to accept whatever she offered. And people certainly associated with her and the causes she pursued, and perhaps more importantly regarded themselves as sharing similar characteristics or styles of thinking. In other words, they identified with her in the manner Basil's research indicated was important – adopting attitudes.

So what Oprah lacked in credibility, she more than made up for in identification. This still doesn't tell us why she worked so effectively for Obama. Jib Fowles provides a clue. "As the star's image cycles back into popular culture, it does so with the new accretions of inferences from the commercial detour," wrote Fowles in his 1996 book *Advertising and Popular Culture* (p. 131). On this account, there is a kind a feedback loop in which qualities acquired in one medium transfer to another, which then transfer back and so on. The very fact of Oprah's appearing in a political campaign added new properties to her persona and enhanced her reputation, which then transferred to Obama. Rather like the process of osmosis. Oprah became more magisterial, while Obama gained respect and the warm approval of Oprah's countless followers.

———

Let me save space: CNN, Fox News, *Time Magazine*, *USA Today*, and umpteen other media have decided that Oprah is the most influential woman of the past quarter-decade. When *Vanity Fair* concluded she has more influence than any "politician, or religious leader, except perhaps the Pope," it should have reflected on the fact that there are only about 1.14 billion Roman Catholics in the world.

The woman who elicits these acknowledgments was born, perhaps not entirely adventitiously – who knows? – in 1954, the year of the historic Brown vs. Board of Education decision that ended legal segregation in public schools. She lived on a farm in Kosciusko, Mississippi (population: 7,372) with her grandmother until aged six, when she moved to Milwaukee to be with her mother. Here she was sexually abused by several relations and friends, an experience she was later to disclose in front of tv cameras. An unruly adolescent, she was sent to live in Nashville with her disciplinarian father, Vernon, who instructed her to read one book per week. He also taught her the value of individual advancement. At a time when many were proposing the historical, ethnic and cultural oneness of black people and the urgent need to unify, Oprah opted to pursue a more solitary venture.

Aged 14, Oprah gave birth to a premature baby, who died shortly afterward. Under the tutelage of her dad, she studied diligently and began to entertain ambitions of a career in journalism. Her first job was at radio WVOL, "Nashville's Heritage station," as it describes itself. At 19, she moved to television at WTVF-TV and built a reputation as a reporter and news anchor. Three years later, she was offered a job as co-anchor at the Baltimore tv station WJZ-TV. *People Are Talking* was a daytime talkshow that effectively showcased Oprah's distinct style of interviewing.

In 1984, Oprah switched to another talkshow, this time WLS-TV's *AM Chicago*, which was changed to *The Oprah Winfrey Show* and, in 1986, went national. The program moved to the epicenter of popular entertainment and remained there for 25 years – and 4,000 shows. Its highlights included Michael Jackson's response to the question, "is your skin lighter because you don't want to be black?" in 1983, Tom Cruise's manic cavorting in 2005, and Whitney Houston discussing her drugs of choice (crack "leveled off with marijuana") in 2009. By the time of the last show in 2011, Oprah's personal wealth was estimated at $2.7 billion.

Television talkshows used to be little different from radio interviews, with hosts asking the questions and guests answering them. Oprah, whether by design or just impromptu, changed this format. Her interviews were chats, relaxed conversations between two friends, often about matters that would, at the time, qualify as personal, if not intimate. It was as if Oprah was inviting viewers to become innocent eavesdroppers. When she talked to the camera, it was not as a tv host but as a confidante, someone with whom they could share a secret and trust them not to repeat it. These stylistic features are commonplace today, but in the 1980s they were innovations that were perfectly in sync with wider cultural shifts. I'll write more about these shifts later, but suffice it to say for now, that they involved public figures appearing less exceptional, more ordinary.

Oprah's ordinariness was palpable: viewers didn't so much watch but shared in her discussions of sex abuse, addictions and infidelity. They participated in her reuniting with long-lost family members and former schoolteachers. Many lived vicariously through Oprah's attempts to diet her way to a svelte body, before just giving in to nature. And countless viewers were emboldened to make new starts, especially after hearing her wax psychologically about the limitless power of the individual.

Oprah used her early success on tv to leverage several business enterprises: her Harpo Productions (spell Oprah backwards) in 1988 took full charge of the show. By the late 1990s, the company had annual revenues of about $150 million with about 200 employees. *O, The Oprah Magazine* started in 2000; its circulation is now around 2.4 million. It was in this period that the Oprah Effect, or the O-Factor, came into force: there was nothing, it seemed, she couldn't do. She even appeared in Steven Spielberg's film of Alice Walker's book *The Color Purple*, in 1985.

Presumably emboldened by her early success, Oprah ventured into dangerous territory. For example, in 1987, she filmed an item in Forsyte County, Georgia, where there had been no black residents since 1912 when three black men, all of whom were hanged, allegedly raped a white teenager. Oprah's bold attempt to assess the mood of the people made for challenging television. Her 16 million viewers daily were testimony to this. Capitalizing on her audience, she ran book clubs and consumer products recommendations, converting sometimes obscure titles or little-known commodities into bestsellers.

In a memorable show in 1996, Oprah examined the then panic-inducing mad cow disease (bovine spongiform encephalopathy, or BSE) and announced that the scare had stopped her eating burgers. The stock market took note and the cattle-feeding industry lost an estimated $87.6 million in days. Cattle producers filed suit against Oprah for false disparagement, though a jury eventually found in favor of Oprah.

The risk-taking element of capitalism was never more evident in Oprah than when she took the enormous professional gamble of launching her own cable television station, OWN: Oprah Winfrey Network in 2010. It was a novel idea: an entire tv channel built on the brand of a single personality. The fare was anything but novel, comprising reality, food, health and self-help shows. The British *Guardian* columnist Hadley Freeman pointed out, "it is arguably precisely this kind of soupy self-help that made Winfrey's talkshow look increasingly dated" (December 31, 2010). By the time of the final Oprah show, its audience had fallen to seven million, under half its peak.

Part-owned by Discovery Communications, the cable channel had unimpressive audience figures initially, and, on closing her Chicago-based show, Oprah moved to Los Angeles to take a more active role in running the network.

———

For the first few years of her striking rise in popularity, Oprah was *noli me tangere* – someone who couldn't be touched, less still criticized. Her nightmare childhood behind her, Oprah had bootstrapped her way through America's social order, defying all her putative impediments. But in 1989, Barbara Grizzuti Harrison raised doubts about the purpose and intent of Oprah.

"The importance of being Oprah" was one of the (if not, the) first critical evaluations of someone who, by 1989, was approaching icon status; "an Horatio Alger for our times," as Grizzuti Harrison called her. Was she a "role model for black women?" Oprah rejected both descriptions. Grizzuti Harrison quoted her "born-again capitalist" response to bellyaching African Americans: "A black person has to ask herself, 'If Oprah Winfrey can make it, what does it say about me?' They no longer have an excuse" (p. 130).

If *they* no longer have an excuse for failing to advance, what were whites supposed to get out of Oprah's excursions into sensitive areas, particularly race? "Oprah Winfrey has always promised her guests ... the opportunity for them to 'release the guilt.' And she promises audiences the opportunity to 'see themselves in others' so as to sidestep guilt," was Grizzuti Harrison's answer (p. 134).

Grizzuti Harrison points out that "exploring people's feelings ... is not equivalent to changing them. There are no guaranteed and automatic epiphanies" (p. 134). "We are encouraged to believe we are doing something, embroiled in something; whereas in fact we are coddled in our passivity" (p. 134). Oprah allows "audiences to feel superior to blatant, uneducated racists, while cherishing their own insidious subtle racism" (p. 134).

By watching Oprah and sharing in her disgust, anger or whatever emotion she expresses, whites could find comfort and assuage their guilt, while blacks could remind themselves that the racist barriers were largely illusory. From this perspective, Oprah expedited the "dissociation from past sins" that Shelby Steele believes is central to the post-civil rights experience. Oprah's greatest service was to penitential whites.

In this early critique, nothing is as it appears: Oprah offered an inauthentic "salve to whites' burdened consciences," and a "quick fix" that provided a temporary feeling of contentment; one that became addictive in the years that followed.

Grizzuti Harrison's article was published in 1989, remember. Denzel Washington was picking up an Oscar for his role as a runaway slave in the civil war drama *Glory. Driving Miss Daisy*, in which Morgan Freeman played a chauffeur to an elderly Jewish woman, was winning the best picture award, and Spike Lee's account of inter-ethnic tensions in Brooklyn, *Do the Right Thing*, heralded a wave of cinematic portraits of the ghettos. On tv, *The Cosby Show*, then in its fifth year, was all-conquering, and *Miami Vice*, which featured a partnership between a black and a white detective, was in its designer pomp. Michael Jordan was treading his immaculate path to sports consecration, while Mike Tyson was still a few years away from damnation.

Miss You Much by Janet Jackson, then rivaling her brother in record sales (this alone sold 4 million copies), was dominating charts all over the world, and Madonna's scandalous good-and-evil video *Like a Prayer* proved to be a gamechanger – it was a cultural item that symbolized a change in the way consumers thought and felt about famous people. I'll explain the reasoning in detail later: for now, let me pull one more quotation from Grizzuti Harrison's evaluation of Oprah: "There appears to be no membrane between the private person and the public persona" (pp. 30 & 46).

Like Madonna, Oprah had no truck with the old-style division of public and private selves that had been carefully constructed by the Hollywood film industry, which jealously guarded the stars' personal lives. Oprah opened-up to audiences – she had no inhibitions about revealing her childhood molestation, for example – and urged audiences to be just as revelatory. Vicki Abt and

Mel Sheesholtz addressed some of the implications: "*Exploitation, voyeurism, peeping Toms, freak shows* all come to mind" (p. 182).

The characterization doesn't sound fierce today, when practically every talkshow is, in some measure, an exploitatively and voyeuristically arranged event, featuring people whose personal lives are made available for public inspection. From the vantage point of 1994 when Abt and Sheesholtz were writing (and when, incidentally, Oprah's annual income was already $146 million, more than either Michael Jackson or Bill Cosby earned), shows such as Oprah's were a "vulgarized version of traditional psychotherapy ... where strangers get to watch and listen to hideous confessions and confrontations" (p. 184).

Stripped out of the discussion are "real contexts of time, place, history, biography and moral judgment" (p. 187). How Abt and Sheesholtz missed all the platititudinizing, we'll never know; but they had a point about the absence of contexts. They took issue with Oprah's focus on "the atomistic individual" and her "search for personal satisfaction, good feelings, freedom from blame, shame or social responsibility" (p. 176).

Abt and Sheesholtz gave an example of an 11-year-old boy on the show who blew the whistle on his drug-user mother and her partner. Oprah's "constant badgering" of the boy "further exploits and exacerbates the family's pain" (p. 188). Abt and Sheesholtz could have wondered out loud what the boy was doing on the show in the first place. This is admittedly not a strong example, though, and it does illustrate the questionable curative aspect of Oprah and, more importantly, the deceptively attractive, but misleading, philosophy being promulgated.

Oprah is hardly likely to turn to her audience and thunder: "You're not here for the contextual or any other kind of analysis, 'cause there really isn't any. You're unrepentant, philistine voyeurs, who derive pleasure from others' misfortunes." She's more likely to point her finger and remind her audience, "Pay attention: this could be you." She promotes a worldview in which individuals are independent, self-reliant and capable of changing themselves. That applies not just to people on the show, but to everyone watching. Perhaps this isn't so misleading, after all. But it does simplify the power of other people, circumstances and institutions to licence or restrict individual freedoms; and it does eliminate the role of history in influencing how freedom is distributed. For example, in discussing racism, Oprah takes the individualist approach "by defining racism as a psychological 'illness' for which individuals, and, by extension, society need 'healing,'" wrote Janice Peck in her "Talk about race" article (p. 100). "Subjective rather than objective change." (It's almost possible to imagine Oprah sitting next to former British Prime Minister Margaret Thatcher, saying: "You were right: there is no such thing as society.")

Racial issues are not blotted out; far from it. Oprah's treatment or interpretation of racism implicates everyone either in or watching the show in a self-examination. The frequently painful excavation of other people's lives and Oprah's own reminders of her lamentable past ensured that the show never flinched.

In every respect, Oprah became the personification of her own philosophy. A rugged individualist who not only preached but practiced self-help, she began as survivor and continued that way, adapting to her changing environments. As Patricia J. Williams commented in her 2007 article "The audacity of Oprah": "Oprah reinvented herself by sheer will and rose against all odds to the very top of the phantasmagorical bubble machine we call the entertainment industry" (p. 8).

While Oprah didn't openly espouse the "lifting as we climb" maxim of the National Association of Colored Woman, she clearly practiced something similar, helping others to help themselves. There is much to admire in this stance. Much to criticize too: opprobrium has multiplied in recent years. One of the sharper censures is Tarshia L. Stanley's "The specter of Oprah Winfrey," which argues that, in her passion to extol the virtues of individualism, Oprah just hasn't grasped the limits of self-improvement. "Although it is true that we are all responsible for ourselves, it is also true that there are real and inherent hurdles in society that effectively work to thwart the efforts and undo the bootstraps of certain individuals as they attempt to struggle upwards" (p. 47).

Many share the sentiments: Oprah's conception of racism is similar to Robert Johnson's – like rain. The instruction is not to stay indoors or gripe about the bad weather, but to grab an umbrella and get on with life. For some, this makes Oprah a symbol of conservatism. "She can never admit the need for systematic structural change and collective political activity," grumbles Dana L. Cloud (p. 129).

Maybe Oprah doesn't "admit" it because she identifies the individual rather than the collectivity as the catalyst of change. If so, she invites a related criticism, this time from Valerie Palmer-Mehta: "By favoring the individual over the social, Winfrey is not only acquiescing to the status quo but also promoting it" (p. 73).

To repeat an earlier point, Oprah coddles consumers into passivity, but not inertia: people are encouraged to recognize some of the more unpleasant and disagreeable aspects of American society and work toward changing them. It's how Oprah's philosophy translates into action that's drawn the fire of recent critics.

—

Oprah implores her followers to remake themselves, not the world around them. Critics may thrust their fingers in their mouths and pretend to be sick when they hear her entreaty "dream it, do it," but Oprah's incessant stress on individual aspiration and self-reliance has endeared her to vast audiences. It's as if she has prodded black people and asked them: "Why wait for society to help you when you can help yourself?" Or: "Why waste effort trying to move mountains when you can move your own butt?" Oprah didn't ask these exact questions, but the inquiry is implicit in everything she's done as a public figure.

This is an enormously convenient motif, politically speaking. It discourages the type of mentality that fed black political alliances of the 1950s and 1960s; movements that eventually changed America's social landscape. Individuals acting *ad hominem* couldn't have done this. It averts the kind of thought promoted by radical Black Power activists, such as Eldridge Cleaver (1935–98), who identified white-dominated institutions as the causes of blacks' subordination. And it most definitely deflects any philosophy resembling that of the Nation of Islam, which saw all whites as incorrigibly evil and insisted on a separation of all black people from whites. Oprah's politics, such as they were, were based on practical rather than moral or ideological considerations. Obviously, time changes the direction of political winds.

It's also convenient in a different, more disguised way. For Timothy Aubry, there is "a paradoxical double gesture" at work. Aubry means that, by engaging with Oprah's show and her various other enterprises, whites familiarize themselves with and immerse themselves in the travails of black people, investigating, commiserating, even empathizing. "Employing a liberal ethos of individualism [whites] can deny the barrier of racial difference in order to identify with black characters," writes Aubry in his 2006 article, "Beware the furrow of the middlebrow: Searching for paradise on the *Oprah Winfrey Show*" (p. 362).

This has an ideological suasion: it permits a miniaturization of racism, reducing its scale to insignificance. It also raises doubts about the potency or even virtue of measures intended to benefit black people. Why have affirmative action or related policies, when racism has almost disappeared and the only thing holding black people back is themselves?

We saw in chapter 1 how Earl Ofari Hutchinson suggests how Tiger Woods has been fabricated as "final proof that America is a colorblind society." He might suggest that Oprah was first evidence. Certainly, she offers a kind of narrative, a visible account of connected events, each leading to her present exaltedness. When Oprah urges individuals to take control of their individual lives, or control their own destinies, she isn't issuing maxims: she backs up her claims with her own story, demonstrating that everything she preaches, she has practiced. In this sense, she is functioning, circulating proof that the racism remaining in America is annoying, but not necessarily deleterious.

Palmer-Mehta goes even further, arguing that Oprah's effect is "to place the blame for problems such as poverty and crime on individual failings" (p. 75). So, the only impediments to attaining the goal, or the "dream," are individual weaknesses. Malin Pereira believes there is even a strategy designed to protect this ideal from errant attacks. Her detailed inspection of Oprah's book club concludes that some of the literature reviewed was critical and occasionally troublesome to contain in the framework of the tv show. "The narrative of possessive individualism that sustains the idea of the American Dream as accessible is increasingly challenged," wrote Pereira, who argues that skilful editing served to "evacuate or suppress" critical elements. In effect, the book club delegitimized critical evaluation of America.

On these accounts, Oprah and the order she personifies help perpetuate a popular impression of America as inclusive, embracing a multitude of ethnic groups, respecting difference and diversity and relentless in its effort to eradicate racism. She personally attests to its success in this effort and confirms that, if traces of prejudice still exist, they are like revenants – returning from the dead. If blacks continue to underachieve, it is their own fault. I repeat: this has ideological suasion. Even if you don't accept Steele's thesis in *White Guilt*, you can understand the concept that propels his argument: whites of whatever generation are reminded daily of their connivance in a great historical abomination. Oprah's presence, her life story and her messages help assuage the shame associated with this.

Where is the method, then? We can respect the force of Oprah's overall narrative: everyone can dream, everyone can follow that dream, everyone can overcome what remnants of racism are left behind in the trail of civil rights. We can appreciate the guiding philosophy that individuals are makers of their own destinies and, as such, shouldn't succumb to any kind of theory, metaphysical or sociological, that suggests there are forces compelling us to think and act in certain ways. And we can acknowledge that individuals work best when they work as individuals, each with their own identity, and not as anonymous members of groups, movements or other kinds of collectivities. This is all part of the realization or fulfillment of one's talents and potentialities that Oprah encourages us all to pursue – self-actualization. But again, where is the method?

In the Introduction to their book *The Oprah Phenomenon*, Jennifer Harris and Elwood Watson offer an answer: "Winfrey links the need to value oneself with the consumption of goods." They go on: "This message of uplift via consumption is ... if I am self-actualized and work hard, good things will come to me" (p. 8).

The argument echoes the one I will convey in subsequent chapters: that African American celebrities, wittingly or not, advance the intoxicating prospect that a particular form of the good life is available to all. It is an admittedly narrow conception of the good life, one based on the value of commodities. But Oprah both lives it and embodies it. She lays the scent of consumerism and her acolytes follow it.

Buying products, especially ones that radiate success, is a way of asserting one's own worth in a way that, as Harris and Watson put it, "proclaims taste and sentiment." And perhaps in a way that proclaims racism has been, if not defeated, then bypassed, dodged or in some way got around. Oprah promotes personal change, but the real change she instigates is in spending habits. Not only does she market her own tv network, magazines, DVDs and miscellaneous other items of merchandise, but, in a way, she markets a way of life. This is probably the most telling effect of Oprahization: devotees are so dazzled by the glamor and opulence of Oprah that they confuse their pursuit of self-actualization with the pursuit of commodities. In the process, they become absorbed in a narcissistic search for inner happiness and disregard wider issues that impinge on their lives and the lives of others.

Oprah, in common with other celebrities who will appear in this book, is of her time, both a product and producer of a culture that seems to promise universal consumption and an endless supply of must-have items. More fundamentally, it is a culture in which anything – literally anything – can be bought in the marketplace. That includes the end of racism; or, more specifically, an end to the effects racism has personally on any consumer who can afford to follow Oprah's advice.

"How can you say racism is still a big problem in America?" has begun to look like a rhetorical question. The mere presence of Oprah is an answer of sorts. To recap her own submission: "If Oprah Winfrey can make it, what does it say about me?' It's a hypothetical reaction, but one with too much credence among whites and blacks to be dismissed entirely. When Christopher Holmes Smith in his analysis of Diddy-like hip-hop moguls wrote: "His trade is purely in the realm of socially mobile aspirations – the quintessential pixie dust of the postwar American dream," he hinted at why all African American celebrities seem to exercise an influence and authority that appears disproportionate to their status (p. 80). "Pixie dust" was the magic powder that enabled humans to fly in J.M. Barrie's fantasy *Peter Pan*. In the book, it worked. In reality it's just another commodity.

5

A black family that tv hadn't seen before

'Cosby would have been damned if he didn't make
The Cosby Show. In the event, he was damned because he did.'

Bill Cosby presented us with television's equivalent to one of those ambiguous images that can look like more than one thing: like a skull that also resembles a beautiful woman gazing in a mirror, or the drawing of an old hag that could also be a young woman. They are full of double meanings, so we apply our own interpretation. Many sat back in wonderstruck admiration at Cosby's innovative *The Cosby Show*; others raged and ranted at the monstrosity Cosby had helped create. They were all looking at the same thing: they'd just seen it differently.

The amiable Cosby excited and astonished many, who hailed him as a representative of a new black America. Pamela Browner White, chair of Philadelphia's Anderson Award committee, paid tribute to Cosby's long career as an inspiriting entertainer, calling him the "face and voice of the African-American middle-class family … a man of strong values, [he] has inspired thousands of young adults to achieve their dream of a college education." The comic actor, who, as Jamal Eric Watson put it, "single-handedly changed the way African-Americans were portrayed on television," was the creator of *The Cosby Show*, which Patricia A. Bell maintains "opened up a new era in television, leading the way for other shows to depict upwardly mobile and successful black people."

The show drew less respectful responses from, for example, Sut Jhally and Justin Lewis, who complained that Cosby introduced a "new and insidious form of racism." And, according to John Fiske: "Others have claimed that Bill Cosby is a contemporary Uncle Tom, or Afro-Saxon." (Afro-Saxon usually refers to whites, who adopt black cultural styles; but we see what Fiske is getting at.) His show exasperated countless others. Clearly, Cosby was – and, indeed, is – someone who arouses not just strong passions, but fiery intellectualism too.

Herman Gray believes he knows why: "Much of the reason for the critical suspicion and celebration of *The Cosby Show* is, of course, its focus on a black upper-middle class family." Gray's inclusion of "of course" makes this seem more self-evident than it actually is, but he has a valid point. At the center of Cosby's illustrious, pioneering show was a black nuclear family that lived far away from the hood, had no obvious dysfunctions and no money worries. There's no logical reason why that should satisfy and infuriate simultaneously;

Cosby's achievement was in smashing a commonly held, but hideously distorted, image of black people. His offense was in replacing it with a less commonly held, but according to some, equally distorted image.

Next question: did Cosby succeed in changing conceptions of African Americans enough to make a Barack Obama candidacy possible? By now, the reader will have inferred that I believe in the role of popular culture as an agent of social and political change. I started this book by positioning Obama as the figurehead or emblem of a significant shift in American culture, and, in this and chapters to follow, I'll examine the parts played by black celebrities from entertainment and sports in effecting that shift. Entertainers and athletes portended the arrival of a black president. Oprah is the most conspicuous and influential figure on the landscape. Few can doubt this. There are many others whose precise roles I will scrutinize in chapters to come. Bill Cosby's part is unique and of its own kind.

———

In many respects, Cosby was like Oprah: an advertisement for himself, someone who used his own life as a means of recommending something – in this case, ambition. Cosby aimed high and wished other African Americans would follow his example. Like Oprah, he had a relatively humble background, in his case in Philadelphia (where he was born in 1937), and joined the navy, completing his high school studies through a correspondence course. He won an athletics scholarship to Temple University, Philadelphia, and supported himself through part-time work behind a bar. He tried his hand at some standup work in local clubs and, in his early twenties, began to do spots on television shows. Cosby's imperturbable stage presence and his languorous delivery caught the eye of the producers of the NBC tv show *I Spy* and, in 1965, Cosby started playing the role of Robert Culp's sidekick. The show ran till 1968, after which Cosby moved to his own show, *The Bill Cosby Show*, playing a teacher. He created an animated series called *Fat Albert and the Cosby Kids* and featured in a number of movies in the 1970s, all the time pursuing academic study.

"Black viewers," Jennifer Fuller discerns, were "underserved" by the major broadcasters in the 1980s. "They [the tv networks] limited black programming to a single night" (p. 290). But Cosby's appeal was broad enough for him to avoid television's equivalent of a ghetto. *The Cosby Show* began on NBC in 1984 (ABC was offered, but rejected, the series). Cosby played the paterfamilias of the Huxtables, described by *Ebony* magazine as "a Black family that tv hadn't seen before." Actually, it might have added that black families hadn't appeared on US television at all until 1968 – I'll return to this shortly, as it's important to understand Cosby in historical context.

The Huxtable family lived in a New York City brownstone that teemed with affluence. Cosby's own original idea was for the husband to be a limousine driver and the wife to be a carpenter, but the roles were changed to an obstetrician and lawyer respectively. The fictional grandfather lived in a time of segregated armed forces, and segregated music clubs where he worked as a musician. His son had become a doctor and married another professional and his grandchildren were in college. While *The Cosby Show* was character-driven, Cosby himself never claimed its characters were representative. Actually, he could have: in the 1980s, America's black population was variegated, so the fictional family was representative of a relatively small but growing affluent and upwardly mobile class.

The themes or topics of the show were generic rather than specific to the black experience – if, in the 1980s, there was a uniform black experience: friendship, dating, college, and family tensions were typical fare. The audience was persuaded to think of the Huxtables as a family, which happened to be black, rather than a "black family." But that in itself was unusual. Black families were rarely depicted as ordinary: they were much more likely to be funny, eccentric, pathological, or, in some way, uncommon. In this sense, Cosby offered television's equivalent of what's called in baseball a change-up: a deceptive pitch intended to throw off the batter's timing.

There were other notable surprises. In 1977, for example, ABC television broadcast *Roots*, a twelve-hour dramatized documentary, based on Alex Haley's 1976 *Roots: The saga of an American family*. The story traced the author's family line from his ancestors' enslavement to his descendants' liberation. It was a bold initiative, though Haley's book was a bestseller even before the show. Haley was the co-executive producer of another show, *Palmerstown, U.S.A.*, which told of a friendship between a black boy and a white boy in the 1930s South. Haley's co-executive producer was Norman Lear, who was also instrumental in bringing *Cagney & Lacey* to the screen in 1981. CBS was hesitant about featuring two female detectives as leads in a cop show, but, after two changes of actor, the series became, like *The Cosby Show*, one of the defining tv series of the decade, engaging with the sexism of the eponymous pair's mostly male colleagues in the 14th Precinct of the New York Police Department. The show is also credited with boosting recruitment of women into police forces across the US and Britain. So, *The Cosby Show* was not quite as out-of-kilter as recent commentators have assumed; though it certainly divided critics and prompted arguments like no other show of the 1980s.

From 1985 to 1987 the show broke viewing records, with Cosby becoming the strongest audience-puller in television. At its peak, *The Cosby Show* drew 70 million American viewers (about 30 percent of the nation's population) and became one of the most popular series in television history; it is still shown in syndication in the US and abroad. The show closed in 1992, the final episode being about the only son's graduation from New York City University. At the time there were 537,000 black males in college or university – only 3.5 percent of the total enrolment, according to James Earl Davis (p. 620). There were 583,000 black males in prison.

Cosby himself was a stalwart supporter of education as a channel of mobility for blacks (his own son was a graduate student at Columbia University when he was shot to death while in Los Angeles in 1997.) In 1988, Cosby and his wife had made the largest contribution ever from a black donor to any black college when they donated $20 million to Spelman College, Atlanta. Even after the show had finished, Cosby continued to barnstorm the US to talk about the problems that affect black children and families, always "encouraging an ethic of personal responsibility," as Watson notes (p. 8). Cosby had a parallel career as a pitchman for Kraft Food's Jell-O pudding, and appeared in tv commercials from 1974 till 1999, later assuming the executive producer's role for an advertising campaign in 2010.

After the 2008 presidential election, Dr. Alvin F. Poussaint, a psychiatrist and professor at Harvard Medical School who was a script consultant on *The Cosby Show*, sketched out a possible connection between Cosby and the president: "There were a lot of young people who were watching that show who are now of voting age."

The thread seems tenuous, but there is logic in Poussaint's reasoning: Cosby's depiction of black family life as recognizably *normal*, changed the way whites viewed blacks. The show itself was not as important as the way viewers, in particular white viewers, interpreted it. "It's what people have done with themselves by watching that show and believing in it," said Poussaint to *New York Times* journalist Tim Arango (November 8, 2008). This is essentially why audiences loved the show, but many commentators hated it: it was too believable.

———

"*The Cosby Show* offered viewers the comfort of seeing characters with whom they identified enjoy the spoils of Western capitalism," observed Timothy Havens. He meant *most* viewers: many were made to feel deeply uncomfortable by the show's depiction of black life in the 1980s and early 1990s. For example, Jhally and Lewis agreed, "The Huxtables proved that black people can succeed," but they pointed out that one of the effects of the show was to "encourage white people, looking around them at the comparative prosperity of whites over blacks, to believe in an imagined cultural superiority" (p. 97).

Actually, there is an interesting backstory to Jhally and Lewis's research. In a classic case of biting-the-hand-that-feeds-you, Jhally, a professor of communications at the University of Massachusetts, in 1994 asked Cosby (by then a well-known philanthropist) for $16,000 to fund a project on why his show had been so popular among black and white viewers alike. Cosby had no influence on how the research was conducted, nor any editorial prerogatives. The researchers used focus groups and in-depth discussions, consisting of black, white and Hispanic participants, subdividing the black and white groups by social class. The two main questions they used as a starting point for discussion were: how much the image of the Huxtable family reflected viewers' conceptions of black people; and how "real" were the characters and events in the show. The results, as I alluded to earlier, suggested the show purveyed an insidious form of what the researchers called "enlightened racism."

Put simply, the researchers argued that whites regarded the show as a slice of American life: anyone, black or white, could navigate their ways up the social hierarchy. But they also recognized that the well-to-do Huxtables were far from typical of African Americans. Conclusion: blacks who have not managed to clamber as far as Cosby's make-believe characters, have probably failed because they are too lazy or feckless. "The Huxtables proved that black people can succeed; yet in so doing they also prove the inferiority of black people in general (who have, in comparison with whites, failed)" (p. 95).

In a separate piece of research, Leslie B. Inniss and Joe R. Feagin concurred with the first part of this: "The overall impression is that the American dream is real for anyone who is willing to play by the rules" (p. 709). Inniss and Feagin never explicate those "rules," but let's guess they involve not grumbling about discrimination or getting involved in radical politics, and certainly not getting mixed-up in the kind of misdemeanors associated with rap artists in the 2000s. Rules change.

Inniss and Feagin also add: "We are left with the impression that they will not face any barriers or obstacles in their quest for the good life. They are decidedly upper middle class and can only go up – no discrimination or downward mobility for the Huxtables or by extension for Blacks as a group" (p. 709).

So, we have at least two conflicting, if not competing, representations, or models of Cosby's show and its legacy. One is nicely summarized by Havens, who suspects he knows why audiences took such comfort: "Integral to their enjoyment was the show's representation of a dignified blackness, which broke with centuries of popular Western images of blacks" (p. 387). The positive impact of seeing prosperous, attractive African Americans on screen was uplifting and affirming. Black people were emphatically not handcuffed to history.

The other model is the one Jhally and Lewis believe has more strength. The show worked as a cultural bulwark, fortifying an American mainstay: that the hierarchy is open to all and, to scale it, an individual needs talent, hard work and a certain stubborn streak that prevents him or her buckling at the experience of misfortune. Racism was so rarely mentioned, it was easy to forget or ignore, leading Andrea L. Press to declare: "The show, as a piece of ideology, works to obscure its viewers' understanding of the structural limits to individual mobility in our society" (p. 220).

The limits Press refers to are both racial and class-based. "White viewers in particular become convinced of their own, and society's, lack of racism when they find themselves viewing, and liking, the obviously successful Huxtable family" (p. 220). One of the show's many implicit messages was that affirmative action and, for that matter, any other race-specific policy is superfluous. In the Cosby worldview, individuals progress on their own merits. "Racism will end when blacks become successful," is how Press reads the policy implications of *The Cosby Show*.

Yet, for Press, "most will by definition not succeed on this level." Cosby's narrative deftly elides America's class structure, which, on Press's argument, condemns the majority of African Americans to lives of poverty, and functions to exacerbate racial disharmony. She concludes: "Even if blacks were to achieve economic equality, much racism would persist" (p. 221).

The one character in the show who, it might be assumed, emerged untouched by criticism was Clair Huxtable, played by Phylicia Rashad. A partner in a law firm, Clair, like her husband, escaped traditional stereotypes. In many ways, she embodied feminist ideals: independent, ambitious and sassy, she was able to play both mother and professional without breaking stride. And yet, as Jennifer Bailey Woodward and Teresa Mastin report: "Viewers saw her as overly aggressive, not maternal enough, too outspoken, and overly controlling toward both her husband and children" (p. 272).

The Cosby Show has been vested with more importance than any television series in history – and I'm not forgetting *Roots, The Wire,* or the show that took over from Cosby at the top of audience ratings, *The Simpsons.* None of the others has hefted so much social and political weight as *The Cosby Show.* Aficionados and detractors alike agree that Cosby tried and succeeded in conveying a new and unfamiliar image of black people that owed little to historic stereotypes.

Whether they praised it or damned it, everyone agreed that this depiction of African Americans as educated, aspirational and family-oriented was a development in popular culture. The viewing figures suggested another basis of agreement: blacks and whites alike watched the show in their millions. The fact that whites flocked to their tv whenever the show played indicated that its influence went farther and wider than any previous show featuring black people as central characters.

But what exactly was its influence? This is where we find critics and commentators circling and squabbling. Much of the discord seems to be about whether Cosby is judged against an historical background, or in the context of the day. Cosby's supporters recognize his service in breaking a long-hardened mold: as I will soon show, blacks were woefully under-represented on American television and, arguably worse, forced into such a narrow spectrum of roles that a complete absence would perhaps have been preferable.

Fault-finders consider his show to have performed a disservice to black people by portraying them in a way that was representative of only a minority; and, in doing so, to have deflected attention away from the genuine hardships and suffering of the majority of African Americans. While he didn't state this in the early 1980s, Cosby might have said that it's better to aim high and miss than aim low and hit the target.

Ten years after the end of the show, Cosby himself decided to speak out, not only on the show, but on the condition of black people in America. The squabbling then became a full-blown war of words.

———

One feature of *The Cosby Show* about which all agreed was that it gave succor to whites by offering an image of black people that was clearly at odds with popular ideas. African Americans were great athletes and gifted entertainers, but not much good at anything else. Less than two years after the end of Cosby's show, the publication of *The Bell Curve* reopened a century-old but still box-fresh discussion about whether intelligence is inherited and, if so, is the disparity between blacks' and whites' educational attainments attributable to nature rather than nurture? The implication of Richard J. Herrnstein and Charles Murray's thesis was that the USA was and is a genetic meritocracy and seemingly intractable social problems were not actually soluble. "If nature disposes, the argument goes, there is little to be gained by intervening," as *New York Times* writer David L. Kirp put it in his "After the Bell Curve" (July 23, 2006).

In one way, *The Cosby Show* was refutation: far from being intellectually impaired or inferior to whites, the whole Huxtable family was conspicuously bright and disposed, if not by nature then by culture, to progress as far as their talents would take them. But, in another way, it was supportive of some of the crucial policies implied by *The Bell Curve*. Affirmative action and compensatory education, while superficially laudable, are futile and profligate. Herrnstein and Murray's reason was that no amount of social engineering could change what nature decrees. Cosby's reason, by contrast, would be that policies like this are just not necessary: black people are individuals and, as such, they will, or at least should, take responsibility for their own lives and not rely on assistance from government or anyone else.

After *The Cosby Show* completed its run, Cosby must have grown restless with a social contradiction that his show, in its own way, helped bring about: at a time when black people had more legal freedom than ever, a record number of them had sacrificed that freedom and ended up behind bars. Cosby's show had resisted the fatalistic style of thinking that black people have the odds stacked against them and will invariably fail to achieve anything of note. And yet, he must have agonized over the manner in which schools were re-segregating and black neighborhoods were recrudescing into ghettos where dope-dealing and prostitution were viable career options. Even worse: ghetto culture was being valorized by an entertainment industry fascinated with pimps, bling and rock (cocaine, that is; not music).

Cosby was moved to clarify his own views, at first in a speech to commemorate the fiftieth anniversary of the *Brown vs. Board of Education* decision of 1954, and later in a series of "Conversations with Cosby" held in cities with large urban and poor populations. "We can't blame white people," Cosby argued. African Americans were not "holding up their end of the deal" and should take "personal responsibility" for their problems. The "Blame the Poor" tour, as it became known, allowed Cosby to voice his concern over unplanned pregnancies, high crime figures, dropping out of education and the urban slang that proliferated. He even fulminated over black names "like Shaniqua, Shaligua, Mohammed and all that crap."

Gone was the affable Cliff Huxtable, replaced by a grouchy, barely recognizable 67-year-old. "Please don't give me anything about systemic racism," he urged an audience in Detroit (where 87 percent of the population is black). "Yes, it's there," he acknowledged. "But why is your mouth not working?" (reported in *Black Issues in Higher Education*, February 10, 2005, p. 20).

In a searing rebuke, Cosby insisted blacks needed to stop blaming whites and take control of their children and their communities. Singling out lower-income blacks, who prioritize the right kind of sports footwear over education, he pointed out: "Nine hundred kids enter many of these high schools, and 35 walk out with diplomas ... The rest are in prison, pregnant or wandering around doing nothing." At the time, only 30 to 40 percent of black men graduated from high school; African Americans were three times as likely as whites to be in prison and their sentences likely to be six months longer; young black women aged 15 to 19 had a pregnancy rate of 123.8 per 1,000, against the national average of 70.6 per 1,000; and black unemployment was 10.8 percent, compared to 4.7 percent for whites.

"Cosby spoke the truth," wrote Julianne Malveaux in a 2004 response, "but he spoke it without context." She explained: "It's easy to blame parents of children gone wrong without examining the context in which parents raise children, the wages they are paid, the employment opportunities they have, and the malicious way that public policy has affected these parents and children" (p. 122).

Other responses also took note of Cosby's obliviousness to social context. Michael Eric Dyson's riposte was the most acerbic: he disagreed with practically everything Cosby said. "For instance, the belief the poor are lazy and don't work; that the poor don't have a desire to be in education; that the poor are fundamentally satisfied with their condition which is why they are poor, and basically they're poor because they want to be poor," as Dyson told Ronald Roach in 2005 (p. 15). Dyson's book *Is Bill Cosby Right?* pointed out that, as a member of an elite, "the Afritocracy," the actor-turned-social commentator was disengaged from the majority of African Americans and experienced "embarrassment over the bad behavior of the poor"(p. 182). Cosby may have belonged to the same ethnic group as African Americans, but he was a class apart.

Dyson also took issue with the philosophy that undergirded everything Cosby advocated: "The appeal to internal self-explanations reflects the embrace of the dominant ideology of individualism and makes it more like likely that its advocates will stress personal responsibility to the strongest degree in blaming people" (p. 208). Similar observations were made of Oprah, who encouraged reliance on one's own powers and resources rather than those of others. "Since the myth of romantic individualism still strongly grips the culture, it is unsurprising that the individualistic explanation for poverty is most widely favored," wrote Dyson (p. 203).

And, as if to ensure that he didn't let any detail of Cosby's argument go unpunished, Dyson reckoned Cosby's disdain for non-European names said more about him than the people who owned them. "Names like Shaniqua and Taliqua are meaningful cultural expressions of self-determination."

"Cunning lies and garbage" is how Paul R. Griffin described Dyson's argument, in *Diverse Issues in Higher Education* (November 3, 2005). Dyson's text was cluttered with factual errors, many picked up by the magazine *Education Next*, which concluded: "These and other misstatements of fact, tales, and quotes out of context are used to impugn the reputation of a public figure who dared to ask black parents and students to exercise a greater sense of responsibility"(vol. 6, No. 1, 2006).

Cosby continued to challenge black parents rather than abstractions like dominant ideology or systemic racism, and he maintained his sense of individualism. With Poussaint, he authored a book with the imperative title *Come On, People* and, in 2009, went door-to-door in Detroit to talk to parents about the city's troubled schools. So he could claim quite literally to have walked the walk as well as donating millions to educational institutions and other causes. Dyson mentioned only the $20 million Spelman College gift in his book, and likened Cosby to a fairytale character. "People who give a bunch of money are deferred to, even when they are wrong. The emperor cannot be shown to have no clothes," he told Deborah Robinson of the *New York Times* (March 27, 2007).

The reference is to Hans Christian Andersen's children's story of 1837, *The Emperor's New Clothes*, in which a clothes-obsessed sovereign ruler walks among his subjects naked after being conned into thinking he is wearing clothes that are visible to all but the stupid and those "unfit for office." A conspiracy of silence prevails until an unknowing child's shout of "The emperor has nothing at all on!" serves as a reality check. Cosby is cast as a credulous, conceited poseur, showboating for the benefit of sheeplike followers, but bereft of anything material. A strained analogy; or is it?

———

"Truly, *The Cosby Show* is unique. In its day (in 1968), so too was *Julia*, but it was still a case of Black images being created by white hands" (p. 141). So writes Linda K. Fuller in her 1992 book *The Cosby Show: Audiences, impact, and implications*. She refers to an intelligent, if issues-heavy, piece of television that deserves some attention, especially in the context of the medium itself. *Julia* was a weekly show based on a single widowed mother (the husband was killed in Vietnam) and nurse, played by Diahann Carroll. In its way, this was a groundbreaking show: Carroll's character was a self-starter, motivated to pursue her career without the help of others. Too glamorous to be a "mammy" figure and too independent to be a "welfare queen," she didn't fit into any of the established racial stereotypes that had populated tv previously.

Challenging conventional portrayals as it did, *Julia* could have become a teledramatic event, adventurously tackling social issues. But it turned into a frustrating curio; what Darrell M. Hunt in his essay "Black content, white control" calls an "assimilationist show." He intends this pejoratively, meaning that the black characters in the show were "tokens in a white world disconnected from the realities of the rest of the black community" (p. 270).

Just prior to the show's run, 1968–71, there was civil unrest across the United States. Starting with the explosive six-day conflict in South Central LA in 1965, the rioting spread to several other major cities, culminating in 1967 when police raided Detroit gambling clubs used by blacks, provoking major disorder. The period was marked by severe discontentment, and an official inquiry, published as the Kerner Report, concluded that the cause of the riots lay in racism and the resulting poverty suffered by blacks, leading to their being undernourished, underpaid, badly clothed and poorly housed. None of this was mirrored in *Julia*. Then again, where in television was it mirrored? Only on the news.

Sanford and Son, 1972–77, *Good Times*, 1974–79, and *The Jeffersons*, 1976–85, were all black shows produced by "white hands," to use Fuller's phrase. High-spirited comedies, companionable in tone and with time for sardonic cracks amid the family crises that were common occurrences, the shows were commercial successes, lasting at least five years. Reason: "They were controlled by white producers to appeal to the largely white television audience," as Hunt points out (p. 270). The appeal lay in the depiction of "the gritty realities of inner-city urban life." Why should this be appealing to white audiences?

"Containment" is Helán E. Page's answer. She means that whites have long regarded black people, especially black men, as potentially harmful and so keep them under control or within safe limits. Traditionally, whites contained blacks both physically and aesthetically. The idea of presenting images of safe and friendly blacks for the delectation of whites isn't so new.

Minstrel troupes featuring white performers, their faces blacked-up to resemble blacks, began to appear on the American eastern seaboard in the 1820s, offering a distorted image of black life. It's been argued by many historians, including Joseph Boskin and Robert Toll, that, during the Jim Crow era of segregation, there was an oblique function: whites were assured that the inoffensive "plantation niggers" or "coons" known generically as Sambo were childlike, but happy in their servitude. There was no reason for whites to feel guilty, less still afraid. A black grinning visage with thick lips and wide eyes was a reminder of blacks' contentment – and containment. ("Jim Crow" was actually used as a song title by white entertainer Thomas Dartmouth "Daddy" Rice, 1808–60.)

The arrival of *Sanford and Son* and the other black-themed comedies prompted murmurings that "the medium had regressed back to the buffoonish portrayals of the 1950s," according to Hunt (p. 270). Back then, shows such as *The Amos 'n' Andy Show*, which ran from 1951–53, and *Beulah,* 1950–53, were like lineal descendants of minstrel shows, furnishing viewers with black characters who were lazy chumps or dependable servants. (Both began as radio shows, the former starting in 1928 and sometimes drawing 40 million listeners – a third of America – six nights a week, making it the longest-running and most popular radio program in broadcast history.)

The black comedy shows of the 1970s and early 1980s were well-crafted and sharply-written comedies, but they seemed from the same boilerplate as the earlier black shows. *Sanford and Son* was derived from the much-lauded BBC show *Steptoe and Son*, while *The Jeffersons* was spun off *All in the Family*, which was also derived from a BBC comedy *Till Death Us Do Part.*

The Cosby Show did have, to extend Fuller's metaphor, white hands on it, but Cosby himself was a co-creator of the show and had a writing credit on all 200 episodes, several of the other writers being African Americans. Cosby himself had executive-produced his earlier *The Bill Cosby Show*, though Marcy Carsey and Tom Werner exec-produced the bulk of *The Cosby Show.* Cosby appointed Poussaint as a script consultant, his brief being to assess the impact the show was having psychologically on audiences, particularly black audiences. "It changed some attitudes and perceptions," Poussaint later reflected.

The political climate was not auspicious: in 1984 Ronald Reagan was re-elected by a landslide vote, signaling a significant lurch to the right in the US. Part of Reagan's appeal was in taking up the cause of disaffected whites, who attributed many of their own problems to affirmative action and other policies seeming to favor minorities. Reagan famously opposed every major civil rights initiative and so contributed to an environment in which racism became, if not acceptable, then tolerable.

While he became outspoken later, Cosby himself was not a controversial figure during the Regan era, 1981–89. Anything but: he was arguably the most popular entertainer on American television, if audience figures are a gauge. For a black person to occupy this position in the 1980s was something of a distinction. At the time, Cosby brushed aside questions about why his show didn't include racial issues by wondering out loud why similar questions were not raised about other shows with predominantly white casts. Perhaps the frustration of constantly fielding questions like this drove him to his pronouncements on personal responsibility, systemic racism, Shaniqua and so on.

Ron Howard's 1982 movie *Night Shift* is about two morgue attendants, played by Michael Keaton and Henry Winkler, both white, who start a sideline prostitution racket. Andrea Press recalls a comedy sketch in which Eddie Murphy, on hearing Howard describe the plot, snaps back: "It was a story about two pimps and there wasn't no brothers in it? I don't know whether to thank you or punch you in your mouth, man!" (p. 219).

The equivocation reflects the response to Cosby and *The Cosby Show*. Were Cosby to have followed obediently the pattern of previous black-centered sitcoms, he would doubtless be remembered fondly, and possibly admired, but probably not respected. "Why didn't you use your popularity and your leverage with the tv networks to break away from the old-fashioned characterization of blacks?" critics might have asked.

Instead, they asked: "Why did you characterize blacks as so well-off that everybody is running away with the mistaken idea that all black people are like the Huxtables?" Admittedly, not everyone pointed fingers at Cosby. But, as we've already seen in this chapter, critics eventually rounded on him. It seems that Cosby would have been damned if he didn't make *The Cosby Show*. In the event, he was damned because he did.

Dyson's diatribe against Cosby – an emperor without clothes, remember – included the judgment: "There is significant disadvantage still to black skin in an American culture that proclaims the virtues of individualism while denying it to blacks, *as a group*" (p. 211).

Cosby wouldn't recognize any validity in this. His credo was based on the fundamental humanity and individuality of blacks, and the illegitimacy of any attempt to conceive of black people otherwise – either as a group, as Dyson suggested, or as a race, as many whites, then and now, maintained.

6

Please be black, Michael

'Looked at one way, Jackson is a bizarre but freakishly gifted misfit.
Looked at another, he is one of the most illuminating figures
to stand on America's postwar landscape.'

The record sales were promising. The biggest grossing record of 1983 was in prospect. Epic Records executives were bowled over when they saw the glossy new video for "Billie Jean." The video featured a jheri-permed Michael Jackson wearing eighties-style shoulder pads, a red bowtie and correspondent shoes sliding across a road surface that lit up as he passed across it. The single from the *Thriller* album was already a charts success, but the video would give sales new momentum. The execs' delight quickly turned sour with the news that MTV was refusing to feature the video. Why would the then fledgling 24-hour music-only cable channel reject one of the world's most popular artists from its playlist? Could it be something to do with the fact that Jackson was black?

Jackson (1958–2009), then 25, was on his way to the stratosphere after a childhood in showbusiness and adolescence in no-man's land. A prodigious singer and dancer, Jackson had been performing theatrically practically since he was old enough to walk. His father Joe had organized Michael and his brothers into the Jackson 5 and signed them to a small independent label called Steeltown Records, which released two singles in 1968. Although neither sold well, they caught the attention of Berry Gordy, the owner of Motown, then a major force in the music industry with a roster that included Diana Ross, Stevie Wonder, the Temptations, and several other leading African American artists of the time. In the Jackson 5, Gordy must have seen the kind of raw material that could be dropped onto his well-calibrated assembly line for immediate processing. The Jackson 5 was punchy enough to accommodate the bass-driven rock impulses that were running through black music and which came to be called funk.

Gordy introduced the band as Diana Ross's discovery, titling the first album *Diana Ross Presents the Jackson 5*, which was released in late 1969 and contained the memorable "I want you back." Always a man with his finger on the pulse, Gordy felt the Jackson brothers were perfect for the 1970s. He'd watched the way the Monkees, a band comprising four white actors, had been put together to feature in a tv series and make records – which they performed in the series. It was, in the 1960s, an impudent and transparent marketing strategy. But it worked like a charm. Gordy envisaged a similar career for the

Jackson 5. By 1971, he had placed the band at the center of a cartoon series, which aired on Saturday mornings and which featured actors speaking the dialogue of the brothers. Jackson 5 merchandise proliferated. The age span of the band members (seven years separated the oldest, Jackie, from Michael, the youngest) meant the band appealed to a wide spectrum of fans.

Joe sensed his sons had even more commercial potential than the usually prescient and always opportunistic head of Motown realized. In his autobiography, Gordy wrote that, from 1973, after four years with Motown, "Their [the brothers'] father, Joe, went from being quietly behind the scenes to having many complaints and demands. It was everything from wanting a say in how they were produced, what songs they did or didn't do, to how they were being promoted and booked" (p. 347).

In 1975, Jackson moved his sons from Motown to CBS's Epic label (later acquired by Sony). By then, the band had been recording and performing for four years; Michael had detached himself temporarily for solo work, but was not yet a star in his own right; record sales for both him and the band had sagged in the previous two years. There was every reason to suppose that consumers had grown tired of the precocious child and his competent but unspectacular brothers. Yet, the move suggested that major media corporations like CBS were aware of the commercial potential of African American performers and were eager to exploit a mass market rather than the more specialist market Motown was able to reach.

As well as working with the band, Michael continued to pursue a parallel career as a solo performer, though with indefinite results. His collaboration with the trumpeter, bandleader and producer Quincy Jones proved a turning point. The first fruit of the collaboration was *Off the Wall*, an album described by Barney Hoskyns as "a triumph of studio-crafted miscegenation ... the first real mass-audience black/white album" (p. 301). (Miscegenation refers to the interbreeding of people considered to be of different racial types.)

Released in 1979, the album effectively relaunched Jackson as a newly matured entertainer. It was his fifth solo album and has, to date, sold 20 million copies. On the sleeve was an image of a formally attired Jackson, his nose narrowed slightly by a rhinoplasty, but his face not yet blanched. Coincidentally, around the same time, Chic's "Le Freak" became the biggest-selling single in Atlantic Records' history (4 million copies); the band, like Jackson, projected the image of unapologetic middle-class black sophisticate. (*En passant* the gay subtext of Chic's "Good Times" was also consistent with the liberating mood of the period: "Boys will be boys/better let them have their toys".)

And, also coincidentally, there was a change in the aspirations and social mobility of black Americans. Against a backdrop of Reagan-inspired cutbacks in federal regulation and intervention, a warrantable black middle class emerged. These were people who were not prepared to camp on the edge of society, but wanted to get involved. The market took note. In 1985,

Clint Wilson and Félix Gutiérrez wrote, "Advertisers promote consumption of their products as a shortcut to the good life, a quick fix for low-income consumers (p. 128).

Their book *Minorities and Media* was an analysis of how and why the media's portrayal of ethnic groups changed in the period: "The message to their low-income audience is clear," they wrote, referring to the manner in which advertisers had begun to take notice of previously ignored segments of the market: "You may not be able to live in the best neighborhoods, wear the best clothes, or have the best job, but you can drink the same liquor, smoke the same cigarettes, and drive the same car as those who do" (p. 128).

Later Alan J. Bush and a research team were to reveal: "African Americans are more favorably disposed [than other ethnic groups] toward advertising, watch more tv, and rely on advertising to help choose the best product" (p. 22).

Jackson, as much as any other visible figure of the time, symbolized not just unmistakable affluence and conspicuous consumption, but an extravagant, flamboyant prosperity. His lavish eccentricities, though not yet the stuff of legend, were beginning to surface. He'd also shown a willingness to submit to and operate within white parameters (he'd left a black-owned label to join CBS), while remaining defiantly and incomparably individual.

———

When Rick James died in 2004, MTV featured an obituary on its webpages. It described James as "an American funk and soul musician from Buffalo New York, who worked as a singer, keyboardist, bassist, record producer, arranger, and composer during his long career." It referenced James' associations with Motown in the late 1970s. "James was famous for his wild brand of funk music and his trademark cornrow braids." There was no mention of James' dispute with MTV over the cable channel's refusal to play his track "Superfreak," which was a big seller in 1981 (and which was sampled for MC Hammer's 1990 hit "U can't touch this"). James criticized MTV for excluding videos by black artists, using the phrase "blatant racism" to describe the practice.

Actually, it wasn't that blatant; the channel had featured black artists, including Tina Turner. But many of the artists featured were from England, where music videos were made to accompany practically every new single. This explains why so much of MTV's early playlist had an English quality. Duran Duran was the most conspicuous English act, but there were also black artists like Joan Armatrading and Eddy Grant on MTV in its first two years. Another English artist, David Bowie, joined James in asking for more black artists. Three decades later, black music had become a rich profit center for the record industry and a key source of cachet for the now-global tv channel, which had improbable origins.

Not being a businessman, I often marvel at the ingenuity of entrepreneurs who can conjure up what must strike most people as laughable ideas and turn them into moneymaking endeavors. Imagine this, for instance: two tv execs leave a movie theater in 1977 after seeing John Badham's *Saturday Night Fever*. With a perfunctory plot and almost ceaseless disco music and dancing, the film sounds irritating beyond belief, but became a huge global success and launched the career of John Travolta. Impressed by the music that throbbed throughout the film and the nifty footwork of Travolta et al., one exec suggests to the other that they start a tv channel on which they show nothing but the kind of material they've just witnessed. The other scoffs: "Look, that was 118 minutes and it was held together by a plot, even if it was a pretty thin one. Why would anyone want to watch music clips nonstop without even a story to sustain their interest?"

Four years later, in 1981, MTV began transmitting. Fanciful as the *Saturday Night Fever* scenario seems, it actually isn't too far from the truth: MTV was started by John Lack, who worked for Warner Cable, Robert W. Pittman, an NBC radio programmer, and Les Garland; together they dreamed up the idea, having taken note of a similar set-up in New Zealand, which showed pop videos and, in turn, promoted record sales. In fact, the distinction between promotional material and entertainment was smudged if not erased by MTV, which showed only music clips, including concert footage, interspersed with chat from video jockeys, or VJs.

The program content came from record companies, which were eager to grab what was effectively free advertising from the new cable outlet, owned by Warner Amex (i.e. Warner Communications and American Express). Pop videos were not then at the point where every commercial single was augmented by a video, but they were moving in that direction, especially in the British recording industry. MTV's income came from advertising revenue, which went up in proportion to their viewing figures, and its share of cable subscriptions. So all parties benefited from each other.

While it seems a perfectly brilliant concept today, in the late 1970s it must have seemed preposterous. In fact, it must have seemed that way in the first year of operation, too: fewer than one million viewers subscribed to the channel. Now, there about 350 million viewers, mostly aged 18-25 with no dependants and with disposable income – the kind of demographic that advertisers yearn for. MTV's global venture started in 1987 with MTV Europe and continued with such stations as MTV Mandarin, MTV Japan and MTV Africa. It has more imitators than the iPad: other channels have hijacked the all-music idea, leaving MTV to mutate into a reality tv station.

One of MTV's abiding images is a mockup of the moon landing, with a flag bearing the MTV logo being planted on the moon's surface. The allusion is direct: in 1969, the Apollo 11 satellite beamed images from the moon's surface into people's living rooms. Over the next decade, technological developments made it possible for television companies to distribute globally by bouncing signals off satellites. HBO, for example, began its service in 1976, transmitting from the Philippines the heavyweight title fight between Muhammad Ali and

Joe Frazier known as the "Thrilla in Manila." Other channels to use satellite broadcasts included The Christian Broadcasting Network, later to become the Family Channel; the Star movie channel, CNN, which specialized in news; Nickelodeon, which featured only children's programs; and ESPN, the sports-only channel. MTV was part of the proliferation. Spot the odd one out: only CNN offered hard news; the others provided content for leisure, relaxation, enjoyment – in other words, entertainment.

A year after MTV's launch, a newspaper adopted a similar brief: downplay politics and world events and concentrate instead on material that amused, indulged and gratified consumers. Seven years after the resignation of President Richard M. Nixon amid the Watergate scandal, six years after the end of the Vietnam War, and two years after the seizure of 52 American hostages in Iran, Americans were in need of some lightening news. At least, Al Neuharth thought so. Ergo *USA Today*. It had four digestible sections, News, Money, Sports, and Life, each packed with short (300 words tops) articles, eye-catching graphics, color photographs, advice columns, film and music reviews, extensive sports coverage and even some political news. The newspaper struggled at first, but now outsells the *New York Times* and has an international edition. *USA Today*, like MTV, both reflected the changes in both popular taste and the market and, as powerful media in its own right, catalyzed further changes. One of the more important ones was the multiplication of entertainment-centered media that were also fully functioning advertising vehicles.

———

"The point I always made was that MTV was originally designed to be a rock music channel," said Buzz Brindle, the channel's director of music programming in the early 1980s, who must have grown weary of explaining the absence of African Americans. "It was difficult for MTV to find African-American artists whose music fit [*sic*] the channel's format that leaned toward rock at the outset."

Maybe MTV had an agenda for its music. But it also had an agenda for its customers. No, not the people who watched the tv for pleasure: the advertisers who paid MTV to screen commercials and so provided it with its raison d'être. "In the 1980s and 1990s, advertisers could reach desired consumers instead of addressing a mass market," Jennifer Fuller points out (p. 290).

Media markets segmented, enabling a specialist tv channel like MTV to offer its advertisers a direct route to the youth market at a time in history when young people were becoming the most sought-after consumers (sought-after, that is, by ad agencies and their clients). Fuller again: "The most coveted demographic was young urban whites" (p. 290). One of the most revealing acknowledgments of this is an ad for MTV that ran in the business sections of newspapers, and was quoted by Thomas Frank in his essay "The new gilded age": "BUY THIS 24-YEAR-OLD AND GET ALL HIS FRIENDS FOR ABSOLUTELY FREE," its headline read (p. 150).

When Garland eventually decided to allow "Billie Jean" onto the MTV playlist, he didn't explain his change of heart, though it was thought to have been influenced by the prospect of CBS, the owner of Jackson's label, murmuring that it could withdraw its full roster of music. "CBS Records Group President Walter Yetnikoff had to threaten to remove all other CBS videos from MTV before the network agreed to air the video for 'Billie Jean'," Nadra Kareen Nittle summarized the circulating story in her "MTV and Black Music: A Rocky History" (May 9, 2011).

Garland dismissed this as myth: "There was never any hesitation," he was quoted by *Jet* magazine in an article titled "Why it took MTV so long to play black music videos" (October 9, 2006). Garland claimed: "I called Bob (Pittman, MTV co-founder) to tell him, 'I just saw the greatest video I've ever seen in my life. It is off the dial it's so good'." Yetnikoff has been silent on the issue. But, *if he did* make the threat to Garland, real or imagined, it was one of the most influential statements of intent in cultural history.

The commotion kicked up by James was probably embarrassing, but containable. Yet it ensured that there was at least awareness that MTV did not feature black artists, certainly not in proportion to their presence in popular music. MTV would certainly have become sensitive to criticism, especially at a time when the African American population was evolving into an exploitable market for consumer goods. To snub a conspicuous and, by common consent, talented performer such as Jackson could have been fatal. "Fortunately, Michael Jackson helped us to redefine the musical parameters of MTV," reflected Brindle. Whether his use of "fortunately" suggests MTV made an auspicious decision, or was just lucky, we can't know. But the meaning of his statement is clear enough.

Within months of screening Jackson for the first time, MTV received another video from Epic, this time an extended 14-minute film directed by John Landis, featuring former *Playboy* centerfold Ola Ray and a voiceover segment from Vincent Price, best-known for his starring roles in Hammer horror movies. *Thriller* became a classic of the new pop video genre, though in many ways it was a gamble. The album from which the track was taken was released earlier in 1983 and sales, while impressive, had begun to plateau.

MTV was in its third year of operation and was far from a proven commodity. The model of coupling a record with a video was still relatively new; today, of course, it would be unthinkable to release one without the other. CBS saw no purpose in making a video so long after the release of the album and with sales already at a respectable level. Jackson offered to pay Landis out of his own pocket. "But I wouldn't let him," said Landis. "He was still living with his parents in Encino behind a supermarket." Landis raised the $500,000 production costs by filming a 45-minute documentary called *The Making of "Thriller"* that he could sell for theatrical release. Like a movie, the video had a première in December 1983.

Thriller became the top-selling album in history (110 million copies to date) and turned Jackson into one of the world's leading entertainers. *Bad*, his follow-up, was considered a virtual failure, selling 30 million copies. The tour to promote it in 1987 was watched by a total of 4.5 million people. The video of his single "Black or white" was simultaneously shown to an estimated 500 million television viewers in 27 countries in 1991. A six-album deal with Sony was worth up to $1 billion. Jackson's rare public appearances, though fleeting and uneventful, were accorded a status akin to a royal visit. Measured on any scale, Jackson was the biggest pop act in the world. He was well known, but not known well.

There were no headlines about booze-and-drugs, rehab, sex parties and the now familiar antics we associate with celebs. If anything, Jackson eschewed these kinds of activities. As far as we know. If anything, he took the Greta Garbo (1905-90) approach, jealously guarding his private life. This disinclination to open himself for public inspection played no small part in deepening the fans' interest in him. One of the most perplexing aspects of Jackson concerned his physical transformation: as well as changes in several features of his face, his complexion seemed to be growing pale, at times even ashen. In a 1991 interview with Oprah, Jackson said he suffered from a skin condition called vitiligo, but few accepted that he hadn't undergone some sort of treatment: his face seemed to be in a state of perpetual alteration. Was he a black man trying determinedly to become white?

We'll never know whether Jackson actually wanted to rid himself of all traces of his ethnicity. An African American so successful that he could have almost anything in the world, he seemed to pursue the one thing he couldn't have and, in the process, confirmed that whiteness remained a precious commodity in the land of plenty. In his book *Michael Jackson: The Magic and the Madness*, J. Randy Taraborrelli quotes Don King, the impresario, who promoted a world tour for Jackson and his brothers, and sensed Michael's unease: "It doesn't matter how great he can sing and dance ... He's one of the megastars in the world, but he's still going to be a nigger megastar" (p. 377).

———

Have you ever thought what's happening when you watch a music video? Are you being entertained, or held captive in front of a three-minute commercial? You could ask a similar question of sports: does enjoying the competition implicate you in witnessing advertisements for cars, beer, razor blades, and all the other kinds of products aimed at the sports fan market? Does it really matter? After all, television keeps us engrossed, absorbed and amused. We usually have little inclination to analyse whether the hidden persuaders are surreptitiously bending our shopping preferences to their own requirements. Advertisers and tv companies figured this out long ago. MTV was, in its own way, a prototype. As its imitators proliferated, blurring the difference between entertainment and marketing became passé: making the two one and the same thing was the task. The band Dire Straits satirized the tightening relationship between pop music, television and consumerism in their 1985 track "Money for nothing," in which they boast of getting to "play the guitar on the MTV" while acknowledging their unwritten responsibility: "We gotta install microwave ovens/custom kitchen deliveries/we gotta move these refrigerators/we gotta move these color TVs."

Dire Straits reaped the benefits of MTV when their record reached the top of the charts, though the band was far from the biggest beneficiary of exposure on the channel in the 1980s. Madonna profited from being banned by MTV. This is not nearly as ironic as it sounds: a prohibition makes something or someone immediately more fascinating than they were before. Madonna was already pretty fascinating by 1990 when her "Justify my love" was considered too risqué. Already one of the world's most successful entertainers, Madonna was intent on transforming herself into a brand. As *Forbes* writer Allen Adamson reflects in his "What Madonna can teach Lady Gaga": "She was a genius at knowing how not to be too far out in front of the curve, and being able to sense when her current brand of entertainment had run its course." At the time of Adamson's article, February 14, 2011, Madonna was a 52-year-old mother of four and had just completed directing the film *WE*. Her first album *Madonna* had been released 28 years before, in 1983. Her rise coincides perfectly with the ascent of MTV; theirs was a most exquisite symbiosis.

If someone at MTV had looked to Madonna's divination for guidance, their faith would have been well-served: her genius – I follow Adamson's usage – was not so much for predicting the future as for shaping it. Morphing from one persona to another with each new album, she sensed consumers' appetite for endless novelty, change and excitement of the senses. Scandals were an effective way of satisfying all three criteria. In 1989, for example, the year before the MTV ban, she had drawn the wrath of the Catholic church with the symbol-laden video for the title track of her album *Like a Prayer*. The track became a *cause célèbre*, especially after Pepsi, outraged by the video, cancelled a $5 million endorsement contract with Ms Ciccone.

MTV must have hesitated about screening "Like a prayer," but erred on the side of abandon. Madonna's videos were, like Jackson's, events rather than just visual accompaniments to music. The music video's spectacular rise through the 1980s was in no small part attributable to her genius, though we should consider whether Madonna would still be influential today were it not for MTV. Perhaps she would have become another Streisand, or Cher, regardless; or even continued performing like Annie Lennox, or Debbie Harry. Equally, she may have slipped out of the popular consciousness in the way of Pat Benatar or Linda Ronstadt, both admirable singers, but neither as well known or as influential as they were in the early 1980s.

Let's keep perspective: MTV pushed advertisements at its audiences in the guise of entertainment. Perhaps that's harsh. MTV's output didn't just appear to be entertainment: it was. After all, we, the consumers, define what is or isn't entertaining. During the 1980s, our tastes changed so radically that we started to appreciate what might have been regarded as irrelevancies in earlier times. In the golden era of Hollywood (1930-1960s), fans were interested in stars *qua* stars – in their capacity as performers, not humans with predilections, fallibilities and foibles like everyone else. Madonna, with her invitations to inspect her body or discuss her sexual preferences, played no small part in changing that. She was vigorously abetted by a media – a *global* media – switching focus away from hard news to entertainment in the way instigated by *USA Today*.

As the media changed focus, so did we. This sounds like I am arguing that the chicken preceded the egg, whereas, in actuality, I am just groping for a new way of asking "which came first?" The media certainly changed focus, examining the hitherto private lives of the rich and famous, presenting consumers with what, in previous years, might have been dismissed as insignificant tittle-tattle or, at best, tangential to other, more interesting topics. If consumers hadn't been interested, the media would have found little traction. *The Oprah Winfrey Show*, as we saw in chapter 3, was a conduit of the irresistible new voyeurism.

———

A global television audience of over one billion watched the memorial service for Michael Jackson in July 2009. It was smaller than the 2.5 billion television witnesses to the funeral of Diana, Princess of Wales, in 1997, but a gargantuan gathering nevertheless. It offered an index of Jackson's near-mesmeric power to fascinate, even in his death. When Jackson died in June 2009, at the age of 50, it seemed as if people momentarily lost the ability to differentiate the flesh-and-blood mortal from his icon – the public representation that had been part of the popular imagination for the nearly four decades.

Everyone in the world was familiar with Jackson. Even those who had never heard a note of his music (and that probably means no one) would know of his extraordinary reputation – as the self-styled King of Pop, whose idiosyncratic habits accreted as he matured; the religion-hopping son of Jehovah's Witnesses, who embraced Islam but spoke for all religions; the artless lover of children who might also have been a cunning seducer of innocents.

Those who loved him, loved him in the kind of way fans in the late twentieth and early twenty-first centuries were wont: with a mixture of affection, attachment and idolization not for a person, but for an image of a person. Few people knew Jackson, the man; the world knew Jackson the icon. Few performers and certainly no African American performer had ever commanded a following like Jackson's: in one remarkable decade, Jackson sold 110 million records (over 75 million as a solo artist); and sales surged again in the aftermath of his death.

Jackson's response to this adulation was to become a virtual recluse, giving interviews sparingly and making infrequent public appearances. During the 1990s, Jackson made three albums; though interest in him centered less on his music, more on his weird, self-indulgent lifestyle and unusual choice of companions. As his enigma deepened, questions multiplied. Did he sleep in an oxygen tent? Why did he want the bones of the Elephant Man? Was he so obsessed by Diana Ross that he actually wanted to look like her? Did he seriously believe he was an emissary for God? "He's just using me as the messenger," he told *Ebony* in May 1992. And, how come he always seemed to be in the company of young children? This last question was asked too many times to remain unanswered.

In 1994, Jackson agreed to pay Jordy Chandler, then 14, an undisclosed sum, thought to be more than $25 million, to stop a sex abuse lawsuit ever reaching court. Jackson was never put under oath for a civil deposition, which could be used in a criminal trial. The deal was negotiated on Jackson's behalf by his lawyer, Johnnie Cochran, Jr., later to represent O. J. Simpson. Part of the agreement reached was that the payment did not constitute an admission of guilt by Jackson. After the charges, Jackson was forced out into the open and made to defend himself, whether he liked it or not. In the process, the qualities that were once integral to his appeal became implements of immolation. Was he weird-unusual, or weird-sicko?

The more rumors circulated, the more Jackson seemed to insulate himself from the world outside his 3,000-acre California residence, Neverland, which he appeared to have turned into his own gigantic playground where children could visit and stay and share the same bedroom as Jackson. He confirmed as much in a startling tv interview in 2003. Jackson's astonishing naïveté in talking about his love of children was, at once, touching and disarming. For some, it was a genuine expression of deep affection for children from someone so unworldly that he had no conception of the furor he was initiating. For others, it was the admission of a predatory pedophile, slyly attracting children for his own depraved ends. Charged in California for child molestation, he was obliged to defend himself in court. Joan Smith, of the *New Statesmen*, argued: "The Michael Jackson trial has been a paradigmatic moment in American cultural history" (June 13, 2005).

Smith argued of Jackson, "for all his weirdness, his fantasies and his perpetual quest for transformation have deep roots in the American psyche." She means that Jackson's rise from-rags-to-riches, his attempts to remake and reinvent himself and his "monarchical fantasies" are constituent parts of American ideology. His plastic surgery was no more than an extreme version of what more and more Americans engage in every year.

Jackson was acquitted. He never made another studio album. Jackson's *Invincible* was released in 2001. His appearances on stage also became fewer: in 2006, he disappointed fans by singing just a few lines of "We are the world" at the World Music Awards in London. It was his first performance since being cleared of the child molestation charges. There were suspicions that Jackson had acquired a dependency on prescription drugs.

In 2008, Jackson attempted to reprise his career as the King of Pop: it was announced that he would play at London's O2 Arena, the concert intended to coincide with the 25th anniversary of the release of *Thriller*. It did not materialize, though in March, 2009, more definite plans surfaced when promoters confidently publicized a ten-concert residency at the same 20,000-seat arena, scheduled to start in July. Jackson's motivation for undertaking such a punishing schedule was unclear, though the running costs of Neverland, which amounted to $3 m (£2.1 m) per year, were possibly a factor. It was reported by the BBC that Jackson would earn $400 m (£283 m) for the concerts, which sold out in minutes.

Jackson died before they began. Investigators concluded that a powerful concoction of prescription drugs ingested by Jackson at his Los Angeles home was the cause and Dr Conrad Murray, Jackson's personal physicial was charged and later found guilty of involuntary manslaughter. La Toya Jackson, Michael's sister, maintained that her brother told her shortly before his death: "I'm going to be murdered."

———

"White Americans prefer being lied to – a kind of fact-free zone they choose to live in – about any topics they disagree with." Quincy Troupe was furious about the media's coverage of Jackson's death. Writing for *Black Renaissance* in 2009, Troupe noticed how Jackson's idiosyncrasies overshadowed his musical achievements in most of media (actually, Troupe would probably object to my use of "idiosyncrasies," though I mean the mode of behavior peculiar to Jackson).

Troupe tries to make sense of this in group-psychological terms. "Many white people in this country," he argues, "are projecting their own feelings of inadequacy, their inferiority complexes and insecurities onto African-Americans through the manipulation of the mass communication media apparatus, which they own and control" (p. 5).

"*It works!*" declares Troupe, not just for whites, but for African Americans "who believe themselves inferior to whites, especially when it comes to standards of beauty, intelligence, achievement or other important areas" (p. 5). It's a pungent argument, lessened in its power by lack of evidence, but worthy of attention.

Susan Fast advances a different understanding of why Jackson excited ambivalence on a grand scale: "It was really his more substantive, underlying differences that were most troubling," she writes, listing Jackson's apparent refusal to stick to "normative social codes." Fast means Jackson didn't fit easily into racial or ethnic categories (we could add that he appeared to transfer across them), or into a recognizable gender role: he favored the companionship of children and young men. "Please be black, Michael, or white, or gay or straight," Fast imagines people pleading (p. 261).

Interesting propositions. But did people really want Jackson to conform to a recognizable status? It's at least possible that Jackson's ambiguities, far from being troubling, were the very source of his humongous global popularity. And did whites really project their own inadequacies onto him, as Troupe contends? From a different perspective, he validated whiteness by trying to erase his own blackness. I'll explain.

Taraborrelli relates an incident when the Jackson 5 was caught between conflicting demands. Berry Gordy taught them to assimilate in such a way that they'd be appreciated by the lucrative white market. This meant that they couldn't be seen to endorse the black power ethic that pervaded not only America, but vast portions of the world in the late 1960s and early 1970s. Yet for African Americans to be devoid of any kind of political awareness would have looked phony. The very fact that they all wore Afro hairdos hinted at an identification with what was going on about them. When a journalist asked a Motown publicist if the brothers' hairstyles "had something to do with Black Power," there was a sharp riposte. "These are children, not adults," snapped the publicist. "Let's not get into that." There were no more words, but the subject wasn't closed. "Michael – a media master at the age of thirteen – understood that his lack of social consciousness would not look good when the writer's story appeared. Before he left, he gave the writer a soul handshake and a big wink" (p. 79). After that, Motown's press department insisted that anyone who wanted to interview the band had to agree not to ask any questions about politics or drugs.

In spite of the Afro, the winks and the brothers' handshakes, Jackson was in no way reflective of the mood of the 1960s and 1970s. Quite the contrary: he came to represent a detachment from the mood, a young black man who looked like he was into black power and soul but was, in reality, a complete innocent. Even in his teens, it was easy to imagine he was a child, a gifted child; confirmation perhaps that blacks were naturally compensated for their lack of achievements in education, commerce and politics. In manhood, Jackson was even more comforting: an African American who had risen to the top on merit. Not all blacks, he seemed to be saying, were preoccupied with racism and the obstacles it strewed in their paths. Some were interested only in progress as individual people, not as members of a group that claimed a special status.

Off the Wall, the album that announced the arrival of Jackson as a mature 21-year-old artist, was released in 1979. Oprah was hosting a local talk show in Baltimore, Bill Cosby was fronting a Saturday morning cartoon show, Barack

Obama was graduating from high school, and Stevie Wonder was reaching the end of a creative period that had established him as arguably the world's pre-eminent popular musician. Jackson conformed to none of the existing stereotypes. Yet he was black. The importance of this was clear: he was silently making a statement about America's ability to accommodate black progress; about the possibilities awaiting black people with talent and determination enough to make it to the top; about the disappearance of the age-old American Dilemma. As a child, Jackson may have affected an Afro hairstyle, but, in the 1980s, he was a black man who could almost make you forget he was black. You could almost forget he was a man.

Celebrity can be a dangerous thing: it can flatter its incumbent with delusions of infallibility. Had Jackson heeded Don King's warning, he would have realized that his status was granted by a culture dominated by white people and by white values. As such, his acceptance was destined to be conditional. Here was a boy, a cornucopia of natural talent, who developed and expanded that talent in manhood. His dancing could mesmerize people, his singing could enchant them. He didn't talk politics and his comments about the condition of black people were so fluffy as to be meaningless. Christopher Andersen believes his fans – and, by implication, all of us – played their parts in "infantilizing" Jackson: "We were happy as long as he played Peter Pan and never grew up" (p. 356).

At a time when America was almost embarrassed by its seemingly never-ending racial problems, it was comforting to know that blacks, however humble their origins, could soar to the top. Even more comforting to know that, however high they soared, they still wanted to be white.

Sexually, Jackson was puzzling but not threatening: in his adolescence, he fraternized with older women, such as Elizabeth Taylor, or sought the companionship of escorts like Brooke Shields for celebrity functions. In 1994, a year after the first glimpse of his doubtful interest in young boys, he married Lisa Marie Presley. Jackson reportedly proposed over the phone four months after they had met. Their relationship was short-lived and Presley filed for divorce in January 1996, leaving many to ponder whether the marriage was a subterfuge. Jackson then married Debbie Rowe, a nurse who had been treating his skin condition. They had two children, rumored to have been conceived *in vitro*.

As an asexual figure, Jackson remained innocuous – to use Helán E. Page's phrase again, containable. The dread that might have been engendered by a virile young man who commands the fantasies of countless young women of every ethnic background didn't apply to Jackson. He was, to use Jan Nederveen Pieterse's evocative term, a symbolic eunuch. Actually, Ellen T. Harris compares Jackson to an actual eunuch – Carol Broschi, aka Farinelli (1705 –1782), the eighteenth-century castrato singer, who was also "idolized" (p. 183).

When, in 1993, Jackson's sweetness-and-light conception suddenly went darker, his public humiliation may well have functioned as a lynching – a symbolic lynching. As JoAnn Wypijewski, of *The Nation* wrote: "The definition of sexual danger has become endlessly elastic." She concludes: "It cannot matter that Michael Jackson was acquitted of child molestation, since he was frequently remembered in death as a pedophile" (p. 7).

However people remember Jackson – a wondrous talent, a scheming deviant, a manchild lost in Neverland – no one can deny that, in cultural terms, he will remain a compelling subject: an icon of the late twentieth century, he reflects not only the changes in the circumstances of the African American population, but changes in white America. Jackson was idolized, perhaps even reified and, for many, objectified into an extraordinary being, an Other, for whom there were no established reference points in whites' conceptions. Looked at one way, Jackson is a bizarre but freakishly gifted misfit. Looked at another, he is one of the most illuminating figures to stand on America's postwar landscape.

7

A desire for buffoonery and song

'Whites have been fascinated by blacks and have paid to
watch them perform in one way or another since
at least the early nineteenth century.'

Joice Heth. Ever heard of her? Her name isn't up there with Rosa Parks
(1913–2005) or Billie Holiday (1915–59), Shirley Chisholm (1924–2005)
or Angela Davis (b.1944), all black women who, in different ways, set their
impress on American culture. Heth did make her mark, though not as an
inspiration behind the civil rights movement, or a chanteuse of the Jim Crow era
(1876–1965), or as an indefatigable politician with designs on the presidency.
Heth was a freak – an exhibit at a show in which unusual or grotesque people
were displayed and customers paid to see them. In the first half of the nineteenth
century, this counted as entertainment.

Entertainment is never *just* the provision of amusement or enjoyment: it's
an opportunity to learn, if we know what questions to ask. For example: why
were white audiences entertained by white performers pretending to be black
who toured America and England in burlesque shows that ridiculed blacks?
Blacks and their culture fascinated whites in the nineteenth century; they still
do, it seems. Why? In a way, the whole of this book is an answer. But the source
of the long-lasting fascination lies in the early nineteenth century, which is
where Heth's story unfolds.

In 1835, Heth went on display in Manhattan, where she was advertised
as THE GREATEST NATURAL & NATIONAL CURIOSITY IN THE WORLD. Born, it
was said, in 1674, when slavery was in full force, Heth was held in captivity
by the family of George Washington (1732–99), the first president of the
US. The Emancipation Proclamation, which brought the end of slavery,
was not until 1863. Thousands of customers were invited to spend their
pennies to gawp at a 161-year-old woman, born in bondage. If they so
wished, they could even prod her. Collecting the pennies, Phineas Taylor
Barnum (1810–91) was starting what was to become a career of heroic
proportions. Later, he would open his museum of freaks in New York City
and, in 1871, launch an extravagant circus known as "The Greatest Show
on Earth."

Barnum may not have legally owned Heth, but he treated her as his
property, exhibiting her publicly for up to fourteen hours at a stretch. In fact,
the exploitation continued after her death in 1836: Barnum turned her autopsy

into a public event, 1,500 spectators paying for the right to witness the post-mortem examination of her body, which revealed that she was actually about 90 years younger than her advertised age.

In his book *The Showman and the Slave*, Benjamin Reiss remarks on the media's dehumanizing coverage of Heth: "Many early reports favored grotesque images of her body over accounts of her life story" (p. 39). She was displayed as a "human commodity," a product worthy of whites' curiosity and perhaps more. Barnum, though strictly an impresario, in staging the autopsy inadvertently offered a contribution to an emerging racial science aimed at discovering the source of the manifest physical and moral differences between blacks and whites.

Heth wasn't the first black woman to be placed like an object on public display. Saartjie Baartman (*c*.1789–1816) was taken from her Griqua tribal homeland in South Africa, enslaved, and then, in 1810, exhibited as a freak in London. Like Heth, she was displayed as an unusual physical specimen that observers were allowed to touch. Sold to a French animal trainer, she came to the attention of the prominent anatomist Georges Cuvier (1769–1832).

Baartman died penniless, aged 26. Cuvier was especially interested in her genitalia, the labium of which he considered a "special attribute of her race." After dissecting her body, Cuvier published his findings in 1817 as *Le Règne Animal Destribué d'Après son Organization*, which included his conclusions on the specimen he called *La Vénus Hottentote*. He compared the structure and functions of her body to those of the great apes. The comparison extended to the way he discharged her dismembered cadaver: preserved in formaldehyde-filled bell jars and either sold, loaned or donated to natural history museums. The 2010 film *Vénus Noire*, directed by Abdellatif Kechiche, tells Baartman's story.

Baartman spent her life in bondage of one kind or another, though Heth probably volunteered her services to Barnum. She may even have connived with him to develop a routine, or a little performance designed to amuse whites. Consider the arrangement. Barnum was a showman whose mission was to divert people's attention so pleasurably that they'd be persuaded to pay and so provide him with an income. Joice Heth was probably, as Barnum's publicity claimed, an ex-slave and she was certainly a black woman, her only prospect of a living being in domestic labor of some kind. So there were reciprocal interests.

Depending on your perspective, Barnum was either insightful or opportunistic in sensing whites' curiosity. But, perhaps this was not such a feat in the 1800s, when interest in black people appears to have been widespread. Quite apart from the scientific discourse on the concept of "race" and its ontological status, there were discussions on the natural disposition of black people: why did they always seem to be full of fun? In the mid-nineteenth century, the respected English geologist Charles Lyell observed the fondness of "Negroes" for music and dancing and concluded that this was not due to what he called "external influences," meaning it was part of their inherent qualities – it was natural, in other words.

Lyell is quoted by Joseph Boskin, whose historical study *Sambo: The rise and demise of an American jester* traces the origin of an enduring and adaptable characterization of black people – as carefree buffoons devoid of the intelligence or sensibility of whites. Blacks grinned a lot, danced a lot and loved singing. The reason for this could have been more expedient that Lyell imagined: looking unhappy or angry could earn a slave a beating; beaming could make life slightly less unpleasant. Also, as Ronald Takaki points out in his *A Different Mirror*, "they might have been playing the role of loyal and congenial slave in order to get favors, while keeping their inner selves hidden … many slaves wore masks of docility and deference" (p. 115).

African American slaves probably wore the sambo mask for pragmatic reasons, but its functions for whites were many. The apparent happy-go-lucky demeanor of black people persuaded whites of the essential childlikeness of black people, perhaps reassuring them that they were morally justified in keeping a paternalistic control of their dependants. It may even have created the impression that blacks actually benefited from their dependence, and that their obedience was a reflection of devotion rather than coercion.

Whites were convinced that blacks were incapable of their own level of sophisticated thought and emotion, and the joyous manner with which blacks accepted their servitude would have supported this. It would also have assuaged any residual fears that whites would not be in control forever, a point that leads Jan Nederveen Pieterse to call the sambo figure a "cultural talisman" through which masters sought to "choreograph reality." The phrase suggests composition, planning and the element of theater, all designed for the amusement of whites.

Boskin writes of the "incongruity of play and circumstance" that propelled whites toward a conception of blacks that explained the apparent contradiction between the inhuman conditions in which slaves lived and their pleasant, comical mien. "It was a conception that attempted to encompass all the facets of blacks' playfulness: their cheerful and lighthearted manner, penchant for frivolity, rhythmical movements, unusual mannerisms, even their patter of language." Blacks were "mirthful by nature" (p. 54). Even if the conception existed only in whites' imaginations, its effects went far beyond. It became the basis for a form of entertainment.

———

The minstrel show, or the Ethiopian Opera, was the most popular entertainment in the early nineteenth century, ceding place to vaudeville after the end of the American Civil War (1861–65), before motion pictures took over in the twentieth century. The minstrel shows consisted of white singers and dancers in "blackface," meaning their faces were covered in theatrical makeup, or burnt cork. They would sing, dance, play banjo and clown around, creating crude caricatures of inoffensive "plantation niggers," or "coons," the popular name for southern blacks. Daddy Rice (1808–60) was the most famous of these minstrels.

White audiences loved them, probably because they affirmed what they wanted to know: that there was no need to feel guilty, or afraid. This appeasement was especially comforting against a background of slave rebellions, many of which were inspired by Christian beliefs – the Virginia insurrection of 1831 organized by Nat Turner being the most celebrated.

These uprisings suggested a different image of African Americans from those expressed in both the minstrel shows and popular literature of the day. "Responsive to kindness, loyal, affectionate, and co-operative," is how the typical slave was depicted in many of the popular novels, according to George M. Frederickson. In his *The Black Image in the White Mind*, Frederickson reports on what he calls a "romantic racialist image" that circulated through literature and popular thought.

One of the stock characters of the shows was the bumptious, mock-important fellow forever embarrassing himself as he tottered toward a freedom that seemed in sight after the abolition of the slave trade in 1807. It was, of course, farce: blacks, the audience was agreeably reminded, could not survive without the protective care of whites.

In his history of the minstrelsy, as the theatrical tradition was known, Robert Toll points out that African American beliefs, songs, dances and folklore were taken by the white minstrels. "The presence of these distinctively Afro-American themes supports the view that minstrels borrowed from black culture," writes Toll (p. 50). He sees significance in this "because it was the first indication of the powerful influence Afro-American culture would have on the performing arts in America." However, he is careful to point out: "It does not mean that early minstrels accurately portrayed Negro life or even the cultural elements that they used. They did neither" (p. 51). But they did have enormous effects on cultural change.

"Minstrel caricatures of slaves served not only to define African-Americans in the minds of the dominant culture," writes Richard L. Hughes, but, "also contributed to the growing sense of 'whiteness' among an ethnically diverse population" (p. 29). This is a valuable point and I'll return to it: the minstrels "helped define what was white and, consequently, what was American."

The impresarios were white: men such as Charles Callender, George Christy, and Sam Hague, an English promoter who, in the 1860s, took the unprecedented step of featuring black performers on stage. White minstrels stretched and distorted aspects of what they considered black culture so that they presented portrayals white audiences found satisfying. Black performers deviated little from the established archetypes and routines. The promoter J.H. Haverly capitalized on Hague's success with black performers and turned his troupe into one of the most successful touring theaters, using similar marketing techniques to those used by Barnum – what today we might call hype, back then, "humbug."

Toll discerns an important difference in Haverly's theatrical approach: he presented his minstrels not as mere entertainers, but as authentic representatives of the black population, or perhaps the black species, "like animals in a zoo" (p. 206). The commercial success of Haverly's enterprise indicated the perverse amusements whites took in having images of blacks presented to them, even if in theatrical form. Black performers themselves profited from the minstrel shows. Those who were prepared to play up to the sambo type, like Billy Kersands, grew prosperous. Others, such as James Bland, enjoyed popularity in Europe as well as the US. Horace Weston (1825–90) "was the first African American banjoist to achieve a significant reputation," according to Robert B. Winans and Elias J. Kaufman (p. 10).

Flanked by white owners and producers in the wings, the minstrels laid on a costumed performance for the delectation of whites. "Coon songs" were popular compositions. A respectful acknowledgment of blacks' musical gifts, their untutored sense of rhythm and their instinctual ability to amuse others might have been offered as compliments. But they were conditional. Blacks were granted access to some, though not all, cultural areas – entertainment being the main one, sports the other. And they were expected to embellish, not compromise, stereotypes; "darkie," "nigger" and "coon" were popularized in their music.

There was a balancing act going on. Black performers "did not just attempt to hook audiences with hokum; they subverted and manipulated stereotypes as they struggled to present black identity." That's the interpretation of Karen Sotiropoulos (p. 105). In her *Staging Race*, Sotiropoulos argues that, while black performers were obliged to comply with white expectations, they were also agents of change, playing roles for the benefit of whites, at the same time distancing themselves from those very roles. In his critical review of Sotiropoulos's book, David Krasner adds, "black performers were media savvy; like the boxer Jack Johnson, they sought publicity to stay in the headlines" (p. 377). In other words: on stage, black people were clowning, dancing and singing in a way that confirmed whites' racist assumptions, but always trying to negotiate enough wriggle space to present glimpses of an alternative experience and identity for black people.

The effect on black audiences is something Jacqueline Stewart ponders in her article, "Negroes laughing at themselves?" "Spectatorship," argues Stewart, "is typically characterized as an activity fraught with social, psychological, and political contradictions for black viewers." In watching hideously disfigured portrayals of black life, African Americans "reconstructed their individual and collective identities." Stewart suggests "feelings of community and race pride" emerged in the common experience of observing and enjoying (p. 653).

There was some debate about whether there actually was or should be a distinct "Negro identity" that was either being represented or misrepresented on the stage. W.E.B. Du Bois (1868–1963), the eminent co-founder of the

National Association for the Advancement of Colored People (NAACP) in 1909, claimed a cultural and racial identity based partially on aspects of the slave heritage. In contrast, as Barbara L. Webb points out: "Some prominent citizens such as Andrew F. Hilyer seemed to fear that the assertion of a distinct Negro cultural identity, especially one founded on slavery, could impede arguments for social and political equality" (p. 72).

This prompts a more general question: how can a theatrical performance convey any sense of cultural authenticity? However convincing, it's arguable that any kind of performance, whether dramatic, comedic, or any other style or genre, is helpless to express experience, except in a distorted or attenuated manner. Entertainment is often enlightening, occasionally edifying, but never veracious. So, if white audiences believed they were getting a clear view of the lives of African Americans, they were deluded. This didn't stop them.

Webb writes of how whites would "vicariously observe" black life, presumably meaning that, through theater, they experienced in their imaginations the feelings and actions of blacks. Nor was it just theater: exhibitions purporting to reveal black folk culture from the plantation past mixed education with spectacle. Depictions were consistent with white expectations, but it seems there was irony, periphrasis and non sequitur in blacks' performances for those who wanted to look closely.

The keenness of whites to learn more about black life, not through study but through entertainment, was a feature of this period that endured through the twentieth century and, arguably, to the present day. While they may once have been satisfied with other whites' interpretations, they later warmed to the authenticity supposedly conveyed by black artists and performers. This opened up opportunities for African Americans to explore their own capabilities as entertainers-of-whites. It also planted the seeds of a tradition deeply in American soil.

—

An elite of African American singers was so outstanding that its members were permitted to deviate from comic roles and even appear on programs otherwise limited to white artists. One such exceptional performer was Matilda Sissieretta Jones (1869–1933), sometimes known as the "Black Patti," in allusion to the late nineteenth century prima donna Adelina Patti. African American concert singers performed primarily for black audiences in churches or blacks-only auditoriums. "Jones initially pursued a different career goal," writes John Graziano. She became "one of the first African American women to associate professionally with white musicians and entertain predominantly white audiences" (p. 545). In short, "she chose to interact with white American culture." Her life illustrates the difficulty black artists had in the entertainment industry.

Touring Europe in the 1890s, she performed in front of all kinds of audiences, sometimes before royalty. In America, audiences were strictly segregated. Her many accolades confirmed she was one of the premier operatic performers of her day. But in 1896, she took a new career path, forming her own company, which she called the Black Patti Troubadours. The name itself was surprising considering she'd previously regarded the "Black Patti" soubriquet as demeaning. The rise of the Ku Klux Klan in the period following the end of slavery symbolized the widespread suspicions about hostility toward blacks. It would climb to a high point of five million in the 1920s.

Even as a "major star," as Graziano describes her, Jones couldn't appear in many whites-only venues. Her repertoire was too highbrow for popular audiences, and she faced the prospect of returning to Europe before her manager, Rudolph Voelckel, and a business partner, John Nolan, offered her the chance to lead a new 40-strong, all-black troupe specializing in "popular" entertainment, mainly – though not exclusively – at black venues. The deal, worth $20,000 per year, made her "the highest paid African American performer of her time," according to Graziano (p. 588).

Voelckel's motives were hardly selfless: Paula Marie Seniors documents how he "could use racism to control people of color" (p. 16). Her options limited, Sissieretta became the head of the touring "colored company" of performers, the titles of her shows evocative of white cultural tastes of the early twentieth century: *A Trip to Africa* toured 1909-10, *In the Jungles*, 1911–12, and *Lucky Sam from Alabam'*, 1914–15. For the last nineteen years of her life, Sissieretta "remained a star and an important symbol," as Graziano puts it. She demonstrated "that black performers were not just limited to minstrelsy but could sing in opera and other genres of art music" (p. 589). She died in 1933.

Graziano believes Sissieretta represented the "New Negro," a term usually associated with the Harlem Renaissance, a literary and artistic movement in the 1920s, which produced the likes of Zora Neale Hurston and Langston Hughes. In 1919, Oscar Micheaux became the first African American to make a film when he wrote, directed and produced *The Homesteader*. Six years later, Micheaux's *Body and Soul* featured "Paul Robeson, the world's greatest actor of the race," as the *New York Age*, a black publication, put it in 1925 (quoted in Pearl Bower and Louise Spence's 2000 essay on Micheaux). Robeson (1898–1976) was the pre-eminent black performer of his generation, though he became a deeply divisive figure. Like Sissieretta Jones, he found the pressures of being a serious and, in his case, politically involved artist too much to bear.

Educated at Rutgers and Columbia, Robeson distinguished himself as a football player, but opted for the theater, appearing in England and the US, in several Eugene O'Neill plays, but most notably in Shakespeare's *Othello*. A bass-baritone, he memorably sang "Ol' Man River" in the second film adaptation of Edna Ferber's paean to the traveling Mississippi theaters, *Show Boat*, directed by James Whale in 1936 (the first was in 1929). Robeson's "success brought him celebrity in both worlds, black and white," observes Barbara J. Beeching. But his affairs with white women, his acquaintance with intellectuals, royalty and other distinguished personages, as well as his achievements in sports and his world travels "gave him a self-confidence that irritated whites, who resented 'uppity Negroes'; and African Americans, who resented those who moved on to better circumstances, leaving their fellows behind" (p. 349).

Robeson spoke out against fascism abroad and racism at home. When he heard of the plight of Welsh miners who went on hunger marches in 1927, he aligned himself with their cause and began to visit Wales, where he performed concerts. Ever the controversialist, Robeson visited the Soviet Union in 1934 and thereafter identified with leftwing politics. The FBI and Britain's secret service MI5 both had files on him, the implication being that he was an agent of a subversive organization and so a danger to America. He was not a member of any organization. The black baseball player Jackie Robinson (1919–72) publicly denounced Robeson, probably in the interests of his own reputation.

Robeson's stance was at odds with the policy of piecemeal reform known as gradualism that characterized the period 1940–49: he had no time for slow, incremental change and insisted his human rights were inalienable. "A good piece of that American earth belongs to me," he claimed. Robeson advocated Black Nationalism, meaning the self-sufficiency of and separate national status for black people.

When, in 1950, Joseph McCarthy (1909–57) started his infamous investigations into alleged communist infiltration in American public life, Robeson refused to sign an affidavit disclaiming membership in the Communist Party, prompting the US State Department to revoke his passport. The decision had uncomfortable resonances with a code of practice that stood before 1865 and prevented freed slaves from possessing passports. (W.E.B. Du Bois had his passport denied in 1952 following a speech in which he was critical of the Korean War, 1950–53.)

Robeson's star fell abruptly: forced to pull out of international engagements, he was eschewed by American promoters. By the time his passport was reinstated in 1958, the civil rights movement was picking up pace and Robeson was a forlorn figure in poor health. He traveled and, for a while, settled in Europe, but returned to the US where he died in 1976. His experience seemed cautionary: conform or perish. When faced with a comparable dilemma, Sissieretta chose to conform. Robeson could have kept his political views to himself and his own affiliations private; his decision not to cost him his career, as well as his passport.

———

Robeson's imperious, flamboyant and tempestuous reputation contrasts with that of his equally distinguished contemporary Duke Ellington (1899–1974), who was born a year after Robeson and died two years before him. Pianist, composer and bandleader, Ellington rose to fame after his *Mood Indigo* in 1930. As Robeson was the "greatest actor of the race," so Ellington was the leading "race man" in the field of music. When direct expression became perilous for black people, there was always indirect: "Ellington did not fight for civil rights in the manner of political activists, but he contributed much to that cause, most of it unrecognized," writes Harvey G. Cohen (p. 1,004).

Cohen refers principally to Ellington's suite *Black, Brown and Beige* (1943), which the artist intended as a musical portrayal of African American history. It was the first in a series of suites he composed, usually consisting of pieces linked by subject matter. Ellington began playing professionally in 1916, inspired by the syncopated music known as ragtime, which had emerged in the 1890s. Ellington realized that the new bluesy jazz sounds emerging from New Orleans called boogie-woogie represented a potent source of new ideas. His collaboration with the trumpeter James "Bubber" Miley produced the "jungle" sound, for which he was known in his early phase. "Many of Ellington's titles from this period reflect the 'jungle' motif," James Haskins reminds us in his *The Cotton Club*, a book about the Harlem club where Ellington's band played its most famous residency between 1927 and 1931 (p. 53). The Harlem Renaissance was in full swing.

Cohen argues that in the 1940s, Ellington, by then renowned internationally, reappraised his contribution and "wondered if delivering the message about the need for equal rights exclusively through the medium of music was sufficient" (p. 1,020). Robeson was forbidden to travel abroad. The Klan's membership had slid to around 30,000, though legal segregation was in force and would stay that way until 1964. At the time, "Ellington commanded center stage in a way that no black artist ever had," Cohen tells us (pp. 1,021–22). But: "Did his insistence on staying within the musical realm only play into the old stereotypes that viewed music as one of the few areas blacks were skilled in?" Cohen imagines Ellington asked himself a similar question.

We can't know whether he actually did, of course. But we know Ellington never expressed his views on what was, for all but his final ten years, a racially segregated society. At least, not explicitly: music is a subtler though infinitely more ambiguous medium than language. And, by using it exclusively, Ellington escaped the kind of privations of Robeson. Nor did he compromise his art, conform to arch stereotypes or play the excessively servile roles – the masks of docility, as Takaki calls them. Perhaps being a man made a difference; for comparison, let me outline the experiences of some prominent black female performers of roughly the same period.

In 1935, Ellington played in a short film, *Symphony in Black: A rhapsody of Negro life*, in which a number of African American artists appeared. One of them was the brilliant but tragic Billie Holiday (1915–59). Seldom less than good, sometimes brushing greatness, Holiday began recording in 1933, aged 18. Her success with bands – including those of Count Basie and Artie Shaw – was tempered by human failings and she had long periods of dependence on drugs and alcohol. Holiday was also affected by the particular problems she faced as a black woman. She performed at clubs where she was not allowed to talk to the audience, stayed in hotels where she was told to use freight elevators rather than share with white guests. Acclaimed by critics and audiences, she reached a public few African Americans approached and, as such, ventured into a world where she was welcome as a singer, but not as a human being. Her manifest disorientation was no doubt a product of this. She was 45 when she died in 1959.

Earlier in the twentieth century, Ethel Waters (1896–1977) started out singing "coon" songs but found white audiences congenial. This was the first of what Donald Bogle, in his 2010 biography *Heat Wave*, reveals as series of racial breakthroughs. She was one of the first (if not the first) black women to sing on radio. She was the only major black actor in Irving Berlin's *As Thousands Cheer*, a white Broadway show in the 1930s. She was among the first black women to star in a Broadway drama, *Mamba's Daughters*. She was the first black woman to have her own network tv sitcom, *Beulah*, which went on the air in 1950, and to which I will return shortly. Stylistically, her scat singing foreshadowed Louis Armstrong and Ella Fitzgerald.

Waters' dealings with promoters, agents and colleagues were often affected by her perception that she was underpaid. Maybe she was, but, in the depressed 1930s, she was the highest-paid artist on Broadway, earning $2,500 per week. Her legal victory over MGM turned out to be Pyrrhic: she didn't work for six years after.

Earlier, in 1925, when she was unavailable for a European tour, Waters' understudy Josephine Baker (1906–75) stepped in. Baker, an exotic dancer, fascinated audiences at Paris' Folies-Bergère, but found America altogether less hospitable. Her periodic returns to the USA were never easy; audiences were wary of a black female whose mission seemed to be to break every rule. Baker was one of several black entertainers, including the prodigiously dexterous Nicholas Brothers (Fayard, 1914–2006; Harold, 1921–2000), to find greater success in Europe than in the USA.

Three different women with three different experiences, though all united by a special kind of struggle that challenged African Americans either to bend or brawl. There are less obvious instances of struggle. Lena Horne (1917–2010), for example, was the first African American, man or woman, to secure a long-term contract with MGM, then the most powerful Hollywood studio, and by the mid-1940s was reputedly the highest-paid black actor. But she too paid a price; as she famously said: "I didn't get much of a chance to act." She usually appeared – looking vivacious – and sang, as she did in Andrew L. Stone's 1943 film *Stormy Weather*, which featured an all-black cast.

Horne acquired a sound working knowledge of why her acting was often edited out of movies: she was expected to look good and sing well; that was the limit of her contribution. No one expected her to act particularly well. She was Hollywood's version of an expensive ornament: pleasing to the eye, though not integral to anything. In Vincente Minnelli's 1943 movie *Cabin in the Sky*, Horne played an overtly sexy handmaiden of the devil; in the original film she sang while taking a bubble bath but the scene was deleted before the film was released — not for racial reasons, as her stand-alone performances in other MGM musicals sometimes were, but because it was considered too risqué.

In fairness to MGM, the studio had broken with tradition when it signed Horne and afforded her the kind of treatment usually reserved for white sex symbols. Baker had been banished for her eroticism twenty years earlier. Studio chiefs presumably felt the world was now ready, their decision no doubt influenced by Horne's pale skin, straight hair and narrow nose (picture gallery at: http://bit.ly/-LenaHorne).

The NAACP took an interest in MGM's initiative and monitored Horne's career, presumably wary of the wider implications. Horne avoided clichéd roles, but was never offered the kind of parts available to white contemporaries, such as Betty Grable (1916–73), Rita Hayworth (1918–87) or Ava Gardner (1922–90). Fortunately for Horne, she kept her career as a recording artist alive. At 83, she sang on Simon Rattle's 2000 *Classic Ellington* album.

When Horne married Lennie Hayton, a white man – a prominent arranger, conductor and pianist who was for many years both her and MGM's musical director – the marriage, in 1947, took place in France and was kept secret for three years. Interracial marriage, as it was called, was forbidden in some US states until the *Loving v. Virginia* case of 1967, which resulted in a Supreme Court ruling that antimiscegenation laws were unconstitutional.

Although she wasn't expected to think for herself, Horne did exactly this and claimed that her friendships with Paul Robeson and W.E.B. Du Bois were responsible for a long period of inactivity after the end of her Hollywood tenure in 1950. She was blacklisted and unable to make films or tv shows for seven years. In the early 1960s, Horne became increasingly active, participating in numerous civil rights rallies and protests.

Horne's career invites comparisons with that of Dorothy Dandridge, four years her junior, also strikingly good-looking, also married to a white man, and also a singer – though not in Horne's class – who sought to transfer to the movies. Often cast as a nymphet, Dandridge is credited with having participated in the first "interracial screen kiss" when she embraced British actor Michael Rennie in Robert Rossen's 1957 film *Island in the Sun*. Frustrated at her failure to find serious acting roles, Dandridge turned to nightclub singing, though with no success. She was made to file for bankruptcy. In 1965, she overdosed on antidepressants and died, aged 41. (Biographer Donald Bogle talks about Dandridge at: http://bit.ly/-DorothyDandridge.)

———

Ethel Waters brought herself up from destitution, working for a time in domestic service. So when, in her fifties, she was offered a job in the title role of the tv series *Beulah*, she presumably thought acting as a maid was preferable to being one. The television series was based on a successful radio show that had started in the 1930s, and which had originally featured a white actor as the eponymous housekeeper-cum-cook. In his book on Waters, Donald Bogle notes how the black press condemned her and contrasted her with Lena Horne, who "refused to lend her talents in roles that will reflect 'badly' upon her people." Stung by this type of criticism, Waters quit the show, though it wasn't the first time she had played a servant role: she had appeared in the 1934 musical *Bubbling Over* as a washerwoman.

Hattie McDaniel (1895–1952) took over. She'd been playing Beulah in the radio show after finding film roles scarce. McDaniel had endured protests in front of cinemas in 1939 when civil rights groups, including the NAACP, objected to her depiction of Scarlett O'Hara's devoted slave, Mammy, in *Gone with the Wind*. The role was her specialty: she had virtually made a living out of it since the 1920s, when she toured on the vaudeville circuit, usually spoofing the plantation mammy caricature. Her biographer Jill Watts reckons, though typecast, McDaniel tried to subvert stereotypes of black docility and simple-mindedness; though this never persuaded her critics that her career was anything but a disservice to African Americans.

McDaniel fell ill – later diagnosed with breast cancer – after filming only six episodes of *Beulah*, which were not screened until much later. She died in 1952, three years before Rosa Parks' refusal to give up her bus seat to a white man in Montgomery, Alabama – an act that inspired the civil rights movement. Watts observes that even McDaniel's legacy prompted controversy: in the 1960s and 1970s, when black power was at its peak, images of McDaniel's grinning, rolling-eyed caricatures were held up as reminders of blacks' mortification.

This was a ruthless assessment: viewed in context, McDaniel's contribution is more varied. She was born and lived entirely amid Jim Crow segregation, so just having a presence in film or on tv was an achievement in its own right. While Hollywood was hardly insulated from the rest of America, it did afford black actors the chance to cross racial lines, even if temporarily and somewhat artificially.

In 1934, five years before the release of *Gone with the Wind*, Clarence Edouard Muse (1889–1979), himself an African American who had managed to make a living as Hollywood actor, self-published a pamphlet entitled *The Dilemma of the Negro Actor*. In it, he reasoned that the black actor has the choice of being responsible to black audiences in his or her screen portrayals, or being a successful black stereotype for "the white audience with a definite desire for buffoonery and song." Was it better, Muse asked, for black actors to achieve success in mainstream roles as loyal maids and fawning darkies, or to risk not working at all by insisting on better parts and more equitable representation?

Muse had no compunction about accepting parts that he considered devaluing: he needed to earn a living in an industry that was driven by commercial dynamics. Only cultural change would open out roles for African Americans. Later, in 1972, with serious black film roles still at a premium, he gave an interview to *Ebony* writer B.J. Mason, in which he predicted: "Popular demand will cause producers to make good black films" (p. 54).

Film studios cast actors, whether black or white, by type. There were few black directors, no producers and, at many studios, facilities were segregated, reflecting social arrangements elsewhere in America. Those who challenged paid with their careers. Often even those who didn't challenge suffered, as we've seen in this chapter.

There are a number of conclusions that can be drawn from the material covered in this chapter. By maintaining a strictly limited array of roles, or types, that African Americans were allowed to play, entertainment has reflected wider social arrangements. Entertainment has also performed what might be called an ideological function, disseminating ideas, or more accurately, ideals that lie at the heart of the ethos of the nation. America was, and is, first and foremost a white society, and its artistic and cultural representations convey this just as reliably as its political and economic institutions.

Perhaps there is a more surreptitious process at work. After the first slaves arrived in Virginia in 1619, slavery became the single most important component of the American economy and thus the source of its prosperity. After nearly 250 years, the cultural patterns carved by slavery were deep and, in the eyes of many, ineradicable. Yet somehow, the nation had to make what must have seemed an accommodation of gargantuan proportions. Entertainment, as I've traced, offered a gratification: it showed black people in the way whites wanted to see them – as fools, minions, or primitives governed by sexual impulses rather than rational thoughts. Casting black actors or other kinds of entertainers in these roles was not an accident, but nor was it the result of the pernicious scheming of racist producers: audiences sought amusement rather than provocation or confrontation. Amusement often derives from comfort. The entertainment industry was responsive.

I started this chapter with a case that illustrated a historical interest in blacks, whether as people or as specimens, that has continued in its peculiar, serpentine way right to the present day. Whites have been fascinated by blacks and have paid to watch them perform in one way or another since at least the early nineteenth century, and probably in less organized fashions previously. I wrote before: entertainment is never *just* the provision of amusement or enjoyment; it's an opportunity to learn. In this instance, it offers us an understanding of the ways whites have managed and preserved their own sense of superiority in the midst of evidence that repeatedly challenged it.

8

Black models don't sell

'Tyra Banks is nobody's fool and certainly no pawn of patrician white executives. Yet she operates in a way that complements perfectly the colorblind code of postracial America.'

Jewel Ciera Washington was 15 when she appeared on the *Tyra Show* late in 2009. She had apparently responded to a request on the show's website. "Are you obsessed with sex and unable to control your sexual impulses?" read the solicitation. "If so, share your story and maybe we can help." The following year, Washington's mother Beverly McClendon alleged that Banks' producers got in touch with Jewel directly to arrange for her to appear on the talk show and discuss, among other things, how she lost her virginity at the age of nine, had sex with over 20 men by the time she was thirteen, and had been pregnant three times. Beverly filed a $3 million federal lawsuit, claiming her parental permission should have been sought.

It was a rare, perhaps unique, contretemps for Tyra Banks, a woman whose rise was not so much smooth as velvety, whose bewitching amalgamation of extreme glamour and unstoppable ambition captured the imaginations of a legion of young women, and whose buzzwords "fierce" and "smize" (smile with your eyes) were not just babble, but babble *à la mode*. When she told Lynn Hirschberg, of *New York Times Magazine*, "I think I was put on this earth to instill self-esteem in young girls," it was possible to believe that she was actually being serious about her destiny ("Banksable", June 1, 2008).

"We've seen with Tyra that the audience is changing. In the past, her audience would have been primarily African-American, but the television audience in general is becoming increasingly colorblind, and younger viewers are particularly colorblind," reflected Leslie Moonves, president and chief executive of the CBS Corporation – a parent company, along with Warner Brothers, of the CW network on which Banks' show appeared. "It's similar to the pattern we're seeing with voters and Barack Obama — he and Tyra have a similar appeal to the youth audience."

Colorblind is one of those terms that have been around for at least a half-century and probably longer: it means not influenced by racism or racial prejudice. So a colorblind society was one in which no-one was evaluated on his or her color, or any other kind of visible marker of his or her ethnic origin. The term drifted out of the popular vocabulary in the 1970s, when it appeared naïve and idealistic – the colorblind society seemed to exist only in the imaginations of the most optimistic liberals – but roared back into vogue with the election of Barack Obama. Does Tyra really have "similar appeal" to the president?

Banks is a product of Inglewood, an ethnically diverse suburb of Los Angeles and home of the sports and rock venue the LA Forum. She lived in a one-bedroom apartment with her mother and brother. The story goes that, on her first day at the all-girl Immaculate Heart High School, Banks was told: "You should be a model." She wasn't the first young woman to have heard that, of course, but in this case, the person who said it was a photographer and took some shots for the then 15-year-old Banks to circulate around model agencies. A French agency summoned her to Paris, where she began to sashay along the catwalks for the likes of Givenchy and Chanel. She abandoned her studies. By the early 1990s, she was earning a living in Europe, dreaming of becoming one of the future generations of supermodels.

Up to that time, catwalk and photographic models were largely interchangeable. Only occasionally would a prominent figure separate herself from the others: Twiggy in the 1960s, and Elle McPherson and Christie Brinkley in the 1980s were exceptions. But, in the 1990s, a clique known collectively as supermodels emerged, headed by Cindy Crawford, Claudia Schiffer, Christy Turlington and Linda Evangelista, the last of whom famously declared: "We don't wake up for less than $10,000 a day." Even allowing for exaggeration, the point was clear enough: supermodels' earnings were up there with those of movie stars and premier rock performers. This was reflected in the corresponding shift in status from anonymous ambulant coathangers to glittering occupants of the celebrity A-list.

Both magazines and fashion designers were reluctant to employ black models in the 1990s. But there were exceptions. One was the Somalian Iman, who moved to the USA and began modeling for the Wilhemina Agency in the mid-1970s, working for, among others, Calvin Klein and Donna Karan. In 1992, when she was 37, she married David Bowie, and had transferred from fashion to film.

Another was the perplexingly androgynous Grace Jones, who was born in Jamaica but essayed modeling in New York and Paris, where she probably designed or developed her trademark *dominatrice sauvage* image. Jones alternated between singing and acting and still performs, even in her sixties.

Nothing stands still for long in the fashion industry, though some things endure. By 2008, Carole White, co-founder of Premier Model Management, which supplies models to top fashion brands, confessed that finding work for black clients was significantly harder than for the white models. "Sadly we are in the business where you stock your shelves with what sells," she said. "According to the magazines, black models don't sell," White told Rob Sharp, for his article "Fashion is racist: insider lifts lid on 'ethnic exclusion'" in the British *Independent* newspaper (February 16, 2008).

Fashion was anything but colorblind, though in 1987 Naomi Campbell, the London-born model, became the first black subject to appear on the cover of the French edition of *Vogue*. There were echoes of the Michael Jackson/MTV episode covered earlier in this book when the late French fashion designer Yves Saint-Laurent (1936–2008) threatened to break all ties with the publication if Campbell was not put on the cover. Campbell became part of the elite group of supermodels, modeling for the world's pre-eminent designers before, perhaps surprisingly, posing nude for *Playboy* in 1999. Surprisingly in 1999, that is: over the next decade, Campbell became involved in several shenanigans that served to maintain her public profile, not always in a dignified way.

In addition to verbal assaults on hotel and airport staff, she whacked her housekeeper (for which she was sentenced to do community service). Campbell won a privacy case against a British newspaper that had published pictures of her leaving a Narcotics Anonymous meeting in London in 2001, while she was receiving treatment for drug addiction. Her brief appearance at a United Nations war crimes tribunal investigating Charles Taylor, the former Liberian president, was made eventful by impromptu remark that the trial was a "big inconvenience" to her. Campbell's turbulent but supremely newsworthy career was ornamented with serial affairs with some of the world's best-known and most eligible men.

Google "naomi campbell" then select *Past 24 hours* under "More search tools" on the left of your screen, and there will be a fresh story. Campbell seems to have made a career rebelling against blandness and, as such, still commands the attention of the global media. If there is a way of causing outrage, she can find it: in 2009, for example, she modeled clothes by the luxury furrier Dennis Basso. While wearing fur is itself an incendiary act, Campbell's action was near treasonous; in 1994, she had appeared with other supermodels in a campaign for PETA (People For the Ethical Treatment of Animals) in which the strapline was, "We'd rather go naked than wear fur."

———

Banks' career offers comparisons and contrasts, the latter probably a function of the former: in the early 1990s, when Banks was a new recruit to the fashion world, she probably stock-checked the industry in her own mind and realized there was pile of one kind of human merchandise and a scarcity of another. The then upswinging Campbell was usually the only black model on the catwalk at the premier events, and her historic appearance on *Vogue*'s cover was more like a one-off *haute couture* creation than the first of a new retail line. Perhaps Banks thought the way to secure a place in the industry was to be Aphrodite to Naomi's Athena (or, possibly, the lesser known Enyo, goddess of war).

Banks no doubt realized that modeling ranks alongside sports as one of the most ephemeral careers. In both lines of work, a performer depends on her or his body. In the 1990s, with heroin chic the fashion industry's main and only aesthetic, Banks' body began to look too voluptuous for the catwalk. Photographic modeling was still an option and Banks, like Campbell, created her own piece of history when she signed a deal with Victoria's Secret, the underwear and lingerie retail and mail-order company; she became the first black model to feature in the company catalog. Banks was also the first African American woman featured on the covers of *GQ* and the *Sports Illustrated Swimsuit Issue*.

In 1999, having made a foray into film with appearances in the Michael Jackson video for *Black or White* in 1991, and in John Singleton's 1995 feature *Higher Learning,* Banks took a job on *Oprah*. At 25, she was young enough to be a youth correspondent. The assumption was that she was Oprah's protégée – not a foundationless assumption, as it turned out, since she worked on the show until 2001. At this point, the networks were filling up with reality tv shows, *Big Brother* being the most outstanding example of a genre that captivated the world and that would dominate for the next decade. Banks' *America's Next Top Model* – or *ANTM* – sat squarely in this genre, fusing elements of unscripted drama with aspirational young people in cut-throat competition. She sold the concept to CBS, which fed the program to its sister channel UPN, later to become the CW network, which had a target demographic of 18- to 34-year-old women. The show spawned 17 international editions. As Kiri Blakeley, of *Forbes*, put it in her "Tyra banks on it": "The formula clicked instantly: pretty girls crying, fighting and having every molecule on their insecure little bodies brutally critiqued by Banks and her fellow judges" (July 3, 2006).

Banks' only conspicuously unsuccessful enterprise during this otherwise fertile period was a sub-Beyoncé-sounding record *Shake Ya Body* that failed to make any kind of impact, despite being featured on *ANTM*. It remains her only single release. Less conspicuous was a failed Internet investment with hip-hop mogul Russell Simmons.

Another tv series, *Tyra* started in 2005: this one was a more conventional daytime talk show, much like *Oprah*. It lasted until 2009. In one of the shows, she interviewed Campbell. "I was tired of having to deal with you," she told Campbell, accusing her of having tried to sabotage her early on in her career. The implication was that perhaps both of them recognized the limited number of places for black models at the top table. Campbell never acknowledged the rivalry, though it became a matter of public record.

Ever the pragmatist, Banks set up her own production company in 2006; its first motion picture was Michael Lembeck's 2008 *The Clique*. Bankable, as the company is called, has developed prime-time series *True Beauty* and *Stylista* and contributes to Banks' several income streams, which collectively yield $30 million per year, according to *Forbes*. In 2008, as if to emphasize the distance Banks had traveled from Paris' Grand Palais and the Espace Eiffel, where she wore Versace and Dior, she did a deal with Wal-Mart for an *ANTM*-branded line of merchandise. Complementing this line, Banks launched an online fashion and beauty platform "that offers women the personalized style know-how they are looking for" at TypeF.com.

While Campbell continued her ethereal ways, Banks went for more earthly endeavors. She transformed herself from a decorative mannequin to a trader; and what does she trade in? Transformation: through a dramatic change in appearance and, perhaps, form. Banks herself changed from working-class child to supermodel and then to producer-presenter and top earning woman on television.

Banks has never openly acknowledged it, but everything she has done suggests she would have broad sympathy with Whoopi Goldberg, who, in rejecting the label African American, explained, "Rosa Parks did not sit on that bus so that I could put something in front of the word American. She sat on that bus to remind people that we are all entitled to the same thing." In responding to this, Donna Leonard Conger, an author and herself black, wrote a 2003 autobiography with the insistent title *Don't Call Me African-American*. Her argument cuts two ways: it's not just whites who expect black people to act like black people; black people themselves have similar expectations.

Banks, it seems, wanted to be neither African American nor black, or possibly not even human: she wanted to make herself into a brand. "When I was a model, my biggest obstacle was that I was black and curvy," she told Lynn Hirschberg. A strict diet and an exercise regimen kept the latter obstacle under control, though the first was more obdurate, especially if, as she suspected, the world's leading black model enjoyed and protected a kind of queen bee status. Unlike Campbell, who continually forced her way into the media, Banks opted for a less visible presence before she made her attempt at the next transformation: "When I went into producing, my biggest obstacle was that I was a model." Again, she overcame the obstacle and changed.

Like Oprah, Banks made light of the hindrances: the impediments resulting from racism occupy the same kind of status as those resulting from a soft spot for crème brûlée or a few missed spin classes at the gym. A career transition fraught with problems, especially for a black woman with little formal education, no experience in business or media production, is, for Banks, merely another segue. Reading her subtext, her only problem was that, as a model, she wasn't taken seriously (model=dim).

There are other similarities with Oprah, particularly the answer to a question posed by Khary Polk in 2007: "Can we transform social inequality through commodity fetishism?" By fetishism, Polk refers not to sexual gratification linked to inanimate objects (I don't think so, anyway), but to a course of action to which people have an excessive commitment – in this case to consumable products. Polk could be comparing Banks with Oprah, when she writes: "Although they may differ in scope and vision, all these choices carry with them the possibility for radical change" (p. 312).

The scope is different: about half of the viewers Oprah brought to their screens before she left in 2011 were 50 and older; 65 percent of *ANTM*'s viewers are under 50, and Banks attracts a very specific demographic – young women up to the age of 34. The vision is not so different in that both shows are urging self-improvement through honest endeavor and initiative. Banks represents the possibility of limitless change, but the prescribed methods are basically the same as Oprah's.

———

Banks learned the value of appearance in her teens. Modeling is an occupation based on impression: the way someone or something looks is all that counts. Hair is never just hair: it's coiffured, gelled, lacquered, extended, covered, colored and treated with any number of products. Bodies are often augmented or stripped of unwanted parts. A model's face is always adorned with eye makeup, lipgloss, bronzer and a dozen or so other cosmetics. The model's performance comprises facial expressions, body movements, turns, swaggers, struts; her behavior radiates confidence, arrogance, at times a little aggression ("fierce"?). The model's function is not to reveal herself, but to make visible the designers' creations. In a sense, she subordinates her humanness to frocks, shoes, necklaces and other accessories. There may even be a philosophy secreted in this. After all, image creation and impression management sells clothes and jewelry. But is it a philosophy for life?

Banks distinguishes herself from Oprah and Martha Stewart, whose empire included tv shows, magazines, cookbooks and miscellaneous household merchandise, when she defined her specialty as "attainable fantasy." Oxymoronic, perhaps; but we get the point: nothing is beyond anyone's reach. As we saw earlier, Oprah urged her followers to pursue their aspirations individualistically, through perseverance and endeavor. This is Banks' idea of empowerment too. Her targets are young women, the more ambitious the better.

Banks promotes an ethic of attractiveness and health. The therapeutic sensibility serves no one's interest but those individuals with zeal and appetite enough to act on their impulses. America's next top model is not a raging malcontent complaining about her impotence in an environment that persistently devalues blackness and clamps down hard on the working-class. Weakened capability is no excuse for not having strong ambitions, in Banks' philosophy. She is discontented for sure. With herself. Those discontents can be assuaged, not by turning society upside down, but by buying a new outfit, cutting off poodle bangs or applying the latest cream to hide puffy eyes.

The vignette introducing this chapter was about someone who answered the description of sex addict; but, in a sense, everyone on *ANTM*, and everyone watching it, is an addict, unable to live without products and services that promise change, however minor. The imperatives of consumerism are evident not just in the show, but in Banks herself, who admonishes the contestants for their narrowness of ambition, while practically taunting them with her own fabulous clothes, exquisite makeup and killer looks.

The unremitting stress on change, on transformation, on upgrading operates at every level.

In 2008, in *ANTM*'s eleventh season, one of the wannabe models with the exotic name Isis King (aka Isis Tsunami), a 5 foot 7 inch African American with an unusually linear 31-24-34 inch body (the relevance of these measurements will soon become clear). The fundamental difference between her and the thirteen other contestants wasn't apparent: she was equally well dressed, expertly made-up and comported herself with panache. But that straight-as-an-arrow body seemed a bit odd; even spindly Lily Cole, at 5 foot 10 inch, was a curvier 32-25-35.

Isis King was a pre-operative transsexual. It was a first for the first for *ANTM*, though, in several ways, Isis King personified the show's values more meaningfully than any of the contestants in the previous shows. As *Newsweek*'s Joshua Alston reminded readers: "Where the other girls in the competition take their beauty and mannerisms for granted, Isis doesn't."

Nothing came naturally to Isis King, not even her sex. Nor her gender. For clarity: I take sex to refer to the anatomical categories male and female, divided on the basis of reproductive functions; and gender the social and cultural expression of differences between male and females. King had instigated a transformation at the profoundest level of his being; her emergence as a female would represent a chrysalis-like metamorphosis. With one huge difference: this was no spontaneous, or natural, change; it was induced by human will, assisted by drugs and counseling and effected by expertise and medical technology.

The medical and psychiatric professions have followed the same logic of consumerism and the industries that drive it: changing ourselves by whatever means we can. That logic dictates that we should aggrandize ourselves. By this I mean enhance our reputation, increase our status and improve our appearance. In other words, transform ourselves in a way we think and, we suppose, others think is desirable. And how should we do this? By consuming a never-ending supply of new products and drugs and availing ourselves of the services of others. Banks depicts a reality in which we are what others see; we make ourselves visible in our performance: how we dress, accessorize, walk, pose, smile, or rather "smize." We are encouraged, if not compelled, to improve ourselves by treating ourselves as products. And perhaps this provides the first clue to understanding the rise and rise of Tyra Banks, who doesn't appear to have any particular talent for singing or acting (though she has essayed both, of course) but who certainly possesses a talent of uncertain provenance.

In her capacity as the quintessential consumer, Banks sets the tone of American life. Her opulent style, fabulous looks, restless ambition and acute awareness of her appearance are exemplary. Kanye West almost certainly didn't have Banks in mind when he wrote "All Falls Down," but he captures the mindset of her viewers and contestants: "She's so self-conscious ... so precious with the peer pressure ... Single black female addicted to retail" (West and Lauryn Hill, 2004).

———

Between 1968 and 1983, at least three pieces of research arrived independently at what seemed an uncomfortable conclusion: African Americans were more receptive than whites to advertising and less skeptical about its content. Why uncomfortable? Because the implication was that black consumers were more pliable – putty in the hands of advertisers. The studies were by Stephen A. Greyser and Raymond A. Bauer, 1968; Richard M. Durand, Jesse E. Teel, Jr. and William O. Bearden, 1979; and L.C. Soley and L.N. Reid, 1983. Another study by Ronald F. Bush, Joseph F. Hair and Paul Solomon, in 1979, found black consumers responded more positively to ads featuring African Americans than those featuring whites.

In the 1990s, the distinctness of blacks' orientation to advertising, marketing and consumerism was documented in a number of other studies. "According to some surveys, African-Americans are more motivated by quality and status than Caucasian consumers," noted Alan J. Bush and his colleagues in 1999. "For certain products such as boys' clothing and liquor, many African-Americans feel that buying premium brands is a way to make a statement about themselves" (p. 15).

Consumer culture is predicated on the appeal of products, not for their use but for their status as possessions. Commodities are valuable, though not necessarily useful. At least, that's the sense in which we refer to commodities in discussions of consumerism and the preoccupation of whole societies with the acquisition of replaceable goods and services for personal use. In this context, we have a question: why are African Americans' appetites for commodities so unquenchable? West's reference to the "single black female addicted to retail" may be partial: after all, white females too seem unable to do without buying products. But, the evidence definitely points to an ethnic divide: blacks approach shopping with gusto and treat their commodities like silent proclamations about themselves. Next question: why?

In 1990, when the term "supermodel" was just about entering our vocabulary and Banks was peering enviously at the likes of Cindy Crawford, the annual expenditure of African Americans was $316.5 billion. It more than doubled over the next twelve years and was up to nearly $853 billion by 2007, according to Blaine J. Branchik and Judy Foster Davis (p. 37). Even allowing for inflation, the increase reflects the growth and development of African Americans' purchasing power. But Branchik and Foster Davis detect another process at work: "Blacks sought respect and equal treatment in society by engaging in specific consumption behaviors, including activities intended to reduce race-based discrimination" (p. 38).

The authors use the term "marketplace activism" to understand this: activism usually refers to employing vigorous campaigning to bring about political and social change. African Americans' shopping habits, on this account, are "intended to advance social and political agendas" (p. 39).

What might, on the surface, look like a tendency to consider possessions and comfort more important than any other kinds of values – materialism, in other words – is actually something quite different: it's a means of seeking respect and demonstrating some measure of equality. This isn't such a new phenomenon: in 1949, the *Ebony* publisher John H. Johnson (1918–2005) answered the question "Why negroes buy Cadillacs" by explaining that the luxury GM car was a "symbol for many a negro that he is as good as any white man."

"Compensatory consumption" was how David Caplovitz captured the motives of poor or low-income groups who do whatever it takes to buy high-end consumables. "The ownership of such goods is apt to take on symbolic significance of social progress for people whose chances for social mobility are blocked," he wrote in 1967 (p. 20). So, they compensate for their lack of progress – and Caplovitz was writing only just after the civil rights laws – with the desirable commodities that conferred immediate status on their owners, and symbolized, as he put it, social progress.

Another expression of marketplace activism would be to boycott certain types of products or refuse to patronize services that offended or caused distress to a group of people. In 1990, for example, Jesse Jackson encouraged a boycott of Nike after criticizing the ethnic makeup of the sports goods manufacturer's 3,500 employees; he suspected that African Americans, who made up a big portion of Nike's market, were under-represented at senior management levels. An abstention with rather less far-reaching consequences was that of Jay-Z, who, in 2006, boycotted Cristal champagne after interpreting as racist a remark by an executive of Louis Roederer, the drink's producers. The sometimes grotesquely conspicuous consumption of rap artists can appear contemptuous of African Americans, most of whom earn less in a week than the cost of one bottle of Cristal (national average wage in 2011: $814 – about the same as a bottle of Cristal Brut Millesime). The subject deserves more detailed examination and I will attend to this later. But now, I want to persist in my search for the source of Tyra Banks' appeal.

"A Barbie is a Barbie is a Barbie," writes Elizabeth Chin. Like other products, Barbies are articles, designed, manufactured and sold on the marketplace. But Chin adds a caveat: "The Barbie consumed by the poor African American girl in urban Detroit must be understood differently from that same Barbie, consumed by a well-to-do middle-aged male Caucasian collector in Santa Barbara."

Barbies are not just products: they are commodities. Imbued with value, significance and consequence by consumers, who buy or just covet them, commodities mean something to us and express something about us. Advertisers are always trying to persuade shoppers about these things, but, ultimately, consumers determine the meaning of what they intend the commodity to express.

In 2001, Michèle Lamont and Virág Molnár explored such an expression: as they put it, "how a low-status group, black Americans use consumption to express and transform their collective identity and acquire social membership, i.e. to signify and claim that they are full and equal members in their society" (pp. 31–32).

The title of their article, "How blacks use consumption to shape their collective identity," suggests how Lamont and Molnár understood the meanings African American consumers instill in the products they buy. "Consuming rebuts racism," they argued, somewhat puzzlingly (p. 43). It does so by contradicting or at least counterbalancing negative characterizations of blacks: owning a house in a salubrious neighborhood, driving a Lexus and wearing Marc Jacobs signify a status that undercuts notions of inferiority.

Being part of a group that has historically been disenfranchized, dispossessed and, in myriad other ways, pushed to the margins of society, black people have and still do use consumption both to exhibit their status and validate their full membership of society. It isn't simply a question of exhibitionist behavior intended to draw attention to oneself, or massaging one's own ego. All consumers take a certain satisfaction from the status commodities bestow on them, but blacks consume to "transform their collective identity," as Lamont and Molnár put it, while whites presumably just want to improve their image.

The evidence for the argument was gleaned from "marketing professionals who specialize in the African-American market segment," rather than consumers themselves. So when the researchers claim consumption for African Americans "constitutes a collective act," while whites see it "in more individualistic terms," we should probably be wary of exaggeration (p. 37). Consuming can be and is, to use another of the authors' terms, a "cultural tool" that allows individuals to signal their aspirations and their identities. And, to return to Caplovitz, symbolize their social progress.

But do blacks consume as a method "of gaining acceptance to mainstream society," as Lamont and Molnár urge us to believe (p. 39)? Isn't it patronizing to assume African Americans are still looking for a way in? Or maybe it's just out of date. After all, we are in the second decade of the twenty-first century. A black president arrived in 2009 emblematizing postracial society. Prominent African Americans have issued reminders that the time for supplication is over. Yet the suspicion remains: consumption does hold some sort of transformative promise for African Americans.

———

Mark 8:36. "For what does it profit a man to gain the whole world, and forfeit his soul?" You might assume from Tyra Banks' meditations on life, beauty and ambition that she skipped this passage of the bible, or didn't ruminate on it much. Ignoring the gender-specificity, it could be interpreted as meaning that all the money, luxury, glitz, and other appurtenances of the good life promised by a career in modeling are worthless if, in the process, you are forced to surrender your soul. But, in a way, you have to.

Transformation, as I've argued, is implicit in both Banks' own life and in her role as matriarch of a show in which young women grope towards a kind of self-empowerment in their quest to become professional models. The transformation, at one level, yields professional success. At another level, it changes the person into a commodity, a product that, for all the glamor, sells other products. What else do models do? They appear on the runway as awesomely beautiful creatures, true. But their real job is as moving showroom dummies. Their audience consists of customers, not just fawning admirers of great looks and posture. Customers buy clothes, which in turn they will sell to other customers. That's the deal: take the riches, but surrender your humanity. And it's an attractive bargain in a culture in which commodities are highly valued.

Banks struck such a bargain as a young woman and profited. Critics could say she operates at a superficial level, but the prospect of profound change is never far away. The effects of a new hairdo, a pedicure, or a complete makeover can be life altering. Her show *ANTM* holds out the same promise. And yet, she has no time for dreamers: she berates young women who assume their good looks will carry them to riches and insists they acquire a work ethic. The fashion industry, like every other industry, is susceptible to sudden and unaccountable changes, and prospective employees should prepare for it. To outsiders it might seem as if some people are just naturally good looking, while others aren't. Banks has a different message: accept responsibility for the way you look and work at changing it.

So transformation doesn't just happen: the individual makes it happen. And individual initiative is central to Banks' worldview. As she told Lynn Hirschberg: "I feel it is so important that whatever happens to someone – women especially – doesn't have to be their fate. You can, and you must, move forward."

Banks' belief in the transmutative power of consumption corroborates the research quoted earlier about the special value African Americans invest in commodities. Like Oprah and Cosby, Banks' philosophy is one of relentless individualism: take responsibility for your actions, depend on no one but yourself and look out for number one. She never appears to have doubted where her own actions would take her. She wanted to emulate great athletes, though not in their capacity as athletes – in their capacity as peddlers of commodities. As a young woman, she wrote: "If Michael Jordan can sell tennis shoes and Magic Johnson can sell cars, I can sell cornflakes." It seems a wrongheaded ambition, but one with too much truth concealed in it to be ignored. Banks was selling straight out of school. By "selling," I mean, of course, that she was a professional model. She has never stopped selling; only her products have changed. Perhaps the most important item in her mature portfolio is the prescription for change. It's an irresistible product.

Banks has sidestepped racial issues and, apart from the case of Jewel Washington, any kind controversy. Like other black celebrities of today, she has perfected a method of making her audience forget she is black, at the same time gently evoking reminders that she is part of a generation of African Americans to whom race has only historical significance. She is nobody's fool and certainly no pawn of patrician white executives. Yet she operates in a way that complements perfectly the colorblind code of postracial America.

9

Like a jungle sometimes

'How did we move to a position where the most potent of black musical forms has been hijacked, where discrimination is seen largely as a vestige of a bygone age, and where the term racial is barely used save when prefixed by "post"?'

Whites love black life. They don't want to live it; they just want to experience it vicariously. They want the thrill of the internecine strife that implodes in ghetto violence, the intrigue of dealing dope on street corners, the rancor that seems to fire many black Americans. And they don't just want to sit in the audience, like they used to when the minstrels clowned and sang about joy amid misery on the plantations. They want to get on the inside.

It's not hard to see why some black artists are so appealing: they don't just act like thugs or sing about the ghetto; they seem to be the real thing. Take the artist known (variously) as P. Diddy, Puffy, Sean Combs, Sean John and Swag. A night out for a few drinks with him is rarely uneventful. Back in 1999, when he used another appellation, Puff Daddy, and hung with J.Lo, he took her to a Manhattan nightclub to celebrate his protégé Jamal "Shyne" Barrow's new record deal.

At some point during the evening, an argument broke out and someone threw a wad of money at Diddy. Not a gesture, you might think, to occasion vexation, though Barrow took exception and drew a 9-millimeter Ruger from his waistband. Three bystanders were shot and wounded, and Combs spent the day in a police lockup, eventually charged with criminal possession of a gun, though not the one used in the shooting. Barrow was jailed for nine years and deported to his native Belize for the attack. Diddy was cleared of any wrongdoing in the criminal case, but he and Barrow, as well as the now-shut club's owners, were targeted in a $130 million (£81 million) legal battle for compensation in 2008. The case dragged on until 2011, when Natania Reuben, who had been shot in the face, received $1.8 million (£1.1 m), some of which was from Diddy's own pocket. By then, he was worth $475 million, according to *Forbes*, and on his way to becoming a billionaire.

The nightclub shooting happened when rap was earning its reputation as a reliable expression of ghetto life. Two years before, Diddy's friend Biggie Smalls, a former crack dealer and Bad Boy recording artist, was killed in a Los Angeles shooting. The murder remains unsolved, but is still thought to be one of a series of attacks that formed part of a feud between Bad Boy and Death Row Records, a LA-based rival label. Smalls' death came six months after the killing of Tupac Shakur. In 1996, Snoop Doggy Dogg, as he then preferred, was acquitted of first- and second-degree murder charges in a 1993 killing. (First-degree is willful and premeditated; second-degree is not planned in advance.) These and many more incidents made rap seem much more than a musical offspring of hip-hop culture: it was a terrifying guide through the streets, where vengeance is a dish served searing hot and respect is a resource so scarce but so valuable that people's lives often depend on it.

"Rap conforms to many dominant stereotypes of black identity, both negative (e.g. rappers represent the vulgar and violent tendencies of blacks) and positive (e.g. rappers draw on the colorful, verbal style and rhythmic abilities blacks possess to tell the truth about the black experience in America)," wrote the anthropologist Maureen Mahon in 2000 (p. 288).

The central character in this truth-telling was the gangsta, an urban outlaw, scowling scarily out of tv screens, his tattoos or burn marks signaling his membership of a crew or the amount of time he has spent in prison. The gangsta projected "a conscious commitment to otherness and nihilistic responses to the social containment of black men," according to Ken McLeod (p. 223).

Jesse Weaver Shipley adds: "Ideas of 'keeping it real' and 'thug life' imply a unified singular subject produced in opposition to a hostile society" (p. 662). Well, maybe in the 1980s and 1990s, when the rappers celebrated their outcast status and resisted whatever moral codes they suspected had been contrived by whites to restrain them (like: breaking the law is wrong).

Tracks like NWA's "Fuck tha police" from 1988, or Public Enemy's 1989 "Fight the power" spat out contempt for authority and urged a return to the subversive days of black power. "Moreover, as it evolved, rap became more confrontational and unabashedly antagonistic towards America's power structures, suggesting a willingness, a desire even, to draw the scrutiny of the world around it," observed Erik Nielson of the global popularity of music with origins in the American ghettos, but which seemed "to give voice to marginalized people" (p. 1,269).

For a while the truculence reverberating out of the boomboxes grabbed the attention of the police: Nielsen describes how the Miami Police Department kept dossiers on several rap artists and set up a task force to monitor their behavior. Its operations were "reminiscent of the government's COINTELPRO days of the 1950s and 1960s, when Black activists, writers, artists, and musicians were routinely surveilled by the FBI and other law enforcement agencies" (p. 1,255). The forces of law and order were spooked enough to keep a close watch.

Rap music sounded like collective hatred, howling and untamed. And then something happened: it was broken. Like a wild Mustang that becomes accustomed to a saddle and a rider.

—

A fresh-faced young white man drives through spotlessly clean suburbs, pointing at puzzled pedestrians as he lip-syncs, "It's like a jungle sometimes." It looks anything but. His passengers are two middle-aged African Americans, dressed in the baggy tracksuits and bling favored by rappers in the 1980s. The music adds to the bizarreries. Incongruous harsh boomings jar with the residential surroundings, suggesting wormholes to another time, another place. "Makes me wonder how I keep from going under," mimes the driver, who arrives home from the supermarket to be asked by his wife whether he remembered to get diapers.

At the other end of the wormhole, we are in 1982 and in a place that looks like South Central Los Angeles, the archetypal black ghetto. The music is "The message," a six-minute inspection of ghetto life, in which the rapper observes rodents and insects roaming through his abode. Anyone who heard Grandmaster Flash and the Furious Five's influential track knew that it was intended to prompt a feeling of dread. The singer compares his environment to a jungle, complete with baseball bat-wielding predators, and cautions no one in particular, "Don't push me 'cause I'm close to the edge."

"The song contains the type of graphic description of oppressive conditions found in the best Blues and R&B commentaries, and issues the type of subtle warning to external audiences found in some of the more assertive commentaries," writes James B. Stewart in his 2005 analysis "Message in the music" (p. 219).

In the early 1980s, "The message" carried a terrifying portent: African Americans were caught between the salvation promised by civil rights two decades before and the damnation pronounced by a culture steeped in two centuries of white racism. Even the civil rights instigated by the landmark legislation of the 1960s had brought few visible signs of progress. Black people, as the song pointed out, were forced to play their traditional roles, performing for the delectation of whites: "I'd dance to the beat, shuffle my feet."

Hip-hop artists The Grandmaster Flash and the Furious Five recorded the tribulations of black people, the main one being racism-induced poverty. It was a documentary that scavenged for material in the human landfills of North America. The music didn't celebrate the indomitability of the African American spirit: it suggested how it would soon be broken. It was a pioneer of a genre that would morph from cutting-and-mixing into rap.

Chuck D. of Public Enemy, another hip-hop behemoth of the 1980s, described rap as "CNN for black people." He meant that, like the television news channel, his and other black musicians' output entertained people, but was also "a direct source of information" amid a media largely owned and staffed by whites. But it was also "a new community theater project," according to Stewart, "largely unfettered by corporate attachments, fueled by the harsh realities of inner-city life" (p. 219).

Hip-hop was probably the most transparent of all black music: it offered a glimpse into ghetto life in the 1980s replete with "Rats in the front room, roaches in the back, junkies in the alley," as "The message" put it. Sampled and mashed copiously over the years, that track remains one of most powerful, colorful, lurid, uninhibited, shocking and scabrously realistic pieces of musical social commentary ever. So we come to the question: how did it end up in a television commercial for Kia cars (and worse: the "on hold music" of countless phone systems)?

That's what lay at the other end of the wormhole: 30 years after its release, the track was procured by the Korean car company and included in its advertisement for the Sportage vehicle. The two middle-aged black guys sitting alongside the white driver were members of the original band. Some might cry "race treason," the crime of betraying one's own ethnic group for money. When, in 2007, Oprah stood before a gathering of 30,000 at Howard University and declaimed, "My integrity is not for sale, and neither is yours," she appeared to speaking about this very crime. "Do not be a slave to any form of selling out," advised Oprah – who has frequently been accused of doing exactly that.

Were the hip-hop artists of the 1980s treasonous? Did they betray the cause, such as it was, they set out to advance? After all, if you are going to write and record a frighteningly explicit image of black life, you don't allow someone to use it to sell SUVs to white suburbanites (or to pacify callers while they are waiting to be connected). It's like entrusting a biography of Martin Luther King to Pixar: you know they'll do a bang-up job, but you also know a lot of the import and gravitas will be lost in the adaptation.

"Hip Hop culture is the single most widespread preoccupation among today's African American diasporan youth," wrote Pero Gaglo Dagbovie in 2005 (p. 300). Dagbovie considered that the music, the speech, the dress and, generally, the posture of hip-hop engrossed young black youth (which he considers dispersed and divorced from their original spiritual homeland – "diasporan"). While youths of other ethnic backgrounds – white, Latino, Asian – may not have shared the "preoccupation" Dagbovie sensed among blacks, they too were enthusiastically absorbed in the dispatches from the ghetto. "Hip Hop artists," in Dagbovie's view (he doesn't use the hyphen), "recount their own personal histories of resilience, which mirror the overall theme of perseverance against the oppression that dominate the African American experience" (2005, p. 301).

These themes, remember, were the same ones that resurfaced in the car advertisement. What conceivable relevance could they have to well-heeled and, presumably, mainly white consumers? Even the watered-down radicalism, as Dagbovie calls it, wouldn't appear to have much significance in selling $12,000 commodities. Dagbovie deepens the mystery when he offers a personal testimony: "Members of the Hip Hop generation are linked mainly by the fact that we were born after the major struggles of the Civil Rights Movement and have collectively inherited a great deal from the battles waged by our elders" (2005, p. 302).

It's a muscular affirmation, though the writer doesn't specify exactly what has been "inherited," or how it's been used; we can inherit our parents' money and squander it, or our big brother's clothes and never wear them for fear of looking old-fashioned. Dagbovie makes a further observation that from 1995, black people have "not responded collectively to black oppression or made distinctive contributions to the black 'tradition of protest'" (2005, p. 306).

When hip-hop culture and rap music surfaced in the 1980s, it provided audiences with a wiretap on black life – not as whites suspected it was, but as it was lived; that is, without access to the kinds of desirable features afforded to their white contemporaries. This is what gave rap its astringency: other kinds of music with black origins expressed criticism in less sharp, more ambiguous ways. Rap was social critique as music. So here's the conundrum: how, in the space of about 30 years, did we move to a position where the most potent of black musical forms has been appropriated, or hijacked, depending on your perspective, where discrimination is seen largely as a vestige of a bygone age, and where the term "racial" is barely used save when prefixed by "post"?

———

African Americans who are "permitted" by whites to become successful are "bright children," no matter how old. This is the view of Jan Nederveen Pieterse: his version of history suggests blacks who used their talents, whether in entertainment or sport, to delight white audiences were only allowed to do so under certain conditions. If they met whites' popular expectations, they were fine; often, they were infantilized, treated in a way that denied them their maturity either in age or experience. The simple act of calling someone "boy" conceals a psychological stratagem with enormous cultural consequences. African Americans who gave the impression they opposed or even questioned the existing order of things were either banished or subjected to a kind of symbolic emasculation that left them weaker or less effective.

If they were too menacing, their work was expropriated by whites and turned into a more domesticated product. Blues, for example, found its life and heartbeat in the misery and oppression of the South of the 1920s. African Americans migrating north took the music with them: their songs told of sickness, imprisonment, alcohol, drugs, and sex. Unlike gospel or the negro spirituals, blues didn't develop out of the churches and this, combined with its earthly subject matter, earned it the soubriquet "devil's music."

Blues provided an alternative to spiritual music that gloried in God's grace and anticipated a journey to the Promised Land. There was no hope, only realism. In his *Black Culture and Black Consciousness*, Lawrence Levine captures the distinction between the two by quoting the singer Mahalia Jackson (1911–72), who sang blues but refused to give up gospel music: "Blues are the songs of despair, but gospel songs are the songs of hope. When you sing them you are delivered of your burden" (p. 174).

It was the singer, not the song that gave blues its emotional power and, ultimately, commercial appeal. When Ma Rainey (1886–1939), Trixie Smith (1895–1943), or Blind Lemon Jefferson (1897–1929) sang, there was an almost palpable bond with audiences (listen to Jefferson's classic "Black Snake Moan" at: http://bit.ly/-BlackSnakeMoan).

For all its intrinsic qualities, the enduring success of blues came from without: the phonographic recording ensured a wide audience across America – and, later, the world. "It had begun as early as the 1920s," writes Gerri Hirshey. "Scouts and field engineers were being sent out by white companies to find and record black singers down South" (p. 60).

So folk music was turned into a commercial product, mechanically reproduced and traded in the marketplace. In the process it became available to many more people than would have had access to blues before: few whites would have ventured into blacks-only taverns and clubs. Authenticity was a selling feature of blues: early entrepreneurs might have used it as a marketing ploy, but there was a sense in which blues conveyed aspects of the black experience in a way that sounded genuine and unvarnished. Race music, as music performed by African Americans was called, was popularized by a recording industry in search of new products.

The people scouting for music were not corporate types sensing opportunities to make money off the backs of poor blacks: more typically, they were devotees of folk music. W.C. Handy (1873–1958) was a one-time minstrel, then bandleader turned promoter, who became aware of the emerging twelve-bar chord sequences that were the hallmark of black folk music. Teaming up with partner Harry H. Pace, he started the Black Swan Phonograph Company, with W.E.B. Du Bois on its board of directors, in 1923. Its records were an eclectic mix, blues being only one of a number of styles. "The only genuine colored record" was the boast made on its labels. Ethel Waters (1896–1977, whom we covered in chapter 7) was signed to the label, though Pace refused to let her sing the blues and insisted she concentrate on ballads.

Marcus Garvey (1887–1940), the entrepreneur, journalist and proponent of Black Nationalism who encouraged African Americans to return to their African homeland, took objection to Pace, describing him as "a business exploiter who endeavors to appeal to the patriotism of the race by selling us commodities at a higher rate than are charged in the ordinary ... markets" (quoted in Ted Vincent's *Keep Cool*, p. 104).

The other noteworthy label of the era was OKeh Records, started improbably by a German jazz enthusiast in 1918 and which featured Louis Armstrong (1900–71) on several of its releases. A major influence on jazz, Armstrong was a horn player, as well as bandleader and singer, who went on to feature in Hollywood movies, such as 1943's *Cabin in the Sky* (with Lena Horne and Ethel Waters). Miles Davis (1926–91) once pointed out that, "Jazz is a white man's word," and "blues is a white man's invention," his inference being that the genres were only given coherence when packaged in a saleable form by white record companies and impresarios. In its "natural states," the music played by African Americans was not demarcated: white corporations introduced the boundaries.

What we now recognize as early jazz, with its strong two-beat rhythm and improvisation, originated in New Orleans in the early twentieth century and became known as Dixieland. The music swept northwards to the major cities. "The Jazz Age Black music in Chicago appears to have been mostly under the control of African-Americans from 1918 into late 1921," writes Vincent (p. 70). After this, white interests arrived and grew progressively parasitic. Davis himself resisted bowdlerizing his music for record companies and, as a result, became even more compelling. While "cool" is now part of the popular vernacular, its sources lie with Davis and the group of musicians who emerged in the 1950s. "These musicians were less secular stars than quasi-religious figures, and their fans often referred to them with godly reverence," Nelson George discerns (p. 25).

Historians too have religious zeal when competing over the origins of jazz. In his *Blues People*, Leroi Jones argues that, Davis apart, most musicians associated with cool were actually white. Certainly, many of the musicians responsible for popularizing jazz were white innovators. Glenn Miller (1904–44), Tommy Dorsey (1905–56), and Benny Goodman (1909–86) were major influences in swing, a variant that was the dominant form of jazz in the 1940s. Similarly, blues had a surge in popularity after white artists combined its lyricism and simple melodies with a heavy beat to deliver rock 'n' roll. It seems ludicrous now, but when rock 'n' roll first set a generation's pulse racing, it was damned by many for its primitivism: "jungle music," as it was called (even by *Encyclopedia Britannica*), was banned by radio stations and dance halls across America. White DJ Alan Freed (1921–65) was one of its champions and persisted in playing rock 'n' roll on his influential "Moondog" radio show in Cleveland. Whether it was integrity or showmanship, we'll never know, but Freeman promoted the new music to the hilt in the 1950s and is even credited in some circles with coining the term rock 'n' roll. He played race music, as it was still widely known, or rhythm & blues (as distinct from today's R&B), which was an up-tempo variation of blues practiced by black artists.

The aura of rock 'n' roll greatness still surrounds Elvis Presley (1935–77), Jerry Lee Lewis (b.1935) and other white artists who were either giants or dwarves standing on the shoulder of giants, depending on your perspective. Elvis' first commercial recording was in 1954, "That's All Right, Mama," a blues number written by Arthur "Big Boy" Crudup (1905–74) and recorded originally by him in 1946, as "That's All Right." Lewis featured "Good Golly, Miss Molly" and "Tutti Frutti," both recorded earlier by black artist Little Richard. Bill Haley was the white artist most readily associated with rock 'n' roll in the 1950s, though many of his commercial hits, such as "Rocket 88" and "Shake, Rattle and Roll" were covers of black artists' materials, the former often acknowledged as a rhythm & blues track that prefigured rock 'n' roll, and credited to Jackie Brentson and his Delta Kings, written by Ike Turner, in 1951. The latter was written by one-time minstrel Jesse Stone (1901–99), whose friend and bluesman Big Joe Turner (1911–85) recorded it in 1954.

Whatever your perspective, rock 'n' roll was undeniably white, attracting a young, overwhelmingly white audience. Only later did African Americans get credit and, even then, it was due in large part to British bands, like the Rolling Stones and the Yardbirds, who self-consciously modeled themselves on black blues performers and dipped liberally into the back catalogs of artists such as John Lee Hooker (1920–2001) and Sonny Boy Williamson (c.1899–1965). This was in the 1960s, when the civil rights movement prompted a re-evaluation of the cultural contributions of African Americans. Earlier in this chapter, I used *expropriation* to describe the way whites dispossessed African Americans of their music. It's an apposite description, though white artists piqued deeper interest in the original blues and this had the effect of conferring at least some credit on influential bluesmen like Howling Wolf (1910–76) and Muddy Waters (1915–83).

Some argue that the blues throbs in rock music even today. The historical fact remains: white artists took the initial plaudits and were responsible for steering race music, or at least a sanitized version of it, into the mainstream. Black artists were permitted entry only later and, even then, with reservations.

———

"Are you ready for a brand new beat? Summer's here and the time is right for dancing in the street." It was 1964, a time for exultation. A year before, 200,000 people had marched on Washington DC to listen to Martin Luther King's inspirational "I have a dream" speech. The suavely imposing Sidney Poitier (b.1927) became the first black American actor to win an Academy Award for his role in *Lilies of the Field* (1963). Poitier was a substantial character uninterested in playing up to stereotypes and, as such, made a crack in a wall that had stood before black actors, obstructing their progress.

Or was it a time for commiseration? Memories of the killing of three civil rights workers, all members of the Congress of Racial Equality (CORE), by the Ku Klux Klan were still fresh. The murders were later to become the subject of the film *Mississippi Burning*.

On July 2, Congress passed the Civil Rights Act, which banned discrimination in employment and in public places: it was the culmination of a protest that had started in 1955. Was this why people were dancing in the street? Or was "dancing" a figure of speech? Within weeks of the new legislation's passing, rioting broke out in Harlem and Rochester, New York. A year later, there was more rioting in Los Angeles and several other major cities.

Some people were dancing with joy, as Martha and the Vandellas encouraged them to do in their track "Dancing in the street." Others were dancing to a different beat: frustrated by the failure of civil rights to deliver any immediate, tangible change, they took more immediate, violent action. Whether the song itself was intended as anything more than a catchy addition to what was then an expanding Motown catalog, we don't know. Even if it was, it was invested with so much social and political meaning that it didn't matter: it became an anthem of both rapture and rage.

Martha Reeves, the lead singer of the band, had worked at the Motown studios in Detroit since 1962. The owner, Berry Gordy, was a singer, songwriter and entrepreneur, who had worked on the Lincoln-Mercury assembly line and watched cars start out as a frame pulled along a conveyor belt until they emerged at the end of the line as complete cars. He applied the same principles to recording artists. He was aware of several other record labels owned by African Americans, such as Vee-Jay Records, and Peacock Records, specializing in race music, but had a different agenda: he wanted a record company run by black people, with black artists, but with a white market. The music-industry term is crossover.

Other labels, such as Chess Records and Specialty Records, released material by black artists; but at a time when African Americans were sequestered in segregated parts of town and denied many basic human rights, the labels were likely to remain in their niche markets. The civil rights movement had exposed much of the suspicion and hatred many whites still harbored a century after Emancipation. Gordy's Motown assembly line turned black artists into performers who were not considered unpredictable or potentially threatening: safe entertainers.

Nat King Cole (1919–65) could have provided Gordy with a case study. Born in Alabama, Cole recorded for Capitol Records, which had mostly white artists such as Frank Sinatra and Judy Garland on its roster. In 1948, Cole was the first African American to have his own radio series and, in 1956, transferred to the then fast-growing medium, television. NBC featured him in its "Nat King Cole Show," but struggled to find advertisers. "Madison Avenue," said Cole, "is afraid of the dark." (Madison Avenue, in Manhattan, is the center of the advertising industry). Cole wore his hair "conked," or straightened, and, for the tv show, wore makeup that lightened his skin; he also sang duets with white artists, effecting, it seemed, an almost perfect integration. Almost.

In *Crosstown Traffic*, Charles Shaar Murray senses: "The black entertainer succeeds with the white audience either by embodying an aspect of blackness with which that audience feels comfortable, or else by appearing almost tangential to the black community" (p. 79). NBC presumably felt Cole was sufficiently unaffiliated that he fell into the latter category. Ray Charles (1919–2004), who emerged slightly later in the 1950s, would have given form to an aspect of blackness that made whites comfortable: he was conversant with blues, jazz and even country music, played, wrote and performed with virtuosity and was blind. His disability had a symbolic as well as physical character and, from a white perspective, rendered him safe.

Cole, like Louis Armstrong, had made the transition, however incomplete, to the popular market and, in doing so, made accommodations to white tastes. Neither artist was promoted as a bearer of black culture. "Black entertainers were decorative and not necessarily emancipated figures," writes Pieterse. "The figure of the black waiter or bartender melts easily into that of the black performer" (p. 141).

Gordy envisioned his artists as attractive, showy and, like Cole, unrecognizable from a tuxedoed maître d'. The Jackson 5 got the Motown treatment, as did internationally famous bands like the Temptations and Smoky Robinson and the Miracles, though Diana Ross (b.1944) was perhaps the most illustrious product of the Motown assembly line; she is still touring and releasing albums.

As Motown waded into the mainstream, another record label, Atlantic/Stax, stuck to its own tributary with a roster of black and a few white artists whose gospel-fused rhythm & blues was designated soul. (Big Joe Turner's original "Shake, rattle and roll" was released on the label). The music was more gutsy and less processed than Motown's output, leading one of its house musicians and producers, Steve Cropper, to conclude: "To me, Motown was white music" (quoted in Hirshey's *Nowhere to Run*, p. 307). Coming from a white musician, this seems a harsh appraisal, though Gordy may have taken it as a compliment. In his 1994 biography, Gordy recounts how, in the early 1960s, his brother Robert released a single "Everyone was there" under the name Bob Kayli. It sold respectably; so Bob Kayli went on a promotional tour. When he went on the road, sales dropped. "This white-sounding record did not go with his black face," writes Gordy. "I realized this was not just about good or bad records, this was about race" (p. 95).

This realization, coupled, presumably, with a knowledge of Cole's experience, persuaded Gordy that if his black artists were to integrate, they would have to be, to repeat Murray, tangential: appearing to diverge from the path of African American music. In the process, Motown artists were rendered safe: brilliant artists that they were, the likes of Ross et al. were not likely to cause trouble, socially or politically.

Some artists grew to resent this. Marvin Gaye, for example, who co-wrote "Dancing in the street," initially "did everything he could to win a mainstream middle-class audience, crooning the ballads he thought white music lovers wanted to hear," according to his biographer David Ritz (p. 107). He may not have liked it, but he went along with Gordy's strategy, performing on the dinner-club circuit dressed in tux and bowtie. He told Ritz: "Sometimes I felt like the shuffle-and-jive niggers of old, steppin' and fetchin' for the white folk" (p. 106).

Unlike many of his predecessors, Gordy made no claim to authenticity: his music was not sold as if salvaged from a forgotten or neglected culture such as gospel or blues, both of which were rooted in the black experience. Motown was an entirely new and unique artifice: it didn't exist separately from Gordy's Hitsville studios, as they were known. The demise of the many artists after they left Motown added another meaning to this observation.

Soul was dealt a blow with the death of Otis Redding in 1967, though it would survive and adapt in new forms, but with a defined market. By the early 1970s two songwriter/producers from Philadelphia were practically outdoing Motown at what it did best: making black music for white audiences. Kenny Gamble and Leon Huff's Philadelphia International Records produced a sound that was part sedative, part stimulant. Using African American artists, including Barry White (1944–2003) and Harold Melvin (1939–97), they embellished recordings with string accompaniments to make a sound that had moved as far from blues as black music had ever traveled.

Much of the Philadelphia output was absorbed into disco, a celebratory music that, in the 1970s, echoed a kind of communion between gays, straights, blacks and whites: the dance floor was a shared domain. Watch the 1977 movie *Saturday Night Fever*, discussed earlier, and it serves as a frescoed social history of disco. Michael Jackson's *Off the Wall*, his first adult album, was released in 1979. Disco was, by then, approaching the end of its natural cycle, though several Jackson tracks, especially "Don't stop 'til you get enough," were disco-ready.

Less assimilated into mainstream – and, by implication, white – culture were the grittier sounds of bands such as Sly and the Family Stone, the brainchild of Texan multi-instrumentalist Sylvester Stewart (b.1943), who followed in the tradition of Stax soul, and, like James Brown (1933–2006), created a challenging yet compelling sound. Greil Marcus contrasted his project with that of Motown: "Sly was less interested in crossing racial and musical lines than in tearing them up" (p. 81). In a sense, the forerunners of rap were just as unhelpful.

———

All art aspires to provoke; rap music more than most. When C. Delores Tucker (1927–2005) spoke, she spoke with credibility: she boasted a lifetime's left-wing social action and had the backing of several black, feminist, liberal organizations. So, when she teamed up with arch conservative and adviser to Republican presidents William J. Bennett (b.1943), in 1995, it seemed a dangerous liaison. Their shared concern was with what they regarded as the hate and sexism perpetrated by rap and endorsed, albeit indirectly, by record companies, such as Death Row Records. They condemned the lyrics as "sleazy, pornographic smut," and warned that rap music was toxic; among its noxious effects were the promotion of violence and the degradation of women.

The Sugar Hill Gang's "Rapper's delight" was the first commercially successful rap record in 1979. This was sampled from Chic's "Good times," which is still acknowledged as a disco classic. The Sugar Hill Gang's number was a free and easy dance track ("you're rocking to the rhythm, shake your derriere/you're rocking to the beat without a care,") though the character of rap changed dramatically over the next couple of years. "The message," as we saw earlier, was a much weightier and disturbing contribution, and offered a glimpse into how music could radicalize the black experience. Much of the rap music that followed was invective against the police, injunction to challenge authority, and construal of criminal behavior as political action. For example, *AmeriKKKa's Most Wanted* was Ice Cube's first album after he left NWA: it pushed the parameters of rap, integrating various perspectives from law enforcement officers, judges as well as offenders. The album opens with the sound of Cube being led to the electric chair.

In 1991, NWA's second album *Niggaz4Life* entered the *Billboard* pop chart at number two, unassisted by a trailer single, video or the promotional backing of a big record company. By the time of Tucker's intervention, the genre was no longer a subterranean music produced by independent labels. A tier of African American entrepreneurs and producers, the most celebrated being Russell Simmons, had emerged. Others included Andre Harrell, Antonio "LA" Reid, and the man who would become P. Diddy.

Lawsuits, bans, even a Rico (Racketeer Influenced and Corrupt Organizations) suit (intended to combat the mafia) flew in rap's direction. In the early 1990s, it was the most controversial music since rock 'n' roll. Public anxiety was initially about the alleged incitement to hatred, but it broadened as the appeal of rap itself broadened. By the mid-1990s, rap's audience was ethnically mixed and there were signs that an African heritage was not a prerequisite for performers, either.

Eminem, the nom de plume of Marshall Mathers, was an oddity: a white man who could write and perform rap with the best. His 1999 album *The Marshall Mathers LP* was the fastest-selling solo album in United States history. There had been white rappers before, but Eminem enjoyed the respect of rappers and producers like Dr Dre, of NWA, and Snoop Dogg, with whom he toured and performed. From one perspective, Eminem's success was a *reductio ad absurdum* of rap: a white man stretching the genre to a logical, but ridiculous, extreme. From another, it was the remaking of the genre. The common themes of poverty, racism, criminality and sex were still there. But the *enfant terrible* was white and, actually, he wasn't so *terrible* after all.

In 2000, *Entertainment Weekly*'s Owen Gleiberman hailed Eminem as "The first great white rap star – the first to channel, with electrifying obsessiveness, the anger and the strut, the power-lust desperation, the proud sociopathic *hardness* that has become the unholy essence of hip-hop" (December 23). Gleiberman divined that Eminem would "be to rap what Elvis Presley was to rhythm and blues."

In view of the expropriation covered earlier in this chapter, it seemed a fair assessment. And how about the cross-cultural effects of both artists on what were once black genres? Eminem might not have been such a cuddly teddy bear as Elvis, but nor was he as menacing as his black predecessors: his fans didn't hear in his music the dreaded rumble of the coming 2pacalypse.

Like Elvis, Eminem branched into film with 2002's *8 Mile,* not the first rap-themed movie, but the first to feature a white lead actor. And, as if to continue the housebreaking, several rap-themed films and tv shows quickly followed in 2003. These included *Malibu's Most Wanted,* in which Snoop Dogg did a voiceover for a talking rat, and *Bringing Down the House,* in which Queen Latifah, "hip-hop's first lady" as she was sometimes called, had a starring role opposite Steve Martin. Perhaps the animated comedy *Lil' Pimp* in 2005 confirmed that rap was not just domesticated; it had been trained to do tricks to amuse white audiences. The film depicted a world that seemed a long way from the one described in "The message."

Instead of being embarrassed by comparisons with their forebears, hip-hop artists relinquished any responsibility to chronicle, critique or challenge, and opted for voluntary domestication. As 50 Cent certified in his *I'm a Hustler*: "Rule number one, don't go against the grain." The same artist, in an interview with Kaleem Aftab, reflected on the price of fame: "In exchange for not being able to walk around in the mall, you can buy everything in it."

Hip-hop became a market-driven genre. The morality or propriety of a course of action was typically considered, but usually not too deeply. "I'm not just like some green motherfucker that's just doing things to make money," insisted P. Diddy (total wealth: $475 million, according to *Forbes*). "I've never drunk beer, wine, never drunk whisky," he explained to Guy Adams. "Vodka is what I've drunk all my life" (p. 19). Hence, the only alcoholic beverage he promoted was Ciroc vodka.

Business tie-ups with Diageo, the makers of Ciroc, or Coca-Cola (a vitamin-water company part-owned by 50 Cent sold out to the soft drinks corporation) may not be what hip-hop culture was once about, but today's rap artists "frequently speak of ten-figure desires," as Zack O'Mally Greenburg puts it.

When exactly did a rogue culture become an adjunct of consumer culture? On July 19, 1986, according to Steve Stoute, who recalls a Run-DMC concert at New York's Madison Square Garden. When the band performed "My adidas," a kind of exaltation of the German sportswear, the audience responded by hoisting their own adidas shoes in the air. Stoute believes that, after that, commercial companies sensed the music's potential for selling products, and white audiences became curious: "Suddenly it began to appeal and sell to consumers from zip codes where rap wasn't even on the radio, much less being stocked in the record stores" (p. 34).

Adams dates the end hip-hop, or the start of what he calls "commercial hip-hop," later; at May 1997, when Diddy, as Puff Daddy featuring Faith Evans, released *I'll Be Missing You.* After that, rap slipped its moorings. Snoop Dogg (annual income: $8.5 m) proudly wore a gold knuckle-duster, as if in parody of the violent ghetto culture that gave birth to hip-hop. Kanye West ($9.8 m pa) commissioned artist George Condo to design the album cover for *My Beautiful Dark Twisted Fantasy*, requesting "something that will be banned." He confidently tweeted, "Yoooo they banned my album cover!!!!!" Imagine his disappointment when it wasn't banned.

It's as if hip-hop artists were desperately trying to live up – or down – to a stereotype that generations of black people had been striving to destroy. As Armond White uncovers: "There's been a change in the pop perception of black stereotypes that creates rapport for even the meanest black social conditions." He alludes to ghettocentric logic, which I'll explain in chapter 10. White goes on: "Through hip-hop, more Americans come to identify with black public figures than ever before: It's the common ground Bill Cosby shares with Snoop Dogg."

Today, rap is up there with pop, rock, dance and R&B as one the most popular mainstream music genres; even the surfeit of "nigga" and "muthfucka" in the lyrics sounds tiresomely familiar. Diddy and Snoop vie with Jay-Z and 50 Cent in the race to become rap's first billionaire. Where there was once substance, there is now a density of crassness that inflates hip-hop's fatuous subject matter and renders it good for only one thing: selling products. Fratricidal murders are the stuff of history, ghettos are strictly in the imagination, and it's difficult to believe that tracks such "The Nigga Ya Love To Hate" and "Gangsta Gangsta" are torchbearers. *Newsweek*'s Allison Samuels wonders whether rap's enraged and unpredictable young firebrands were really revenants, "minstrels in baggy jeans."

In his *Notes of a Native Son* James Baldwin revealed: "It is only in his music … that the Negro in America has been able to tell his story." Black music, in all of its forms, has echoed the experiences of African Americans. The unruly multiplicity of genres has expressed often coded messages about the meaning of being black. Negro spirituals with lineage traceable to slavery, no less than blues, were mournful cries of a wretched and forlorn people, dispossessed and woebegone.

All the way through to hip-hop, the music has told a story. It is a story that whites have not just wanted to hear, but experience. They will also pay for the privilege. As the saying goes, he who pays the piper calls the tune. Black artists today, no less than the minstrels who clowned for whites 150 years ago, are subject to conditions laid down by whites. If they are prepared to meet them, they survive and sometimes flourish, but the chances are that they will be obliged to make compromises or sacrifices, depending on how you look at it. Remember: one of the most expressive and caustic social commentaries ever written on the black experience ended up on a tv commercial.

10

The ghetto inside

'Where else could you find the irresistible combination of charismatically athletic black men bounteously rewarded for their muscular skills with every toy and stimulant they desired, regressing as if ordained by nature to a more primitive stage of evolution?'

W as it a sign that the rehabilitation was complete, or just a cosmetic show when Nike announced it had welcomed back NFL superstar Michael Vick to its roster of celebrity endorsers? That was July 2011, barely six months since a pundit on Fox News pronounced: "I think personally [Vick] should have been executed." Even if Tucker Carlson later retracted this, the expression suggested how high emotions rode when Vick was the subject of discussion.

In 2007, Vick was in the third year of a contract with Atlanta Falcons, believed to be worth $70 million. At 22, Vick was the second-youngest quarterback ever selected to play in the Pro Bowl, the honor coming after a season in which Vick set four NFL records. He was regarded as one of the most valuable players in the sport. Then, a search of a property owned by Vick in Surry, Virginia, turned up 54 pit bulls, and a later search revealed graves of other dogs said to have been killed during fights organized by members of a group called Bad Newz Kennels. On July 18, 2007, Vick and three other men were indicted on federal felony charges. The indictment charged that Vick had sponsored illegal dogfighting, gambled on fights and permitted acts of cruelty against animals on his property. He was sentenced to 23 months' imprisonment.

By the time of his release in July 2009, Vick, then 29, reckoned his incarceration had cost him a total of $142 million. This included his $2 million endorsement deal with Nike: the sports apparel company even suspended the release of a range of Zoom Vick V footwear. The NFL conditionally reinstated Vick, making it possible for him to resume playing professional football. He signed as a backup player for Philadelphia Eagles. The club's decision to sign Vick drew a response from the Humane Society of the United States, which announced that the group and Vick would work together to eradicate dogfighting among youths. People for the Ethical Treatment of Animals, the animal-rights group, was more reticent: "PETA certainly hopes that Vick has learned his lesson and feels truly remorseful for his crimes – but since he's given no public indication that that's the case, only time will tell."

He played sparingly in 2009, but when Donovan McNabb moved to Washington, Vick assumed his position and played arguably the best football of his life. In 2011, Vick signed a one-year contract with the Eagles, under which he would make an estimated $20 million. The restoration of the endorsement contract didn't square the circle: Vick's offense was unforgivable in a nation of dog lovers. But this is where we recognize Nike's role as a major player in what we could call the racial politics of sports.

———

Nike has, for decades, been a purveyor of easy-on-the-conscience representations of the black urban experience to the middlebrow masses. In 1985, after eight years of steady growth and increasing profits, the sports goods company reported two consecutive losing quarters. Competitors, such as adidas, Puma and, especially, Reebok were taking advantage of the enthusiasm for aerobics, which Nike had missed. Nike's marketing strategy was to use established sports figures to endorse its products. So, when it signed Michael Jordan, there was a risk: he was, like the majority of other NBA players, black and, at that stage, unproven in the pro ranks. The NBA itself had an image problem: it was widely regarded as, to quote the *Los Angeles Times Magazine* writer Edward Kiersh, "a drug-infested, too-black league." Its players were, to use Tyrone R. Simpson's arresting phrase, "excessively libidinal, terminally criminal, and socially infernal" (p. 7).

This had commercial implications summed-up by Kiersh: "Sponsors felt the NBA and its black stars had little value in pitching colas and cornflakes to Middle America." Nike used Jordan primarily as a sales instrument: his role was to move branded footwear and apparel. But, in the marketing process, something else happened: he was presented as an "atypical Black figure," as David L. Andrews and Michael L. Silk call him, "distanced, from the discourses of irresponsibility, hypersexuality, deviance, unruliness, and brutish physicality routinely associated with African American males in general, and NBA players in particular" (p. 1,629).

During the 1990s, the NBA was a one-man show that other players were allowed to crash. Jordan was like air, or, I should say, Air: he was everywhere, all the time. There was no escape from his image, whether on tv, movies, cereal boxes, posters, you name it. It was as if he was a palpable presence. All most people saw was a representation, usually in the context of advertising. Yet, there was a sense in which people not only liked him, but felt they knew this crisply wholesome, indubitably clean-living and utterly harmless dark-skinned, but not dark, man.

There were, on closer inspection, two Jordans. One was the flesh-and-blood mortal who played ball for the Bulls, and, according to a 1992 book by Sam Smith, demanded special treatment at the expense of his teammates and had an unseemly gambling habit (Jordan admitted he'd written a check for $57,000 in settlement of a gambling debt). The other Jordan existed independently of time and space, residing in the minds of the countless acolytes who believed they knew him. This was the Jordan of the imagination. It was the Jordan Nike made and sold – just like a commodity. Jordan was not just the cynosure of 1990s sports, but the first truly modern sports celebrity.

What of his service to African Americans? For some, it was what Roman Catholics call supererogation – doing more than is required by duty and yielding a reserve fund of merit than can be drawn on in favor of sinners. For others, it was pious sales pitch in the service of only the commercial sponsors who paid him to advertise their products. In 1992, Kiersh wrote of Jordan: "Some condemn him for peddling expensive sneakers to impoverished black teen-agers."

By then compensatory consumption had been replaced by something different, as Andrews and Silk discerned: "The acquisition of material goods has become so commonplace that social distinction is frequently sought" (p. 1,631). While the authors are not explicit about this, I presume they don't understand social distinction to be just difference or excellence; perhaps a more basic human striving to express social standing or other qualities.

David Halberstam argues that Nike was the greatest beneficiary of its commercial relationship with Jordan. In 1984, the company had revenues of $919 million and a net income of about $40 million, and by the end of 1997, Nike's revenues were $9 billion, with a net of around $800 million (pp. 412–13). Jordan had made about $130 million from Nike at that stage. In a 1998 issue of *Fortune* magazine, Roy Johnson analysed what he called "The Jordan effect," meaning Jordan's impact on the overall US economy. The Air Jordan line was worth, in sales, $5.2 billion (about £3.2 billion). For that, you could buy Manchester United, Dallas Cowboys, New York Yankees and still have enough change to snap up Jordan's own club from 1984–98, Chicago Bulls. But, the overall value of Jordan-related sales over a 14-year period from 1984 was even more: $10 billion (£6.16 billion).

No figure in history had moved so much merchandise as Jordan. While often described as an icon, it's worth remembering that icons are usually regarded as representative symbols of something: manhood, for example, or freedom, or a new era, and so on. What did Jordan symbolize?

The first point to bear in mind is that, unlike any other athlete in history, Jordan was delivered to his audience gift-wrapped. "It was Nike's commercials that made Jordan a global superstar," Naomi Klein suspects (p. 52). There had been other gifted athletes before Jordan, though none reached what Klein calls "Jordan's other-worldly level of fame."

Klein isn't questioning Jordan's basketball prowess. But, pre-Jordan, sports stars, no matter how good or great, were athletes who happened to do advertising. They weren't synonymous with a brand, as Jordan was. Nike changed all that: the company embarked on what Klein calls "mythmaking," creating an aura around Jordan. "Who said man wasn't meant to fly?" asked one of the early ads, showing the apparently gravity-defying Jordan. The other-worldliness translated smoothly into sales. So, while other figures, such as Jesus, Che Guevara, Marilyn Monroe and Muhammad Ali were icons, none was manufactured as such. Jordan was. His iconic status was designed to sell Nike goods. But somewhere in the manufacturing process, Jordan came to symbolize a new version of blackness, what Helán E. Page, in 1997, called "embraceable male blackness," something with which whites would feel safe.

"When we view black men in our media, their representations generally fall into two reductive, disparate categories," revealed Ed Guerrero in 1995 (by reductive, he means presented in a simplified form). "On the one hand, we are treated to the grand celebrity spectacle of black male athletes, movie stars, and pop entertainers ... conspicuously enjoying the wealth and privilege that fuel the ordinary citizen's material fantasies." On the other, "we are also subjected to the real-time devastation, slaughter, and body count of a steady stream of faceless black males on the 6 and 11 o'clock news" (p. 183).

Guerrero named Jordan, along with Michael Jackson and Bill Cosby, as personifications of the former category. Jackson had, in 1993, been accused of making "sexual offensive contacts" with a 13-year-old boy. Cosby was 58 when Guerrero wrote. Jordan, at 32, was a more apposite reflection of the "grand celebrity spectacle" category.

When Thomas Oates and Judy Polumbaum conclude, "Jordan was able to escape both the patronizing and demonizing extremes often associated with black athletes," they miss the point (p. 196). He didn't "escape" them: he rendered them irrelevant. Here was a black man with none of the usual faults habitually associated with black men; in fact, no faults at all. He didn't talk politics and his comments about the condition of black people were anodyne. Rasheed Z. Baaith condensed Jordan's philosophy thus: "Get the money, don't say anything substantial and, for heaven's sake, never offend white people" (p. 8).

Nike didn't want Jordan to upset *anybody*. That was the whole point: his embraceable quality was intended to be good for all groups, male and female, black and white, old and young. So why, eight years after Jordan's 2003 retirement, did Nike re-sign Vick, a black athlete whose transgressions would appear to make him not just "unembraceable," but detestable? The answer is the arrival of an enthusiasm for clothes, hairstyles, music and language that had their origins in the American ghetto.

———

Sports. Where else could you find the irresistible combination of charismatically athletic black men bounteously rewarded for their muscular skills with every toy and stimulant they desired, regressing as if ordained by nature to a more primitive stage of evolution?

In 2007, just after charges were filed against Vick, Steve Visser, an *Atlanta Journal Constitution* journalist, talked to Vick's neighbors, one of whom invoked an old adage to characterize the football player and his well-to-do friends who enthused over dogfighting. "They moved out of the ghetto, but the ghetto is still in them" (July 19, p. 3B). Think about this saying for a while. Is it uttered in contempt, disrespect, and disgust? Or in empathy, as a way of expressing commiseration with others' inability to rid themselves of what nature endowed? Or is it smugness that colors the sentiment: a sneering satisfaction deriving from the thought that the same gift that brought them their extravagant talent and all the worldly excesses also tethered them to their instincts?

Recall how rap music, once acerbic and challenging, was domesticated in a way that made it exploitable: commodified forms of the black experience were delivered via downloads to consumers' MP3 players, smartphones or tablets. Andrews and Silk argue that the same logic guided basketball and, to push their argument, other American sports. Andrews and Silk describe this as ghettocentric logic, but they don't define it. So let me try: the systematic use of symbolic qualities and principles thought to originate from the viewpoint of people living in black ghettos. While the authors witness its pervasion in basketball, I see it everywhere. In music, cinema, tv shows, advertising – practically all aspects of contemporary culture are affected by "street" or "urban," both terms that thrum with blackness. Not an imagined blackness, either: a commodity that can be consumed from the comparative safety of the bleachers or your favorite armchair, or even while driving.

Jordan provided a new coding for blackness, in the sense that he assigned a meaning that was unusual and surprising: a black man that had none of the usual pathological flaws and did pretty much as whites did – except he played better ball and earned much more money. The trouble was, it contained none of the frisson of the older codes. There was no thrill or fear attached to Jordan. Nor the danger and satisfaction of watching high-earners succumb to the base instincts of their race, or the resurgence of an unruly, primitive force capable of destroying everything conferred by civilized society. Were Jordan to emerge as a prodigiously promising college player in 2012, the likes of Nike wouldn't be twisting his arm to sign endorsement deals; at least not unless he demonstrated a capability for being bad as well as good. He lacked the capacity for regression. And here we're reminded once more of the importance of context: time, place, events that precede and follow and circumstances that form settings for ideas and action – all these influence how we understand and assess practically anything. Imagine, for example, how Mike Tyson (b.1966) would be understood today.

In the late 1980s, early 1990s, Tyson was universally acknowledged the best heavyweight boxer for three decades. His almost primeval ferocity took him from his native Brooklyn streets, where he was a habitual young offender, to one of the most famous men on earth with career earnings from sport estimated at $500 million (£300 million). He had no education to speak of, had little interest in engaging with the media and, when he did, spoke often gauchely. "I try to catch him right on the tip of the nose, because I try to push the bone into the brain," he famously described a punching technique. In 1986, when, at 20, he won the first of three world heavyweight titles, he had no peers. He was unbeaten in 23 fights and seemed set to dominate heavyweight boxing for the next decade. By the end of 1987, he had added two more heavyweight titles and could lay claim to being the most fêted sportsman in the world. PepsiCo, in an uncharacteristically intrepid move, signed Tyson to feature in commercials for Diet Pepsi in 1988. In 1984, the soft drinks company had paid Michael Jackson $6 million to make two commercials, and sales response had presumably convinced PepsiCo that black celebrity endorsements were value for money.

Then came signs of regression. Tyson's marriage to tv star Robin Givens was an ill-starred liaison, a domestic psychodrama often played out in full public view. He got involved in scrapes with the police, nightclub brawls, and undignified episodes with women. His boxing suffered and he was beaten for the first time in 1989 in one of the biggest upsets in sports history (his victor, Buster Douglas, was a 42-1 underdog). In July 1991 he was accused of raping Desiree Washington, a Miss Black America contestant he had met while judging the pageant. On March 26, 1992, after nearly a year of trial proceedings, Tyson was found guilty on one count of rape and two counts of deviant sexual conduct: he was sentenced to six years' imprisonment. A poll, taken shortly before Tyson's release from prison, found 71 percent of black people considered the rape charge false, while just 33 percent of whites thought so. Tyson served three years and was released in March 1995, still three months from his 29th birthday and young enough to resume his boxing career.

No longer an intimidating force, Tyson struggled against the very best and lost unexpectedly to Evander Holyfield. The rematch earned Tyson $30 million and Holyfield $35 million, by far the biggest purse in boxing history (not exceeded until 2007). In the fight for which Tyson is best remembered, his true nature seemed to reappear, this time red in tooth and claw. During the fight, frustrated at his opponent's persistent headbutts, Tyson bit a chunk from Holyfield's ear and was disqualified. He was later fined $3 million and banned from boxing by the Nevada State Athletic Commission. The next several years of Tyson's life were spent leaping from one crisis to another. His troubles with the law continued, his domestic life remained in perpetual turmoil and, to compound matters, he was broke – he filed for bankruptcy in 2003. Somehow, he had managed to blow a half-billion dollars and still end up owing about $11 million in tax. He last fought professionally in 2005, a few days before his 39th birthday.

Appearances in movies, such as *The Hangover*, ensured he stayed in the public eye, though a tame Tyson had far less *appeal* than the terrifying beast. I emphasize *appeal* because Tyson was not a popular figure, at least not across the spectrum. He had his supporters among both African Americans and whites, but, of course, convicted rapists who cannibalize rivals in sports arenas rarely register much of an approval rating. Which is not to say that Tyson did not fascinate virtually everyone. He was a mesmerizing character, who attracted people perhaps as Joice Heth had in the nineteenth century: as a freak of nature.

This was an African American who had dragged himself off the streets and taken advantage of the only conceivable edge nature had given him. He worked like a demon to refine that natural benefit into a tangible advantage and, for a while, had riches beyond his own imagination and a status superior to most rock and movie stars. He had everything, including a glamorous Hollywood wife. And what did he do? Revert to something like an early stage of the evolutionary scale. Early in his career, when people would admire the bestial manner in which he savaged opponents, they presumably thought this was a side to Tyson he confined to the ring. Later, they realized this was a kind of microcosm of the man: he wasn't just like a beast, he *was* a beast.

As his film career indicated, Tyson was, and probably had been for several years, an actor. On his release from prison, he may have sensed that his image was the only thing he had left worth anything. His ring skills were in steep decline and his motivation had long since receded. But he knew his market. Asked to discuss his tactics against an upcoming opponent, Tyson promised, "I'll eat his babies!" He played the beast.

On September 7, 1996, Tyson entered the boxing arena to the sound of "Wrote the glory," a track written in his honor and performed by his friend and fellow New Yorker Tupac Shakur (1971–96), who was in the crowd at the MGM Grand in Las Vegas when Tyson beat Bruce Seldon. At the time Tupac was one of, if not the leading rap artist in the world. He'd spent time in prison for assault, and had himself been victim of an attack, getting shot five times in the lobby of a recording studio during a mugging. He'd also been convicted of a sexual offense. They were the street credentials of a true gangsta rapper.

In 1997, John Hoberman wrote: "The Black male style has become incarnated in the fusion of Black athletes, rapper, and criminals into a single menacing figure" (p. xix). Tyson, like Tupac, was a body part of that figure.

After the Tyson fight, Tupac was shot. He died six days later; his killer has never been caught, though the murder was assumed to be part of the feud between East and West Coast rap that accounted for the life of Biggie Smalls, as I noted earlier. In 1994, Tupac had released an album *Thug Life, vol. 1,* much of its material rugged, expletive-charged disquisitions on the black experience, the culture of criminality with its own moral code and its own values. Tupac was a denizen of Thug Life and, in his way, so was Tyson. They were both representative of an aspect of black America that was both repugnant and enticing. The mixture elicited guiltsploitation, the interest of whites in what they took to be authentic aspects of the black experience.

Let me illustrate this. In Barbet Schroeder's 1995 remake of the movie *Kiss of Death*, Little Junior, an utterly dislikable villain, prepares to beat an enemy to death by zipping up a protective suit to keep the blood off his white tracksuit. The scene offers a way of understanding the secret power of guiltsploitation – the exploitation of white guilt for profit. Imagine that, every so often in the mid- and late 1990s, whites clothed themselves in waterproofs and ventured into the ghettos, where they confront blacks, still angry at whites' historical sins. The ghetto residents then exact their revenge by urinating over the well-protected whites. Cowering under the cataracts, whites observe studiously, admiring the arc, color, even the smell of the urine. Once returned safely to their own neighborhoods, they shed their wax clothing, shower and discuss the experience. So goes a fable of the 1990s.

Blacks wore menacing masks, scowled at lot and made noises that suggested they were boiling with rage. Whites liked to glare, though without actually doing anything – apart from spending money, of course. Both virtually countenanced it, at the same time keeping their distance from one another. Tyson, like Tupac, was a harbinger of what Andrews and Silk call, "the commodified, yet seemingly individualistic, performance of alterity" (p. 1,632). By alterity, they mean the state of being different: Otherness.

They seemed to challenge, but actually offered comfort. Comfort, that is, in knowing that, in America in the 1990s, anybody could make it. Even the most poverty-stricken kids from the projects could become millionaires several times over and enjoy the respect of everyone. But what happens when you cover them with praise and fill their bank accounts?

"They moved out of the ghetto ... "

———

In the early 2000s, "ghettocentric logic" crept into basketball and other American sports. Andrews and Silk detect that, after the Jordan era, in which the NBA became a respectable mainstream sport populated by carefully managed "nonthreatening" figures, there was a shift in sensibility. Tastes and aesthetic influences changed, giving rise to a demand for more authentic and perhaps exotic expressions of blackness than those provided by the virtuous Jordan. Tyson and the other dangerous characters offered serious alternatives, but they were ahead their own time. The transitional figure was Kobe Bryant.

A CNN/USA Today/Gallup poll conducted in July and August 2003 discovered that about 63 percent of African Americans felt sympathetic to Bryant, at that time facing charges of sexual assault, compared to 40 percent of whites. The consistency with similar polls taken at the time of the O.J. Simpson and Tyson cases is striking yet predictable. Whereas 68 percent of blacks believed the charges against Bryant were false, only 41 percent of whites saw it that way, reported Patrick O'Driscoll and Tom Kenworthy of USA Today in August 2003.

Bryant, the Los Angeles Lakers' guard, was eventually found not guilty of sexual assault. He had been accused by a white woman of raping her when she was 19 and, if convicted, faced four years to life in prison. His widely reported reply was: "I didn't force her to do anything against her will." The case against him collapsed in 2004 when she refused to testify against him the day before the criminal case was due to start. Bryant later settled a civil lawsuit with the woman, though the terms were never disclosed.

Bryant was, in many ways, the antithesis of the stereotype black sportsman. Raised in Italy and in the suburbs of Philadelphia, he progressed through basketball without any of the histrionics that typically accompany a black athlete's ascent. No fights, drugs, wild parties, or any of the usual revelry associated with top-flight athletes. If anyone could take over the immaculate mantle of Michael Jordan, it was Bryant. His clean-cut image made him a favorite with advertisers: he had contracts with Nike, McDonalds, Nutella, and Sprite. But the accusation left grubby fingerprints and, while Bryant continued to play for the Lakers, his image was soiled. Coca-Cola pulled his Sprite ads and McDonalds announced that it would not be renewing its contract with Bryant.

As with O.J. Simpson, being cleared of all charges seemed to be of less significance than the initial smear. In 1995, during Simpson's murder trial, two-thirds of whites believed the charges against him were true, while just about one-quarter of blacks concurred. Fifty-five per cent of black respondents said they thought the charges were false; one-fifth of whites answered the same.

The Bryant case "reveals the centrality of race in both the adoration and condemnation of contemporary Black athletes," for David J. Leonard (p. 286). In his 2004 article, Leonard points out how "the simultaneous adoration of Black athletes and entertainers" legitimizes "claims of colorblindness" (p. 286). He means whites' enthusiastic admiration for, if not idolization of, the likes of Bryant and – to use Leonard's example – Denzel Washington permits and justifies their insistence that race or ethnicity are no longer relevant. People are evaluated solely on ability, or talent.

Because of the history of sports, black athletes, more than entertainers, "not only elucidate the fulfillment of the American Dream but also America's imagined racial progress" (p. 288). Leonard means prominent African American figures from sport help clarify or make clear America's advance to a colorblind or postracial society because they operate and excel in a sphere where race is not germane. Yet his argument has echoes of Guerrero's: the attention and values sports stars receive tend to "overshadow the realities of segregated schools, police brutality, unemployment, and the White supremacist criminal justice system" (p. 289).

Leonard goes even further, marshaling evidence from history and other scholars to contend: "Blackness within dominant society and within the world of sports represents a sign of decay, disorder, and danger" (p. 299).

Bryant's celebrity status earned him the kind of honor conferred on Jordan and, before him, Jackie Robinson, reasons Leonard: "The public assumed that Kobe had transcended his Blackness" (p. 301). Like the other black sports stars, Bryant lost his blackness, but only temporarily and, as it turned out, conditionally. Once accused of a serious felony compounded by a sexual element and multiply-compounded by the accuser's ethnic status, the "White imagination" re-engineered Bryant's status; in other words, he became both black and Other, a term I've used before to denote distinctness from or opposition to whiteness. Bryant became just like the mythological black criminally inclined, hypersexual predators, or, as Leonard puts it, "another Black athlete" (p. 307).

Jonathan Markovitz is broadly in sympathy with this view. He reckons public understanding of Bryant was filtered through memories over decades, even centuries. America's racial history bore on the case, as Markovitz states: "The Bryant case cannot be understood without grappling with ways in which collective memories of racist violence and sexist injustice were constructed" (p. 397). While neither he nor Leonard mentions it, shortly before Mike Tyson's release from prison after serving three years for the rape of a Miss Black America entrant, most African Americans still believed the rape charge was false. Only one-third of whites agreed, as we saw earlier.

Both of these arguments were framed in the two years following Bryant's settlement in 2004. They may have seemed plausible at the time, though, in 2006, Bryant was rated the seventh-most popular athlete in America, and, by 2010, he emerged as "America's favorite athlete." Bryant tied with Tiger Woods for top spot, though got pushed into third position a year later when New York Yankees' Derek Jeter took the laurels. Far from being demonized, Bryant was consistently one of the most popular sports stars.

Bryant sidestepped a recurring cycle: African American athlete blessed with an abundance of natural athletic talent draws the loud and enthusiastic acclamation of everyone, especially sports fans, earns as much as the annual turnover of a national gym chain, and acquires a celebrity status on a par with top movie or rock stars; *then* gets enmeshed in action that arouses moral distaste and contempt and winds up either in prison, or near it, and watches his stock plummet.

Bryant did get close and America is not usually forgiving. Had his case been five years earlier, there would have been no forgiveness at all. What Leonard and Markovitz fail to take into consideration is that, by 2003, ghettocentric logic had pervaded sports and many other aspects of popular culture. Writing in 2008 for the *New York Press*, Armond White considered the wide-reaching effects of the enthusiasm for commodified black culture. "More Americans come to identify with black figures than ever before," he concluded. "They [the black figures] are stars who charm rather than challenge."

———

Days before the allegations against him were made public, Bryant signed an endorsement contract valued at about $40 million with Nike. At the time,

Jordan was still under a contract, which would earn him $47 million over five years, and LeBron James, the basketball player, held a seven-year, $90 million contract. But Nike's *pièce de résistance* was a five-year deal contract worth $99 million with Tiger Woods.

Wood's strength, as benefits a broad-spectrum athlete whose appeal spanned all demographics, was in painting his image on a wide canvas and letting us splash goodness, cleanness and wellness all over. His weakness had the same source; given the chance, we daubed the canvas with seediness, licentiousness and the by-now-familiar trait associated with black athletes: regression. Nike signed Woods to the record-breaking endorsement contract in 2002 to help the company break into the lucrative golf equipment market. By 2008, golf accounted for nearly $725 million in sales, dropping to $648 million in 2009, but still enough to make the Woods contract good business.

On November 25, 2009, the *National Enquirer* carried news that the married Woods had been seeing a New York nightclub hostess, and that the pair had recently been spotted in Melbourne while Woods was playing in the Australian Masters tournament. At 2:25 a.m. on Friday, November 27, 2009, Woods backed out of the drive of his home in a gated community near Orlando and drove off, crashing into a fire hydrant and a neighbor's tree. There he lay unconscious until his wife emerged with a golf club, with which she smashed the car window before rescuing her husband. There were initial fears for his career after reports that he had sustained serious injuries. They were well founded.

It's unlikely that any reader will not know of the ensuing *cause célèbre*. But, just in case, here is a simplified timeline (for a more detailed alternative: http://bit.ly/-WoodsTimeline).

November 29, 2009: In a statement released on his website, Woods maintains the accident is a private matter and that his wife "acted courageously;" he describes all other "unfounded and malicious rumors" as "irresponsible."

December 1, 2009: Jaimee Grubbs, a cocktail waitress, alleges a several-year affair with Woods; she claims to have pertinent photos and text messages.

December 2, 2009: Woods apologizes on his website for his "transgressions," but expresses dismay at the tabloid coverage.

December 11, 2009: In a statement posted on his website, Woods admits to and apologizes for his infidelity and announces "an indefinite hiatus" from competitive golf.

December 12, 2009: Gillette reduces exposure of Woods in its advertising.

December 13, 2009: Accenture announces it will end its sponsorship agreement with Woods.

December 14, 2009: Nike and Electronic Arts confirm their continued support of Woods.

December 18, 2009: TAGHeuer announces it will not continue to use Woods' image in its advertising.

December 31, 2009: AT&T announces it will no longer sponsor Woods.

January 16, 2010: Woods is reported to have checked-in as a patient at Pine Grove Behavioral Health and Addiction Services, in Jackson, Mississippi, for treatment of sexually compulsive behavior.

February 5, 2010: Woods checks out of rehab and is collected by his wife, Elin Nordegren.

February 19, 2010: Woods appears in public and affirms he will play golf again.

February 26, 2010: Gatorade ends its commercial relationship with Woods.

April 2, 2010: Woods' wife walks out on him and spends two nights away from their Orlando home.

April 8, 2010: Woods returns to competition at the Masters.

July 21, 2010: Woods remains the richest sportsman in the world, earning a reported $105m in the previous year, according to *Forbes*.

August 23, 2010: Nordegren divorces Woods.

October 31, 2010: Woods loses the world number one ranking to Lee Westwood.

March 21, 2011: Woods is seen with Alyse Lahti Johnston, a 22-year-old aspiring golf pro.

May, 2011: Despite struggling to win tournaments and the absence of new endorsements, Woods continues to be the world's highest-earning athlete; this is, according to *Forbes*, mostly attributable to "two sponsors that stuck with him: Nike and Electronic Arts."

July 25, 2011: Woods drops out of the top 20 in the world rankings for the first time since January 1997.

Throughout the sequence of events, Woods' reputation mutated. Lurid tales of hush money, porn stars, and gambling circulated widely, each new story contributing to a new conception of a celebrity whose every attempt to avoid publicity caused exactly the opposite reaction. But would it be accurate to describe Woods' travails as a Fall, whether of Man, from grace, or to pieces?

In 2010, an unpublished report by Kevin Chung et al., of Carnegie Mellon University, concluded: "Nike's decision to stand by Tiger Woods was the right decision because even in the midst of the scandal, the overall profit was greater by $1.6 million for Nike with Tiger Woods than without him" (p. 1). It's possible that Nike's experiences with Bryant had been salutary: in June 2003, a few weeks before Bryant was charged with sexual assault, Nike signed him to a five-year deal valued at $45 million. It could have invoked a clause in the contract to escape its obligations, but it stood firm. In February 2006, Nike launched the first of its Zoom Kobe range of footwear; in the following year, it extended Bryant's contract and expanded the Zoom Kobe range. The lesson? Scandals, even scandals involving sex, that would have proved ruinous to a black man's marketability as recently as the end of the 1990s, were not so disastrous in the 2000s.

Ghettocentric logic was coursing through popular culture. Maybe Nike considered Woods' philandering added devilry to a hitherto sanctimonious character, thus making him more congruent with "urban African American experiences and associated aesthetics," as Andrews and Silk put it (p. 1,627). The sex scandal changed the way consumers engaged with Woods, but it certainly didn't jettison him to obscurity. If anything it just made him *blacker*, meaning it rescued him from his status as a goody-goody, an obtrusively virtuous figure, who looked like a black man but didn't talk, act, or dress like one – and never owned up to being one. Or perhaps it just made him appear more of a human, replete with the usual flaws and fallibilities.

"Tiger coerced no child, copped no plea, jumped no bail, whacked no white woman," JoAnn Wypijewski reminded her readers. "He had merely to bust up the prison of his own image, and ... became 'the new O.J.'" (p. 7). Or did he? "The new Kobe" might be more accurate: remember, in July 2010, shortly after his return to competition and just before his divorce, he shared with Bryant the distinction of being America's most popular sports star. In escaping "prison," Woods lost his uniqueness, but found universality.

When he won his first major in 1997, America was feeling the effects of *The Declining Significance of Race*, as William Julius Wilson called it. During the 1980s, the Reagan administration appeared to hasten the trend towards insignificance, reining back race-specific policy and entrusting equal opportunity to the market. Occasional incidents were interpreted as isolated episodes rather than reflections of continuing historical unease. The Rodney King beating and the subsequent riots disclosed a less propitious image of America. Rap music supplied what Pero Gaglo Dagbovie calls "personal histories of resilience, which mirror the overall theme of perseverance against the oppression that dominates the African American experience" (p. 301). So, in many sense, Woods' appearance was as a *deus ex machina* – an unexpected arrival saving an apparently disintegrating situation.

By the end of 2009, when the sex scandal erupted, Barack Obama was in office. Halle Berry was the year's winner of the Oscar for Best Actress. Kanye West was the best-selling male recording artist. Rapper 50 Cent had launched his own clothing range known as G Unit. Far from being a passage to oblivion, Woods' transgression, to use his own description, was a route to humanity. But it was also a sign of regression.

Imagine Nike owner Phil Knight's reaction if Woods had walked into his office in 1997, spread out the Tarot cards, and turned over the one depicting a tower – not a good omen. Knight (b.1983) was, indeed is, a man who plays whatever he's dealt. He started selling athletic shoes out of the trunk of his car in 1964 and built a business with a market capitalization of $41.43 billion (£26 billion) by 2011; he did so not so much by responding to market demand, but by creating new demands. Woods may have divined the future and told Knight that, after over a decade of purity and integrity, he, or rather the media, would defile his image. "No problem," Knight would probably have laughed. "By then there will be … let's call it 'the new black.' The popular image of blackness will have changed to the point where, to be popular, black people won't have to conform to either the timeworn image of the gifted but savage brute, or the equally gifted saint."

The two images still evoke memories, of course. But sport's African American *dramatis personae* are no longer forced into roles scripted in slavery and played out for decades after. They're living, breathing people with similar kinds of beauty and grotesqueries as everyone else. But there's satisfaction in watching nature reassert itself over nurture, daring onlookers to smile at the triumph of base instincts over civilized manners. This is surely what White has in mind when he perceives "charm rather than challenge" in prominent black figures. Charm is the quality of giving delight or arousing satisfaction through the fulfillment of expectations. Extraordinary athletes with extraordinary flaws.

Nike didn't go sentimentally moral when it offered Michael Vick a contract that practically certified his re-admission into the celebrity pantheon: it made a sound business decision, an acknowledgment that there was value in an imposing athlete who had all the money and adulation he could have wanted and, in sports terms, had the world at his feet, but who found it impossible to eradicate a defect sown by nature. "They moved out of the ghetto, but the ghetto is still in them."

11

To be spoken for, rather than with

'"I'm not going to put a label on it," said Halle Berry about
something everyone had grown accustomed to labeling. And with
that short declaration she made herself arguably the most
engaging black celebrity.'

Superheroes are a dime a dozen, or, if you prefer, ten a penny, on Planet America. Superman, Batman, Captain America, Green Lantern, Marvel Girl; I could fill the rest of this and the next page. The common denominator? They are all white. There *are* benevolent black superheroes, like Storm, played most famously in 2006 by Halle Berry (of whom more later) in *X-Men: The Last Stand*, and Frozone, voiced by Samuel L. Jackson in the 2004 animated film *The Incredibles*. But they are a rarity. This is why Will Smith and Wesley Snipes are so unusual: they have both played superheroes – Smith the ham-fisted boozer *Hancock*, and Snipes the vampire-human hybrid *Blade*. Pulling away from the parallel reality of superheroes, the two actors themselves offer case studies.

Smith (b.1968) emerged as a kind of antidote to the gangsta rap of the 1980s. In contrast to thug-like creatures, Fresh Prince, as Smith was known, and his partner DJ Jazzy Jeff were "embraceable" black men, who specialized in pleasant and entertaining, if insubstantial, numbers with strictly no mention of muthfuckas, bitches or niggaz. The transfer to television was almost seamless: in 1990 Smith starred in *The Fresh Prince of Bel-Air*, a sitcom in which he played an inner-city kid from Philadelphia (his real home town) who is sent to stay with well-to-do relatives in Hollywood. It was successful enough to last until 1996, by which time Smith had ventured into film, his most commercially successful being 1995's *Bad Boys*, in which he and Martin Lawrence played a pair of mismatched Miami cops. The film grossed $141 million (£91 million) and triggered a sequel.

Bigger-budget movies followed; they included *Independence Day*, and, in 1997, *Men in Black*, which gave Smith's music a boost: he released a tie-in single, as he did in 1999 when his *Wild Wild West* came out to coincide with his film of the same name. He kept recording up to 2005, by which time he had enough boxoffice to play leading men. He did so in 2008: in *The Pursuit of Happyness*. His performance persuaded Armond White: "Movie star Smith is also a political figure. His big screen exploits reflect the way we think about race, masculinity, humor, violence and fantasy."

Snipes is also a political figure – if by this White means someone who motivates, typifies or, in some way, relates to popular ideas in a certain period. By 2011, Snipes had appeared in 50 films; he earned $38 million between 1999 and 2004 alone. The relevance of this figure is that he did not pay tax on any of it. In fact, he claimed several tax refunds. Snipes was far from the first Hollywood actor to run foul of the IRS, but, as Eric Hoyt points out: "The case was remarkable largely because of Snipes's defense: he didn't pay taxes because constitutionally, he argued he was not required to" (p. 18). (Since US federal income tax began in 1913, a small number of individuals have asserted that the 16th Amendment, which authorized income tax, was fraudulently adopted or that no law makes anyone liable for taxes.)

Snipes' case was more remarkable for other reasons, including the actor's celebrity status, his ethnicity and the sums concerned. This was someone who had averaged $7.6 million per year, remember. Snipes was charged with fraud for failing to pay taxes and was found guilty. He was sentenced to three years in prison.

Snipes (b.1962) grew up in the Bronx and attended Manhattan's High School for the Performing Arts. After a series of minor film roles, he appeared in the video of Michael Jackson's *Bad* in 1987. Over the next several years, Snipes distinguished himself, avoiding run-of-the-mill films in favor of, for example, in 1990, *Mo' Better Blues* and, in 1991, *Jungle Fever*, both directed by Spike Lee and both, in different ways, essaying racial themes. In 1997, he played a successful bourgeois married to an Asian American who has a brief affair with a white woman in *One Night Stand*. Snipes camped it up as a drag artist in *To Wong Foo, Thanks for Everything! Julie Newmar*. Even when it seemed he had been cast by type, he ironized the convention of natural black athletes in *White Men Can't Jump*.

If any black actor swerved away from the surfeit of stereotype roles available to black actors in the ghettocentric 1990s, it was Snipes. Even his roles in *Blade* and its sequels were unusual: as I pointed out, black superheroes are a rare breed. Snipes was not alone in challenging racial types, of course: Denzel Washington, Morgan Freeman and the afore-mentioned Samuel L. Jackson were among the others, though no one took on more demanding assignments than Snipes. "I don't like perpetuating the stereotype of black males being drug dealers, and innately criminal," he told Earl Dittman, of *Digital Journal*, in 2010 (July 6).

When pressed to explain his decision to play a drug dealer in Antoine Fuqua's 2010 *Brooklyn's Finest*, he revealed that he played his character as a mature version of a figure he had played in an earlier film, Mario Van Peebles' *New Jack City*, in 1991: "He [the character] learned. Incarceration can change you. So he learned a lot. He had time to reflect on the error of his ways, and the futility of that path and how much death he was distributing to his own community."

Snipes was certainly a member of American Rights Litigators, an organization like its successor company, Guiding Light of God Ministries, that advises its members on how to avoid paying tax. Less certain was Snipes' affiliation with the Nuwaubians, a black, quasi-religious sect apparently descended from the Nation of Islam and based in an Egyptian-themed compound called Tama-Ra in Georgia. According to David Cay Johnstone, of the *New York Times*, Snipes, in 2000, sought a permit to build a military training compound on land next to the Nuwaubian camp; the Bureau of Alcohol, Tobacco and Firearms rejected the request (January 14, 2008). Snipes' associations with the group remain unclear, but add mystery to his case.

In 2010, convicted but still striving to stay out of prison, Snipes acknowledged to Dittman, "I still draw on the close relationships and friendships I found on the streets." He went on to uncover: "There's also this rhythm of the Bronx that's always in me. It's a very competitive environment there, and you're competing to survive." Perversely, this complements the remark from chapter 10: "They moved out of the ghetto, but the ghetto is still in them." It's by no means certain that Snipes would disagree with this. "I grew up in the Bronx where I constantly faced adversities. So, what's new? I think tough times in life are actually a blessing," he clarified his apparent indifference to the prison term he faced.

In December 2010, Snipes began a three-year sentence at a federal prison in Pennsylvania. Smith also had trouble: filming in New York's SoHo district, he was told to move his 53-foot double-decker trailer, complete with marble floors, 100-inch-screen film room and separate gym trailer, rented at $9,000 (£5,000) per week. As a result he had to walk all the way from his apartment– about a mile away from the location.

———

"In the 1970s, there was no cinema equivalent of Motown or the long tradition of U.S. Jazz," writes William Lyne (p. 45). "The seventies blaxploitation explosion is roughly equivalent to the early part of the century when white record companies began to record and market 'race' records." I traced the development of blues, jazz and race music in chapter 9. But what of blaxploitation cinema? This was the term used to describe a genre of inexpensive, independent films made in the early 1970s and featuring predominantly black casts and funky soundtracks. The plots were formulaic and the characters were typically one-dimensional, offering little variation on racist stereotypes. An essential ingredient was, as Lyne notes, "big doses of sex that emphasize macho stud constructions of black masculinity" (p. 44). Lyne counts 50 such films released during 1970–72, "with black audiences in mind," but which became popular with whites.

The most influential film of the genre was *Sweet Sweetback's Baadasssss Song*, directed by Melvin Van Peebles (father of Mario) and released in 1971. It cost $500,000 to make and took more than $10 million at the box office. As Lyne detects: "This led studios to turn away from such fare as *To Sir, with Love* and *Guess Who's Coming to Dinner* and toward the blaxploitation formula to boost black box office" (p. 45).

The two examples of the kind of films eschewed by the major studios both featured Sydney Poitier (b.1927), who was brought up in the Bahamas, but traveled to the US as a teenager and, as I pointed out earlier, won an Oscar for his supporting role in 1963's *Lilies of the Field*. Lyne's point is a crucial one: Poitier refused to succumb to the kind of parts typically reserved for black males and, instead, portrayed unusual characters. Unusual, that is, for cinema. In the two films Lyne cites, Poitier played a teacher at a London school, and a doctor engaged to the daughter of an affluent white San Franciscan couple, respectively. In perhaps his most famous film role, Poitier played a Philadelphia detective helping a murder investigation in Mississippi. *In the Heat of the Night* was another challenging film role for a black actor and Poitier reprised it in a sequel *They Call Me Mister Tibbs*. The film was released in 1970, and Poitier completed a trilogy with *The Organization* in 1971. Thereafter, his parts were either less central or more predictable, or else in television movies.

Poitier was an urbane, cosmopolitan figure, gracious of manner and refined of taste. He seemed freed of provincial attitudes. There was no trace of ghetto in him. If he had a musical counterpart, you wouldn't find it in the Motown studios or jazz clubs, and certainly not among the blues or R&B joints. Perhaps at the Capitol Studios in Hollywood, where Dionne Warwick (b.1940) recorded many of her successful singles and albums, such as *Here I Am* and *The Windows of the World* in the late 1960s. Her career also waned from 1970.

Like Poitier, Warwick was a black artist who subverted typical expectations and, for a while, seemed to offer possibilities for integration. Jason King appreciates her impact: "Warwick publicly emerged in the throes of the Civil Rights movement as a stunning emblem of visibility around black femininity and crossover potential" (p. 425). With requisite changes, the same could be said about Poitier; neither had what King calls an "explicit and contemplative relationship to the politics of black revolution," though both were, in an understated way, harbingers. They signaled the approach of others who, unlike them, satisfied popular expectations of black people and so looked and sounded more *authentic*.

Just as people reinvent the wheel, so they reinvent authenticity. Deborah Root, in her book *Cannibal Culture*, recognizes: "Authenticity is a tricky concept because of the way the term can be manipulated and used to convince people they are getting something profound when they are just getting merchandise" (p. 78). Artists like Poitier, Warwick or other black actors and singers who broke through to mainstream without conforming to popular expectations, were regarded as exceptional, but hardly reliable or accurate exemplars of the black experience. But were the blaxploitation and, later, hip-hop any more authentic, or were they just sold as such? Root describes the "commodification of difference," in which packaged versions of a purported culture are put on the market. The label "black" is slapped on something and it at once takes on all manner of exotic qualities that become eminently saleable.

There was a self-replicating quality in films such as *Shaft* and *Superfly*, both commercial successes featuring predominantly black casts, but in a narrow field of roles – the kind that Snipes later set out to spurn, but which audiences seemingly liked: maverick cops, drug dealers, pimps, hookers and so on. As Beretta E. Smith-Shomade certifies: "Most of these blaxploitation films characterized all African descendants as monolithic balls of anger, trapped within urban jungles and forever banished to the margins of society" (p. 27). They seemed authentic depictions.

—

Eventually, audiences started feeling ghetto fatigue and blaxploitation receded into history, though some writers like Pero Gaglo Dagbovie allege, "variations of 1970s 'blaxploitation films' continued through the 1980s and 1990s" (p. 314). The kind of films he has in mind are John Singleton's *Boyz N the Hood* and Spike Lee's *Do the Right Thing,* the former focusing on South Central Los Angeles, the latter on the Bedford-Stuyvesant section of Brooklyn.

Both films were made by black directors and neither compromised by resorting to stereotypes. In their ways, they were complements to the style of hip-hop music of the late 1980s; what Geoff Harkness calls "cultural products with high resolution," meaning artforms that provided or evoked detailed images of cultural life. There's no presumption that they were authentic representations, however; no more than, say, the minstrel shows.

Smith-Shomade singles out *New Jack City* as the film that disrupted convention, though not in its narrative, which was "standard generic fare," or its black male characters, who were "well-worn cinema stereotypes" (p. 30). While it now seems conventional, director Mario Van Peebles' controversial debut film about the rise of a black New York drug overlord played by Snipes (who, as I noted earlier, consciously avoided similar roles afterwards) was both bold and radical in its day. It was released in the same year as NWA's *Niggaz4Life*, an album that sounded like a portent.

In the movie, one of Snipes' aides who has "a crucial role in implementing all security systems" is played by Vanessa Williams (b.1963), then 28 (not the same Vanessa Williams, who had been the first African American winner of the Miss America contest in 1983, and went on to play Berry Gordy's mentee Suzanne de Passe in the movie *The Jacksons: An American Dream* in 1992, among other roles). Williams' character is, for Smith-Shomade, a complete departure from the usual bitches and ho's that inhabited both black-themed movies and the gangsta rap of the period.

Among the other genre films Smith-Shomade believes dealt with female black characters more complexly were *Sugar Hill*, another Snipes film, and

Set It Off, a 1996 film that gave rapper Queen Latifah (b.1970) her first major role and featured Jada Pinkett (b.1971) in a lead role. Pinkett, in 1997, married Will Smith and became Jada Pinkett Smith. The film didn't exactly launch either actor, though for Latifah it formed a bridge between the rap music, for which she was mostly known, and acting, which was to become her main career. In *Set It Off,* she was masculinized, in the sense that she appeared masculine in speech and manners, playing the lesbian leader of a female gang.

Some might struggle to understand why Smith-Shomade believes the film was so catalytic, but her point is that "hip-hop gangsta films have altered the cinematic landscape for black women." They created more roles – and thus more work – for African American women and gave them more visibility. While Smith-Shomade rates the assertive roles written for women in *Set It Off,* she neglects Pam Grier (b.1949), who had been playing bold, decisive and self-assured women for years. Unusual in their day, her portrayals were precursory. Chris Holmlund acknowledges this: "Grier's 1990s characters are now 'normal,' not exotic or 'other'"(p. 106).

Grier was the leading female of blaxploitation, making her screen debut at the age of 22 as one of several voluptuous inmates in the 1971 film *Big Doll House.* She never quite shrugged her image as a strong action woman and, even after the genre faded, found herself typecast. "Most of Pam Grier's 1990s roles are in some variant of action film," writes Holmlund, suggesting Quentin Tarantino's 1997 *Jackie Brown* was the only film of the period in which she was permitted to expand on her basic role (p. 104). Paradoxically, the film pastiches blaxploitation.

Grier's impact in mainstream cinema never matched her influence on blaxploitation and, while she struggled to make a transition, other African American women drew acclaim. Whitney Houston, a singer, became an actor playing a singer opposite Kevin Costner in *The Bodyguard* in 1992. Angela Bassett, an actor, played a singer (Tina Turner) in *What's Love Got to Do With It* in 1993.

Whoopi Goldberg was nominated for a 1986 Academy Award for her role in *The Color Purple,* in which Oprah Winfrey also played. This was not a first for an African American female: Dorothy Dandridge, Diana Ross, Cicely Tyson and Diahann Carroll had also been nominated. Goldberg, though, branched away from serious roles and specialized in idiosyncratic characterizations: as a medium in *Ghost,* 1990; as a singer disguised as a nun in the *Sister Act* films; and as God in *A Little Bit of Heaven,* in 2011. Goldberg defended Mel Gibson, whom she described as a friend, invoking John 8:7 ("let him first cast a stone") to mitigate Gibson's widely reported racist tirade in 2010. She attacked Donald Trump when he questioned Barack Obama's birth credentials in 2011: "I'm getting tired of trying to find reasons not to think of stuff as being racist."

Unlike other celebrities, Goldberg didn't smother her blackness or refuse to discuss it: in fact, during her criticism of Trump, she acknowledged that she was prepared to play the "race card." The race card is typically "used to explain away racial meanings in the midst of melodramatic challenges to colorblindness," according to David J. Leonard (2004, p. 290). Goldberg had strenuously resisted the appellation "African American" for many years before. "I'm an American. This is my country ... Just call me black," she told the British *Daily Telegraph* (April 20, 1998).

Someone like Whoopi Goldberg, with her fearless preparedness to challenge what she believes is racism, appears to make a strong case: she uses her celebrity status and the cultural authority it brings. She remains popular with film and tv audiences and often elicits agreement for her pragmatism. At no point does she reduce the importance or prominence of her ethnicity, nor dilute her fierce patriotism. She is a woman to be reckoned with.

Or is she? After all, Goldberg is a funny person: while her early work was often earnest, even profound, she broadened her popularity by embracing comic roles in light entertainment rather than drama. Her power as a pedagogic or admonitory figure was vitiated by her funniness. This is not a criticism: it is merely an observation of how entertainers known best for their theatrical work become closely associated with their art, often to the point where they find their onstage persona inescapable. I anticipate the reader's response: what about Arnold Schwarzenegger? He certainly played in comedies, but he was a foil rather than a comic and, even then, the bulk of his work was in sci-fi or action roles. Could Danny DeVito, with whom Schwarzenegger (b.1947) featured in the 1988 film *Twins*, make a successful transition into politics after a career spent making people laugh? Or Eddie Murphy or Cedric "The Entertainer" Kyles?

Cultural authority is not the same as other kinds of authority: it is based on the recognition of aesthetic, artistic or intellectual accomplishments and these are often subjective. Celebrity culture confers authority on figures who may have no qualification or credibility outside their own domain. And this is particularly significant when discussing the effects of mainstream actors, who occupy a special position in the celebrity temple. In many ways, their cultural authority outweighs that of rock stars, if only because it derives in large part from their screen presence. Were James Earl Jones (b.1931, who has played Alex Haley and several political leaders), Morgan Freeman (b.1937, has played Nelson Mandela), or Paul Winfield (b.1939, has played Martin Luther King) to make pronouncements on social or political affairs, the gravitas and credibility of some of their subjects would pass, as if by osmosis, to them. Perhaps they all knew the zeitgeist and could, if pressed, give a lecture on the fate of Paul Robeson. Incidentally, all four actors played *Othello*, a role that requires solemnity and erudition.

Were any of the four contemporary actors to branch in directions other than those signposted by the entertainment industry, as Robeson did, it's possible that we would not know about them. Perhaps the fact that we do demonstrates a truth.

———

"I had lived this woman's life from the age of 15 to 65 as she was sexually abused, beaten, treated like dirt. I really felt the injustice and I was called nigger just one time too many on screen," Halle Berry told Baz Bamigboye (p. 49). It was 1993 and she had just finished playing the title role in *Alex Haley's Queen*, the concluding part of the *Roots* saga. She went into therapy. "I had gone to him thinking I was going to give up acting and become a full-time civil rights activist," she explained. She didn't, of course; she went on to grander roles, more bravura performances and, in 2001, became the first African American woman to win the best actress Oscar for her role in *Monster's Ball*.

Whether the experience of playing the daughter of a slave and a white plantation owner who tries to pass as white in the period after the American Civil War (1861–65) impressed Berry (b.1966) indelibly isn't certain. Eighteen years later, she seemed to draw on it when she fought her ex-partner for custody of their daughter. In the process, Berry crystallized many of the themes scattered through this chapter. They include White's point that all black actors are, in some sense, political figures. Berry's case also reflected the interest in "authentic" black culture that spread across popular culture, leading to a redefinition of roles available to black actors and, indeed, a redefinition of blackness itself. It also resonated with historical memories and emotions.

"Halle Berry opened the lid on one of the thorniest issues that still plagues race relations," writes Earl Ofari Hutchinson in his 2011 article for *The Grio*. After splitting up with her partner, a white Canadian, Berry pressed for custody of their daughter. The custody was contested and Berry based her claim on her daughter's ethnicity: she was black, insisted Berry, drawing on what has become known as the "one drop rule." This is an old idiomatic phrase that stipulates that anyone with any trace of sub-Saharan ancestry, however minute ("one drop"), can't be considered white and, in the absence of an alternative lineage – for example, Native American, Asian, Arab, Australian aboriginal – they are considered black. The rule has no biological or genealogical foundation, though in 1910, when Tennessee enshrined the rule in law, it was popularly regarded as having scientific status, however spurious. By 1925, almost every state in America had some form of one drop rule on the statute books. This was four decades before civil rights. Jim Crow segregation was in full force. Anti-miscegenation laws that prohibited unions of people considered to be of different racial types remained until 1967, when the Supreme Court repealed them completely.

By the time of Berry's invocation, it might reasonably have been assumed that the rule had been exiled to America's ignominious past. But, as Amy I. Kornblau writes, in the 1960s: "The 'one drop rule' experienced a resurgence as black leaders argued for people of mixed heritage to regard themselves, and be perceived by others, as black" (p. 291).

"The debate was ongoing during the 2008 [presidential] election," says Hutchinson, commenting on the public dispute over whether Barack Obama was black, biracial, multiracial, or even American. "Obama mercifully put that debate to rest for most Americans when he made it official and checked the box "African-American" on his Census 2010 form."

Berry herself had an African American father and a white mother, who was from Liverpool. Her parents divorced and she was brought up by her mother in Cleveland, Ohio. Prior to the custody argument, she had declared she considered herself biracial, this referring to a child with a black parent and a white parent: "I do identify with my white heritage. I was raised by my white mother and every day of my life I have always been aware of the fact that I am bi-racial."

Hardly a controversial figure, Berry had occasionally talked about the particular predicament of biracial people, but had never made an issue of it. At various points, she had also used black, African American and woman of color to describe herself. She had, in measured terms, talked of how she never felt accepted as white, despite her white mother. But her appeal to the one drop rule seemed a bit like a physicist trying to explain the movements of celestial bodies by citing astrology. Or perhaps, like Storm, the mutant she played in X-Men: The Last Stand, watching the Weather Channel before deciding what to wear – the character can create lightning, avalanches, heat waves, rain and tornados at will. Actually, while it seemed irrational, Berry's explanation of her actions was far-removed from any kind of faux biology or pseudoscience. "I'm black and I'm her [her daughter's] mother, and I believe in the one-drop theory. I'm not going to put a label on it. I had to decide for myself and that's what she's going to have to decide - how she identifies herself in the world," she was quoted by Chloe Tilley, of the BBC World Service.

In resisting conventional census categories, or labels, such as biracial or multiracial, Berry was not returning to another label, black, as if returning to a default setting. Black, in her argument, is no longer a label: it is a *response* to a label – a response, that is, to not being white. Blackness, on this account, doesn't describe a color, a physical condition, a lifestyle, or even an ethnic status in the conventional sense: it is a reaction to being regarded as different or distinct. As Hutchinson reveals, Berry and anyone who embraces this apparent paradox, "effectively recognize the hard and unchanging reality that race relations and conflict in America are still framed in black and white."

Black no longer describes a designated group of people: it is the way in which those who have been identified as distinct from and opposite to whites have reacted; their answer. When Berry allowed, "that's what she's going to have to decide," she meant that her daughter has some measure of discretion in the way she responds. Blackness is now a flexible and negotiable action; not the fixed status it once was.

This doesn't mean blacks are no longer regarded as Other, as definable objects, "as those to be spoken for or about rather than with," to use a suggestive phrase from Juliana Mansvelt (p. 147). Nor does it mean that the appropriation of cultural practices, images and artifacts such as downloads, movies and concerts are no longer predicated on blacks as continuously and unchangeably different. It means that blackness is not a thing, a category, a group, or even a designation: it is, to repeat myself, a response to all of these. The one drop rule was an incongruous imposition on an otherwise sophisticated argument, an argument that carried added force, coming from someone not known for her outspokenness or her humor.

Berry had shown an awareness of history when she dedicated her Oscar: "This moment is so much bigger than me. This moment is for Dorothy Dandridge, Lena Home, Diahann Carroll. This is for every faceless woman of color who now has a chance tonight because this door has been opened."

———

By now, readers will be anticipating my argument. Berry, no less than any other actor mentioned in this chapter – or indeed, the many who have been missed out – is a political figure in the sense that White described Will Smith. As a person with cultural authority, she excited popular ideas about the way we think about race and, in her case, femininity, among other things. Smith's impression of boyish insouciance, as if he hadn't a serious thought in his head, has probably been a big factor in his success. "Smith can now claim cultural authority even over the equally slick George Clooney," White discerns (unlike Smith, Clooney has a well-documented history of involvement in causes, including famine relief in Africa).

White argues that Smith's status alone means he's no longer a lawn jockey, this being a garden-gnome-like statuette, usually black, symbolizing tameness and docility. His failure to show, as White puts it, "any social consciousness at all," does not lessen his impact. If anything, it enhances it. A silent black man without social consciousness who is, on Whites' account, a "first rate egotist" and shares Barack Obama's "smooth, casual approach to popularity," has made it possible for Americans to identify with him. They not only admire, but like and perhaps even respect him. Or, at least they respect his silence.

I contrasted Smith with Snipes quite deliberately. Also a high-earning movie star and maybe also an egotist, Snipes didn't share Smith's approach to popularity. Still enormously popular, he made his mark with challenging roles, often as unprincipled reprobates. His fall from grace didn't involve sexual transgression or violent behavior, but he went beyond the bounds of established standards of behavior and, as he was a black man, that had reverberations. Like so many other conspicuously successful African Americans, he appeared either unable or unwilling to control the impulse that led him to transgress. He even had a name for it, "this rhythm of the Bronx that's always in me."

Poitier too was political: it was as if Hollywood handed him a live grenade and stood back waiting for him to pull it. When he didn't, everyone lost interest and turned to the self-destructing pimps, studs, dope slingers and comely women who were much closer to popular expectations. The blaxploitation sensibility expressed post-civil rights frustration, though in an internecine way: black people were seen locked in mortal ghetto combat. Stereotype-on-stereotype violence shocked and offended, but comforted all the same.

The interest in authenticity, or ghettocentric logic, filtered through, steeping popular culture in all things black. "Through hip-hop, more Americans come to identify with black public figures than ever before," reflects White. "It's the common ground Bill Cosby shares with Snoop Dogg, and Hancock [the superhero played by Smith]." Think of the number of artists who have transferred from rap music to film or else negotiated a two-way career. Quite apart from Smith and Queen Latifah, there is Ice Cube, formerly of NWA and composer of "Fuck tha Police," who debuted in *Boyz N the Hood*, 50 Cent, whose first album sold 12 million copies worldwide, and who, as Curtis Jackson, appeared with Al Pacino and Robert De Niro in *Righteous Kill*, and several more films. Add to these: Eve, Ja Rule, LL Cool, Ludacris, Mos Def, Tyrese Gibson, and many, many more, including Eminen, all products of hip-hop culture, who went into the movies and became all-purpose celebrities. Figures that might, in the 1990s, be seen as menaces to society, became emblems of "black congeniality," to dip once again into White's phrase book.

Some might argue that it's incumbent on black celebrities in general and actors in particular to use their fame and, where appropriate, credibility to advance the causes of African Americans. Others might respond: why should we expect them to do anything other than entertain us? In any case, there is no universal agreement on what the cause actually is, or on the best way to advance it. This is why Halle Berry became a more interesting figure after she had spoken out on a seldom-reported subject.

In 2007, Karen Bowdre believed: "African American women ... are usually portrayed in an overly sexualized manner." (p. 17).

Bowdre may still have a point: most of the black women who have become visible on our screens do not play homely sorts. Beyoncé, Vanessa Williams, Thandie Newton, K.D. Aubert, Gabrielle Union, et al. specialize in beguiling, sometimes exotic roles. So far, only Berry has revealed evidence of her thought-processes. In doing so, she made herself less reassuring, perhaps even confrontational. "I'm not going to put a label on it," she said about something everyone had grown accustoming to labeling. And, with that short declaration, she made herself arguably the most engaging black celebrity.

12

The death of blackness

'Blackness, no less than whiteness, is an invention: they have both been fabricated from the same historical materials.'

In 1947, Kenneth Bancroft Clark (1914–2005) – the first African American professor at the City College of New York – and his wife Mamie Phipps Clark (1917–83) conducted a psychological experiment with 253 black children, who were asked to choose between four dolls, two black, two white. It was as if the children were psychologically indentured: two-thirds of them preferred white dolls. The Clarks concluded that black children had internalized – that is, accepted, or incorporated into their mindset – the hatred white society directed at all black people. That hatred surfaced dramatically when, in the same year as the experiment, Jackie Robinson became the first African American to sign for a major league baseball club: animosity and resentment came from both fans and Robinson's teammates. (The original study is recounted in Kenneth Clark's *Dark Ghetto*. Kiri Davis' 2006 film *A Girl Like Me* re-creates the experiment.)

The Clarks' study unmasked a feature of American society that was unsettling yet intelligible: being white was a good thing; even those who weren't white agreed. "As early as the 1920s, Josephine Baker rubbed fresh lemons into her face for thirty minutes each morning in order to lighten her skin," reports Ben Arogundade in his *Black Beauty* (p. 167). Many other performers either side of civil rights felt obliged to blanch their facial skin in order either to enhance their appeal to white audiences, or just to find work. Their deeds were driven by expedience more than internalized hatred.

Entertainers as diverse as Nat King Cole, Little Richard and Tina Turner wore heavily tinted makeup in their successful attempts to appeal to mainstream audiences. Even so, it came as a surprise when, in 2011, Beyoncé appeared in Los Angeles at the Grammys looking almost as pale as Gwyneth Paltrow. The buzz started: could the extravagantly glamorous wife of the world's leading hip-hop artist, known for her opulent lifestyle, ranked by *Forbes* as the ninth most powerful woman in the world, with annual earnings $35 million, actually be lightening her skin?

It wasn't the first time Beyoncé's skin tone had been questioned: in 2008, L'Oreal was accused of "whitewashing" her by digitally lightening her facial skin for an advertising campaign. L'Oreal denied it, though research by Julia M. Bristor et al. uncovered: "The advertising industry has historically capitalized on a 'hierarchy of skin color' that often exists among African-Americans" (p. 55). Lighter skin equates to social superiority.

Beyoncé was far from the only contemporary black celebrity to find her skin color under scrutiny. Rihanna, Lil' Kim, and even baseball player Sammy Sosa, were thought to have used skin lighteners, perhaps confirming Evelyn Nakano Glenn's contention: "The yearning for lightness evident in the widespread and growing use of bleaching around the globe can rightfully be seen as ... the internalization of 'white is right' values by people of color, especially women" (p. 298). This is not the same conclusion reached by the Clarks' study; but it is uncomfortably close, considering the six decades that separated them.

Writing in 2008, Nakano Glenn called skin color "a form of symbolic capital that affects, if not determines, one's life chances" (p. 282). She was not alone: a 2005 study by T. Joel Wade and Sara Bielitz, which drew on the earlier Clarks' study, agreed: "Skin color can be considered a commodity" (p. 219). They meant that whites' perceptions of blacks' qualities and capabilities are influenced by the tone of their skin. "Attractiveness" was not affected, but "skin color affects the perceived intelligence of African Americans" (p. 232).

The implication is that, where intelligence is a criterion for advancement, being lighter is an advantage. So why do celebrities, who are already well-advanced and whose success is not usually dependent on intelligence, or at least not intelligence alone, apparently strive to become lighter even though they won't be seen as any more attractive as a result?

This question needs two kinds of answer. Sika Alaine Dagbovie supplies the first when she argues that America, even now, is conflicted "over whether to control blackness on the one hand or encourage racial harmony on the other, or perhaps to abandon race altogether." Dagbovie is skeptical about recent developments: "Like the cliché 'some of my friends are black,' which attempts to prove a supposed lack of racism, the multiracial craze only superficially embraces the dark 'Other'" (p. 232).

On Dagbovie's account, some black celebrities' popularity is "connected to their 'otherness'," as she puts it. America, along with many other parts of the world, celebrates cultural diversity, but Dagbovie interprets this as "exploiting difference." Her argument implies that the success of most black celebrities is predicated on their reluctance to address racial issues. Everything I have presented in this book so far supports this. Black celebrities are content in their "exploitation" just as long as the rewards are proportionate. Recall that, in the year of the Clarks' study, Hattie McDaniel took the role of a maid in the CBS radio show *Beulah* and helped boost the weekly audience to over ten million; she was paid $1,000 per week – almost twenty times the national average.

While Dagbovie doesn't address the issue of skin lightening, her argument suggests that black celebrities mostly de-emphasize rather than accentuate their blackness. It could be passive acquiescence, or it could be rational adjustment, depending on your perspective. Either way, it's career-driven and quite different from the internalized race hatred that impelled the children in the Clarks' experiment to choose white dolls. Or is it?

The second kind of answer to why so many black people, including celebrities, "yearn for lightness" (to use Nakano Glenn's terminology) involves drawing away from the present to make sense of the historical spell cast by whiteness. Ben Pitcher maintains that the spell has been broken: "Obama guarantees the ontological transformation in U.S. culture set out in the last sentence of James Baldwin's *Notes of a Native Son*: 'This world is white no longer, and it will never be white again'" (p. 357). He meant that the nature of America's very being would be changed by the election of a black president. A review of history and an evaluation of the present will test this claim.

Let me start with a premise: there is nothing natural about being white. Not in the sense we understand it today. Whiteness has origins in the second half of the seventeenth century when English, Irish, Scottish and other European settlers in America began to see themselves not as individuals or members of national groups, but as parts of a race. Most occupied a status not greatly above that of black bondsmen; that is, slaves. Lerone Bennett reveals this neglected actuality: "The colonial population consisted largely of a great mass of white and black bondsmen, who occupied roughly the same economic category and were treated with equal contempt by the lords of the plantations" (p. 62).

The English historian Edward Augustus Freeman (1823–92) notoriously mused on what a great land America would be, "if only every Irishman would kill a negro, and be hanged for it." The wishful thinking reflects the contempt in which Irish were held by the English, who colonized Ireland in the sixteenth century, and regarded the Irish as incapable of being civilized.

History is frequently a collision of accident and design. As the anti-slavery movement gathered momentum, its insistence that slaves were sentient human beings and deserved appropriate treatment prompted slaveholders to defend themselves. Slaves were like livestock, the "lords of the plantations" argued, but without anticipating the force of the Quaker-led movement. The need for a sharper, more clearly defined barrier of delineation became more pressing as campaigners grew in confidence. The title of Theodore Allen's 1994 book *The Invention of the White Race* conveys the action that followed.

White skin was imbued with new significance – as a means of control. Europeans, some indentured, were endowed with unprecedented civil and social privileges in acknowledgment of their loyalty to the colonial landowners. Poor whites welcomed the new affinity with their social superiors; it gave them a status above that of black slaves. "You could be an ex-slave but you could not be ex-black," remarks Patrick Wolfe (p. 69). Over time, the newly amalgamated whites "came to define themselves by what they were not: slaves and blacks," writes Peter Kolchin (p. 155).

Whiteness invoked ideas and feelings of superiority; the white race that possessed that vaunted quality maintained it over subsequent centuries.

Maintained it to the point where "whiteness in this society is not so much a color as a condition," as George Lipsitz puts it. "It is a structured advantage that channels unfair gains and unjust enrichments to whites while imposing unearned and unjust obstacles in the way of Blacks" (p. 3).

Lipsitz's diagnosis of whiteness as a condition is accurate, but insufficient. What he doesn't reveal is that it has become a *normal* condition, as Toni Bruce recognizes: "In the USA, whiteness is normalized as that which does not stand out" (p. 862). Jennifer Esposito extends this: "Because whiteness is normalized, anyone who falls outside of whiteness (hence miscegenation or the 'one-drop rule') becomes different or other" (p. 524). Excusing her odd use of "hence" and the lower case in Other, Esposito makes her point.

Whiteness is germane to everything I've written about so far: without an understanding of its historical meaning and prevalence, we can't even reflect on the book's title. Think about it: would anyone write a book on *white* celebrities? Do we ever talk about white sports stars, or white actors, or white anything? The very fact that we use the adjective *black* in these and other contexts alerts us not to its uncommonness, and certainly not to its irrelevance, but to its abiding significance. No book that purports to analyse the social impact of black celebrities can dispense with the property that makes them *black* celebrities.

"The blackness that marks us off for permanent subordination and various forms of abuse is also what gives us a sense of identity, community, and history," writes David Lionel Smith, detecting an apparent incongruity (p. 182). Blackness and the resolution of racism are not just incompatible but irreconcilable: remove the subjection and exploitation by whites, and the reasons for black identity or even blackness disappear. Blackness, no less than whiteness, is an invention: they have both been fabricated from the same historical materials.

——

The concept of a postracial society is illogical. It suggests a time after race, when the concept has disappeared, left behind in the vapor trail of history. Just because we no longer talk, at least not publicly, in terms of race, does not stop us referring to blacks and whites *as if* they were races. Some readers will object. Of course we can, they'll insist: we can take pride in our identity and our culture as black people without allowing any semblance of inferiority or subservience into the narrative. Perhaps so, but they need reminding: blackness was imposed on slaves to distinguish them from a miscellaneous mix of Europeans and Americans, all of whom were considered superior.

"We have invented race as an instrument for identifying and interacting with people," confirms Jonathan K. Stubbs, attaching to this the important qualification: "Humans are separated into groups arranged in a social pecking order" (p. 115). In other words, race was and is not just an instrument for organizing perceptions of different groups of people; it is a hierarchy on which people base their evaluations. As soon as race enters the thought-process, an imaginary ranking or pecking-order shows up. Stubbs could have added that race has proved a serviceable tool for whites wishing to explain, justify or somehow legitimize their superiority over other groups, especially blacks.

There has been any number of successful people who either described themselves or were recognized by others as black, and who seemed to have navigated their way over or around every obstacle. Not only have they been successful, they are demonstrably, prominently and undeniably successful. It's impossible to miss them: they are on our screens, magazines, newspapers; in our imaginations. Black celebrities are visible representations of a new American Dream, one in which anybody, not just whites, can make it to the top. And not just in sports or showbusiness either: "African-American children now know that it is possible to become President," writes Joelyn Katherine Foy (p. 51).

So, why should we even discuss whether race is still a factor? Even when the old conception of race as a category of people sharing distinct physical characteristics has been repeatedly discredited, people persist in keeping the word in their vocabularies, and, indeed, in the minds. As long as they do, race remains central to American thinking. And the reason race remains central is because you, reader, can probably name less than twenty recognizably successful black people, among 41 million or more African Americans who make up 12.9 percent of the total population. You will know about Beyoncé, Oprah, Denzel Washington and many of the other celebrities mentioned in this book. You will probably know about Trayvon Martin, the African American teenager whose death in 2012 occasioned a bitter struggle for justice. So now I will offer a little information on people about whom you will know little or nothing.

"In contradiction to Obama's meteoric ascent, many black Americans are not overcoming but are being overcome," concludes Robert Perkinson (p. 77). His comment implies that, despite the momentous changes initiated by civil rights, African Americans are being defeated, leaving deep social inequalities. Long after the 1954 Brown v. Board of Education of Topeka decision that helped break segregated education, "black children are still almost twice as likely as their white peers to become dropouts," report Marian Wright Edelman and James M. Jones (p. 134).

African American children underachieve with a law-like consistency, leading Edelman and Jones to reason: "Many high schools have become prep schools for jail." Failed examinations and expulsions "create an underclass of children who are ready-made for prison cells rather than dorm rooms" (p. 134). Tracey D. Snipe confirms: "There are more Black males in prison (840,000) than in college (635,000)" (p. 30). In the 1950s, before civil rights, African Americans were imprisoned at roughly four times the rate of whites. "Today, they go to jail and prison at eight times the rates of whites, a development unexplainable by changing crime patterns," Perkinson records (p. 77).

Actually, there is an explanation. Michelle Alexander has offered it: the War on Drugs, initiated during the Ronald Reagan presidency (1981–89), served as "a distraction from more important crimes like murder, rape, and robbery" and pushed up conviction rates. Black men were relatively easy targets; so much so that, as Alexander remarks, "the enemy in the War on Drugs can be identified by race" (p. 101).

The trend isn't quite as gendered as Alexander suggests. "More [black women] are now behind bars than at any time," observes Hutchinson in his "Hardest hit by the prison." "[They] are seven times more likely to be imprisoned than white women." More than 80 percent of women prisoners have children.

Sentencing is also apparently affected by race. Among the many studies on this, that of Mark Peffley and Jon Hurwitz is especially interesting. Though mainly interested in how thoughts and opinions on capital punishment vary by ethnic background, the authors note: "There is now a virtual consensus that black assailants convicted of murdering whites are far more likely to face the death penalty than those convicted of murdering minorities" (p. 997).

Racial profiling – using ethnic affiliation as grounds for suspicion – by law enforcement officials had been practiced widely before and after civil rights, though the Rodney King case of 1991 and the subsequent riots in the following year promised to quash this. More recent research presents evidence not only that it continues, but that it has acquired new expediters. Bill Fletcher Jr. elucidates: "Even black officers can and will racially profile African Americans, pointing to some peculiar ways that even members of an oppressed group can come to demonize their own" (p. 5).

Spatial segregation was legally enforced for much of America's history and, while civil rights made an impact, segregation continues to the present day. Dozens, perhaps hundreds of research projects over the past decade alone have certified how, in the words of Nancy Denton, "laws passed to prevent segregation in public housing and federally assisted private construction have been ignored or modified" (p. 135).

Neighborhoods where there is a clustering of African Americans have, in many cases, become what Robert L. Wagmiller Jr. calls "jobless ghettos," which, in turn, have impacts on "traditional family formation," the prevalence of poverty, the number of "mainstream role models," and the fiscal state of community institutions, such as churches, schools, stores, etc. (p. 539). Wagmiller collects demographic materials to conclude that the jobless ghettos are characterized by isolation, concentration and a "culture of despair."

The cumulative effect of these and related factors lead Linda Burnham to conclude that, even today: "The black poverty rate still hovers between 20 and 25 percent and remains more than twice that of whites" (p. 45). Focusing specifically on black children, Jack L. Nelson et al. report: "Between one quarter and one third of children of color live in poverty; only 10 per cent of white children do" (p. 245).

Overt discrimination in employment is outdated, though Emmanuel K. Ngwainmbi discloses a somewhat surprising pattern in his 2005 report: "60%

of all White-owned businesses in the United States did not employ [ethnic] minorities" (p. 5). Eighty-five percent of American businesses are owned by whites.

Less visibly: "African American workers with the same levels of education and experience as white workers, on an average, find themselves in substantially more dangerous occupations. Examples: steel industry – top of the coke ovens, where workers are exposed to many cancer-causing agents." Jennifer Schoenfish-Keita and Glenn S. Johnson go on to provide a catalog of hazardous jobs in which blacks are over-represented (p. 272). Black workers are twice as likely to be permanently or partially disabled due to a job-related injury or illness.

Even in areas where there is no tangible trace of prejudice, direct or indirect, there are patterns of disadvantage, as Cynthia M. Frisby discerns: "Although the incidence rate of breast cancer is lower for African American women than it is for white women, research shows that African American women, as a whole, have a higher mortality rate and a lower 5-year survival rate when compared to White women" (p. 103). Black women do not receive treatment early enough.

With a troubling symmetry, "African American men are at elevated risk for prostate cancer," according to a research team led by Kathryn L. Taylor: the incidence rate of the disease is about 60 percent higher in black males than in white males, and the mortality rate is about twice as high (p. 591). Again, early treatment is the problem; black men are not encouraged to undergo prostate cancer screening. The life expectancy for black men is six years less than that of white men, while for black women it is five years less than white women.

Rogers M. Smith and Desmond S. King have assembled copious data to present a summary of a postracial America that appears anything but postracial. The authors acknowledge that the gap between blacks and whites has narrowed significantly over the past few decades. But: "The familiar, painful litany of the United States' continuing and severe racial gaps in material well-being encompasses virtually every dimension of life, from economic well-being to health to housing to education to the criminal justice system" (p. 26).

These patterns of inequality are unlikely to be addressed in any ethnically specific program or policy, at least not under Obama or any prospective president on the political horizon. Julianne Malveaux explains in her "What about economic justice?": "The invocation of race is so likely to provoke unremitting hostility that many have looked for 'race neutral' remedies to solve a set of issues that clearly have race at their base" (p. 21).

And here we reach our *Catch-22*: a set of circumstances from which there is no escape because of mutually conflicting and, in this case, dependent conditions. For those unfamiliar with Joseph Heller's 1961 novel, the main character is Yossarian, a bombardier in the US Army Air Force, who feigns madness in order to avoid dangerous combat missions, but whose very wish to avoid them is taken as evidence of his sanity.

Writers such as Malveaux have theorized that America's history of structured *de jure* inequality based on race has left a legacy that can't be removed by race-neutral remedies; that is, the kind of programs that make no particular allowance for ethnic background, color, or purported racial origin. Inequality produced by race needs to be addressed by race. Like Yossarian, she seeks a resolution by using the very subterfuge that will prove the existence of the thing she wants to deny. This is not a criticism of Malveaux. Far from it: she has identified that race has proved a cruelly effectual instrument when used malevolently. The question now is whether it can ever be used benevolently?

——

The demons that drive people to tyrannize and repress others are the subject for another book. Yet, the wrongness of racism, once recognized, was not so easy to put right. Centuries of racist thinking were not washed away like footprints in sand with the arrival of civil rights. Why not? "Americans view race through a prism of culture," is John Hartigan's answer. No American alive is a racist. In fact, they live in fear of being described as such. Yet the paradox is, as we know from the summaries of previous pages, that race continues to matter and its effects are felt, as Hartigan points out, "widely and deeply."

People have been either defending themselves against accusations of racism or boasting their anti-racist credentials for decades, of course. But only recently have they been able to point to evidence that simultaneously supports them and indicts the culture of which they are both part and product. America resolutely refuses to consider the possibility that racism is still a factor. It is as much part of history as Wounded Knee, Japanese internment, and the Ku Klux Klan, they might argue. Hartigan believes this is part of the difficulty: "How do we get Americans to acknowledge and assess the pervasive racial aspects of our public culture if the one thing they know they cannot be is 'racist'?" (p. 16).

Hartigan's argument is that race has long been an organizing principle in American culture. For most of its history it has been a method of what he calls "determining belonging," by which I presume he means identifying the right personal or social qualities to be a member of a particular group. In order to do this, there must be a way of contrasting the right qualities from the wrong ones. Blacks have, historically, not belonged; their function was to remind whites what they were not. Whites could not have regarded themselves as a group, a race, without another group with which to contrast themselves.

The people who were, in the seventeenth century, excluded from the white race have entertained, amused, charmed, engrossed, inspired admiration, and earned extravagant praise. They have served up all manner of dazzling performances primarily for the delectation of whites. Should we expect the latest generation of entertainers, sports stars and all-round celebrities to do or be anything more? Meghan S. Sanders and James M. Sullivan's 2010 research steers us towards an answer.

They predicate their findings thus: "Racism has transformed into a new form of racism called symbolic racism" (p. 202). This involves four beliefs: blacks no longer face discrimination; their lack of progress is due to their unwillingness to work hard enough; they demand too much, too soon; they get more than they deserve. The study by Peffley and Hurwitz cited earlier complements this preference for individual makeup over social circumstances: "Whites ... are much more likely to view black criminality as being dispositionally caused, believing the reason blacks are more likely to be arrested and imprisoned than whites is that blacks commit more crimes" (p. 1,007). ("Dispositionally caused," I dare say, means brought about by people's inherent qualities of mind and character.)

None of this seems new or surprising. But the sources of symbolic racism, say Sanders and Sullivan, are the media: whites respond not to black people, but to representations of black people. Sanders and Sullivan's research shows: "There is a difference of perception for African American groups and African American individuals." They mean that whites see black individuals differently from blacks as a group; they might like, admire and respect certain individuals – actors, athletes, musicians, for example – but fail to generalize the qualities of which they approve to black people as a whole.

When individuals whom whites may admire are represented in the media negatively, as were for example Mike Tyson, Michael Vick and Wesley Snipes, whites regard their cases as "more similar and representative of the group." On the other hand "positive individuals," as Sanders and Sullivan call them, are considered untypical and unrepresentative of African Americans as a group. Several of the figures we have considered in previous chapters, including Halle Berry and Will Smith, are identified as African Americans who are viewed positively and liked but are not understood as representative of blacks. Stereotypes from history continue to infect contemporary thinking.

The researchers may well have explored the influence of *ressentiment,* this being a mental state first introduced by Friedrich Nietzsche (1844–1900) to describe suppressed feelings of envy and hatred that can't be acted on. While their study didn't reveal this, it would be consistent to assume that whites have a grudging rather than unconditional admiration for someone such as music and film producer, rapper and all-round impresario P. Diddy, who has a net worth of $475 million, or Serena Williams, who limped by on $12 million per year in the dog days of a tennis career festooned with thirteen Grand Slam singles titles.

If Sanders and Sullivan's experiment is as secure as it sounds, perhaps the presence of so many African American celebrities has had far less positive impact among the American population than it appears. Black celebrities probably occupy a place in the popular imagination analogous to that of showroom mannequins in a storefront: used for display purposes and not necessarily an accurate reflection of what's inside the store.

The belief that black people's "lack of progress is due to their unwillingness to work hard enough" complements a point made by Lipsitz: "What was once done to them by white racists, this line of argument contends, Blacks are now doing to themselves" (p. 1). So: successful black people are exceptional and reap the bounties of an American meritocracy that rewards ability. But they are hardly representative of the majority of African Americans, who remain in charge of their own destinies and contrive to hinder their own progress even when all the obstructions of racism have been removed.

Esposito's inference broadens the picture. There is, she conjectures, an "image of black people in the white mind" and: "This black image is often informed by prominent 'exceptions' to the rule" (p. 532). While she doesn't include this corollary, I presume she wouldn't object if I add: white self-consciousness is informed by images of blacks, as a painter's subjects are brought into relief by the use of contrasts. I repeat Kolchin's point about whites in bygone time, who "came to define themselves by what they were not."

Esposito discerns how the idea of whiteness-as-normal "makes it convenient to blame people of color, as individuals, for problems that are inherently based on the group's social location" (p. 524). This chimes both with Sanders and Sullivan's findings and Malveaux's conundrum.

———

In 1997, the historian Paul Spickard reflected that, since the 1960s, America had experienced: "A modest softening of the lines between the races." Apart from the word "race" to describe cultural groups, it seemed an unexceptional statement: more than three decades after civil rights, some abatement of the strife and divisions that marked America's prehistory would have been expected. Spickard then added: "This is not to suggest that race is becoming less important in American public life – on the contrary, it continues to shape people's life chances far more drastically than white conservative rhetoric would have us believe" (p. 153).

Dirk Philipsen elaborates: "The entire spectrum of life experiences by Americans not only are perceived, but also processed and acted upon in a way that is pervasively racialized" (p. 190). By racialized, I take it that Philipsen means treated in a way made comprehensible in terms of race. If this doesn't surprise us quite as it should, why is that? Perhaps because it resembles commonsense: a glance at the patterns of inequality I've outlined can be rendered intelligible in terms of a mutant racism that has adapted to changing environments and continues to exert a maleficent influence, or as an expression of blacks' inability or perhaps unwillingness to improve their material positions. The latter seems a more popular option.

Perhaps this has pushed many African Americans into a mood of resignation, if not fatalism. Earl Sheridan sums up their stance: "Racism is irrelevant not because it no longer exists, as the conservatives argue, but because it is unbeatable" (p. 190). At times, it certainly appears so: its obduracy has apparently convinced black celebrities that the most productive way ahead is around it. This has prompted Julie Novkov to enquire: "Could a postracial state be something other than a state in which racial subordination was rendered politically unspeakable though still structurally present?" (p. 658).

The reader must decide whether this is preposterous or profound. Initially, I thought the former, but, on reflection I veer toward the latter: the situation Novkov conjectures is actually a decent summary of today; her speculation about whether it can ever be anything different makes us wonder whether, in a truly postracial society, we could conceptualize black people at all.

What about whites? Matthew W. Hughey reckons whiteness is now "less of a synonym for invisible normality" than it was just a few years ago (p. 1,291). When Bruce argues, "the instability of dominant discourses means that the boundaries of the 'normal' must be constantly marked," she implies there is more transience than we typically assume (p. 862). Hundreds of years of conceiving people as black leaves an impression of permanence. A genuine postracial culture would change this. As I've argued, the term black would be meaningless: postracial would mean dispatching blackness and whiteness to oblivion. This won't happen. More likely we will witness the kind of situation encouraged by Halle Berry, in which ethnicity becomes a matter of choice, people electing their ethnic identities. Note the use of plural identities: Berry's child may change hers as she grows, perhaps opting for several at one time, changing to suit different situations. It will be – probably already is – possible to have multiple ethnicities, all interchangeable and all utterly fluid. We live a "liquid life," as Zygmunt Bauman calls it; today's is "a society in which the conditions under which its members act change faster than it takes the ways of acting to consolidate into habits and routines" (p. 1).

For some, this lack of certainty must sound like a waking nightmare. Surely we can't change identities and switch ethnicities as we change our appearance with cosmetic surgery, replace limbs with prosthetics or restore vital functions with organ transplants from human donors? But I see the day when that will happen: I see it now. That's what is happening and, for this writer at least, it is no bad thing. If this means the death of blackness, then so be it. Baldwin was ahead of his time with his "white no longer" salutation in 1955. He would still be too early if he said it today. But tomorrow, he will be right: the death of blackness will bring with it the demise of whiteness and all the inequity, oppression, bigotry and manifold wrongdoing that malefactor has engendered.

Bibliography

Publications

Abt, Vicki and Seesholtz, Mel (1994) "The shameless world of Phil, Sally and Oprah: Television talk shows and the deconstructing of society", *Journal of Popular Culture*, vol. 28, no. 1, pp. 171–191.

Adams, Guy (2011) "Who's the Diddy?" *Independent Magazine*, January 22, pp. 16–23.

Adams, James Truslow (1931) *The Epic of America*, Boston MA: Little, Brown.

Aftab, Kaleem (2011) "50 Cent – From hip-hop to Hollywood", *Independent*, July 29, p. 30. Available at: http://ind.pn/-50Cent

Alexander, Michelle (2010) *The New Jim Crow: Mass incarceration in the age of colorblindness*, New York: New Press.

Allen, Theodore (1994) *The Invention of the White Race: The origin of racial oppression in Anglo-America*, London: Verso.

Alston, Joshua (2008) "The new transgender reality", *Newsweek*, September 17. Available at: http://bit.ly/-NewTransgenderReality

Andersen, Christopher (1994) *Michael Jackson: Unauthorized*, New York: Simon & Schuster.

Andrews, David L. and Silk, Michael L. (2010) "Basketball's ghettocentric logic", *American Behavioral Scientist,* vol. 53, no. 11, pp. 1,626–1,644.

Arogundade, Ben (2001) *Black Beauty: A history and a celebration*, New York: Thunder's Mouth Press.

Aubry, Timothy (2006) "Beware the furrow of the middlebrow: Searching for paradise on the Oprah Winfrey Show", *Modern Fiction Studies*, vol. 52, no. 2, pp. 350–373.

Baaith, Rasheed Z. (2002) "Tiger Woods and Michael Jackson", *The Broward Times,* vol. 51, no. 5, p. 8.

Bail, Matt (2008) "Is Obama the end of black politics?", *New York Times magazine*, August 6. Available at: http://nyti.ms/-IsObamaTheEnd

Bailey Woodward, Jennifer and Mastin, Teresa (2005) "Black womanhood: *Essence* and its treatment of stereotypical images of black women", *Journal of Black Studies*, vol. 36, no. 2, pp. 264–281.

Baldwin, James (1984) *Notes of a Native Son*, New York: Beacon Press.

Bamigboye, Baz (1993) "'I felt abused, beaten, treated like dirt after this TV series'", *Daily Mail* (London), October 1, p. 49.

Basil, Michael D. (1996) "Identification as a mediator of celebrity effects", *Journal of Broadcasting and Electronic Media*, vol. 40, no. 4 (Fall), pp. 478–496.

Bauman, Zygmunt (2010) *Liquid Life*, Cambridge: Polity.

Beeching, Barbara J. (2002) "Paul Robeson and the black press: The 1950 passport controversy", *Journal of African American History*, vol. 87, pp. 339–354.

Bell, Christopher E. (2010) *American Idolatry: Celebrity, commodity and reality television*, Jefferson NC: McFarland.

Bell, Patricia A. (1993) "Review of *Enlightened Racism*: The Cosby Show, *audiences, and the myth of the American Dream*", *Contemporary Sociology*, vol. 22, no. 5, pp. 741–742.

Bennett, Lerone (1993) *The Shaping of Black America: The struggles and triumphs of African Americans, 1619 to the 1990s*, London: Penguin.

Bogle, Donald (1997) *Dorothy Dandridge: A biography*, New York: Amistad.

Bogle, Donald (2001) *Toms, Coons, Mulattoes, Mammies, and Bucks: An interpretive history of blacks in American films*, 4th edition, New York: Continuum.

Bogle, Donald (2010) *Heat Wave: The life and career of Ethel Waters*, New York: HarperCollins.

Bonilla-Silva, Eduardo and David Dietrich (2011) "The sweet enchantment of color-blind racism in Obamerica", *Annals of the American Academy of Political and Social Science*, vol. 634, pp. 190–206.

Boskin, Joseph (1986) *Sambo: The rise and demise of an American jester*, New York: Oxford University Press.

Bowdre, Karen (2007) "Gender stereotypes in film and media", *Black Camera*, vol. 22, no. 1, pp. 15–18.

Bowser, Pearl and Spence, Louise (2000) "Oscar Micheaux's *Body and Soul* and the burden of representation", *Cinema Journal*, vol. 39, no. 3, pp. 3–29.

Bradley, David (2010) "Misreading Obama", *Dissent*, vol. 57, no. 4, pp. 95.

Branchik Blaine J. and Foster Davis, Judy (2009) "Marketplace activism: A history of the African American elite market segment", *Journal of Macromarketing*, vol. 29, no. 1, pp. 37–57.

Bristor, Julia M., Gravois Lee, Renée and Hunt, Michelle R. (1995) "Race and ideology: African-American images in television advertising", *Journal of Public Policy and Marketing*, vol. 14, no. 1, pp. 48–59.

Brown, Anthony L. and Brown, Keffrelyn D. (2010) "'A spectacular secret': Understanding the cultural memory of racial violence in K-12 official school textbooks in the era of Obama", *Race, Gender & Class*, vol. 17, nos. 3/4, pp. 111–126.

Bruce, Toni (2004) "Making the boundaries of the 'normal' in televised sports: The play-by-play of race", *Media, Culture, Society*, vol. 26, no. 6, pp. 861–879.

Burnham, Linda (2008) "Obama's candidacy: The advent of post-racial American and the end of black politics", *The Black Scholar*, vol. 38, no. 4, pp. 43–46.

Bush, Alan J., Smith, Rachel and Martin, Craig (1999) "The influence of consumer socialization variables on attitude toward advertising: A comparison of African-Americans and Caucasians", *Journal of Advertising*, vol. 28, no. 3, pp. 13–24.

Bush, George W. (2010) *Decision Points*, New York: Crown Publishing.

Bush, Ronald F., Hair, Joseph F. and Solomon, Paul J. (1979) "Consumers' level of prejudice and response to black models in advertisements", *Journal of Marketing Research*, vol. 16, pp. 341–345.

Bynoe, Yvonne (2005) "After Katrina – Is there justice or just us?", *The Network Journal: Black Professionals and Small Business Magazine*, November. Available at: http://www.tnj.com/archives/2005/november2005/feature.php

Capolovitz, David (1967) *The Poor Pay More: Consumer practises of low-income families*, New York: Free Press.

Chin, Elizabeth (2007) "Consumption, African Americans" in Ritzer, George (ed.), *Blackwell Encyclopedia of Sociology*, Oxford: Blackwell. Available at: http://www.sociologyencycopedia.com/

Chung, Kevin, Derdenger, Timothy and Srinivasan, Kannan (2010) *Economic Value of Celebrity Endorsement: Tiger Woods' impact on sales of Nike golf balls*, unpublished report, Tepper School of Business, Pittsburgh PN: Carnegie Mellon University.

Clark, Kenneth B. (1989, originally 1965) *Dark Ghetto: Dilemmas of social power*, 2nd edition, Middletown, CT: Wesleyan University Press.

Cloud, Dana L. (1996) "Hegemony or concordance? The rhetoric of tokenism in 'Oprah' Winfrey's rags-to-riches biography", *Critical Studies in Mass Communication*, no. 13, pp. 115–137.

Cohen, Harvey G. (2004) "Duke Ellington and *Black, Brown and Beige*: The composer as historian at Carnegie Hall", *American Quarterly*, vol. 56, no. 4, pp. 1,003–1,034.

Cosby, Bill and Poussaint, Alvin F. (2007) *Come on, People: On the path from victims to victors*, Nashville TN: Thomas Nelson.

Cross, Theodore (2007) "Barack Obama is the superior choice for African-American voters", *Journal of Blacks in Higher Education*, vol. 56 (summer), pp. 68–72.

Dagbovie, Pero Gaglo (2005) "'Of all of our studies, history is best qualified to reward our research': Black history's relevance to the hip hop generation", *Journal of African American History*, vol. 90, no. 3 (summer), pp. 299–323.

Dagbovie, Sika Alaine (2007) "Star-light, star-bright, star damn near white: Mixed-race superstars", *Journal of Popular Culture*, vol. 40, no. 2, pp. 217–237.

Davis, James Earl (1994) "College in black and white: Campus environment and academic achievement of African American males", *Journal of Negro Education*, vol. 63, no. 4, pp. 620–633.

Denton, Nancy (2007) "Review of *The Geography of Opportunity: Race and housing choice in metropolitan America*", *Contemporary Sociology*, vol. 36, no. 2, pp. 135–136.

Dickerson, Debra J. (2007) "Colorblind", *Salon.com*, January 22. Available at: http://www.salon.com/news/opinion/feature/2007/01/22/obama/

Dittman, Earl (2010) "Wesley Snipes returns to NY's mean streets in 'Brooklyn's Finest'", *Digital Journal*, July 6. Available at: http://bit.ly/-WesleySnipesreturns

Durand, Richard M., Teel, Jesse E. Jr. and Bearden, William 0. (1979) "Racial differences in perception of media advertising credibility", *Journalism Quarterly*, vol. 56, no. 3, pp. 562–566.

Dyson, Michael Eric (2005) *Is Bill Cosby Right? (Or has the black middle class lost its mind?)*, New York: Basic Civitas Books.

Esposito, Jennifer (2009) "What does race have to do with *Ugly Betty*? An analysis of privilege and postracial (?) representations on a television sitcom", *Television and New Media*, vol. 10, no. 6, pp. 521–535.

Fast, Susan (2010) "Difference that exceeded understanding: Remembering Michael Jackson (1958–2009)", *Popular Music and Society*, vol. 33, no. 2, pp. 259–266.

Ferber, Edna (1981, originally 1926) *Show Boat*, New York: G. K. Hall & Co.

Fiske, John (2005) "Hearing Anita Hill (and viewing Bill Cosby)", pp. 89–136 in Hunt, Darnell M. (ed.) *Channeling Blackness: Studies on television and race in America*, New York: Oxford University Press.

Fletcher Bill Jr. (2010) "Racial profiling and the 'presumption of guilt'", *The Skanner*, vol. 33, no. 3, p. 5.

Fowles, Jib (1996) *Advertising and Popular Culture*, Newbury Park CA: Sage.

Foy, Joelyn K. (2010) "I hear you now: How the Obama presidency has raised expectations and inspired truth-telling", *Race, Gender and Class,* vol. 17, nos. 3–4, pp. 51–63.

Frank, Thomas (1997) "The new gilded age", pp. 23–28 in *Commodify Your Dissent: Salvos from* The Baffler, Frank, Thomas and Weiland, Matt (eds), New York: Norton.

Frederickson, George M. (1987) *The Black Image in the White Mind: The debate on Afro-American character and destiny, 1817–1914*, New York: Oxford University Press.

Frisby, Cynthia M. (2006) "A matter of life and death: Effects of emotional message strategies on African American women's attitudes about preventative breast cancer screenings", *Journal of Black Studies*, vol. 37, no. 1, pp. 103–126.

Fuller, Jennifer (2010) "Branding blackness on US cable television", *Media, Culture and Society*, vol. 32, no. 2, pp. 285–305.

Fuller, Linda K. (1992) *The Cosby Show: Audiences, impact, and implications*, Westport CT: Greenwood Press.

Gafford, Farrah D. (2010) "Rebuilding the park: The Impact of Hurricane Katrina on a Black middle-class neighborhood", *Journal of Black Studies*, vol. 41, no. 2, pp. 385–404.

Gaines, Ernest J. (1971) *The Autobiography of Miss Jane Pittman*, New York: Dial Press.

George, Nelson (1988) *The Death of Rhythm & Blues*, New York: Pantheon.

Gleiberman, Owen (2000) "Is Eminem the Elvis Presley of today?", *Entertainment Weekly*, December 23. Available at: http://bit.ly/-EminemElvis

Gordy, Berry (1994) *To Be Loved: The music, the magic, the memories of Motown*, London: Headline.

Gray, Herman (1993) "Black and white and in color", *American Quarterly*, vol. 45, no. 3, pp. 467–472.

Graziano, John (2000) "The early life and career of the 'Black Patti': The odyssey of an African American singer in the late nineteenth century", *Journal of the American Musicological Society*, vol. 53, no. 3, pp. 543–596.

Greyser, Stephen A. and Bauer, Raymond A. (1968) *Advertising in America: The consumer view*, Cambridge MA: Harvard University Press.

Griffin, Farah Jasmine (2009) "Children of Omar: Resistance and reliance in the expressive cultures of black New Orleans cultures", *Journal of Urban History*, vol. 35, no. 4, pp. 656–667.

Grizzuti Harrison, Barbara (1989) "The importance of being Oprah", *New York Times Magazine*, June 11, pp. 28–30; 46–48; 54; 130; 134–136.

Guerrero, Ed (1995) "The black man on our screens and the empty space in representation", pp. 181–189 in Golden, Thelma (ed.), *Black Male: Representations of masculinity in contemporary American art*, New York: Abrams.

Halberstam, David (1999) *Playing for Keeps: Michael Jordan and the world he made*, New York: Random House.

Harkness, Geoff (2011) "Backpackers and gangstas: Chicago's white rappers strive for authenticity", *American Behavioral Scientist*, vol. 55, no. 1, pp. 57–85.

Harris, Ellen T. (1997) "Twentieth-century Farinelli", *The Musical Quarterly*, vol. 81, no. 2, pp. 180–189.

Harris, Jennifer and Watson, Elwood (2009) "Introduction: Oprah Winfrey as subject and spectacle", pp. 1–31 in Harris, Jennifer and Watson, Elwood (eds) *The Oprah Phenomenon*, Lexington KY: University of Kentucky Press.

Harris, Jennifer and Watson, Elwood (eds) (2009) *The Oprah Phenomenon*, Lexington KY: University of Kentucky Press.

Harris-Lacewell, Melissa and Junn, Jane (2007) "Old friends and new alliances: How the 2004 Illinois senate race complicates the study of race and religion", *Journal of Black Studies*, vol. 38, no. 1, pp. 30–50.

Hartigan Jr., John (2009) "What are you laughing at? Assessing the 'racial' in US public discourse", *Transforming Anthropology*, vol. 7, no.1, pp. 4–19.

Haskins, James (1984) *The Cotton Club*, New York: New American Library.

Havens, Timothy (2000) "'The biggest show in the world': Race and the global popularity of *The Cosby Show*", *Media, Culture and Society*, vol. 22, no. 4, pp. 371–391.

Haley, Alex (1976) *Roots: The saga of an American Family*, New York: Doubleday.

Hedges, Christopher (2010) "Celebrity culture and the Obama brand", *Tikkun*, vol. 25, no. 1, pp. 33–72.

Heller, Joseph (1996, originally 1961) *Catch-22*, New York: Simon & Schuster.

Herrnstein, Richard J. and Murray, Charles (1994), *The Bell Curve: Intelligence and class structure in American life,* New York: Free Press.

Hirshey, Gerri (1994) *Nowhere to Run: The story of soul music,* New York: Da Capo Press.

Hoberman, John (1997) *Darwin's Athletes: How sport has damaged black America and preserved the myth of race,* New York: Houghton Mifflin.

Holmlund, Chris (2005) "Wham! Bam! Pam! Pam Grier as hot action babe and cool action mama", *Quarterly Review of Film and Video*, vol. 22, no. 2, pp. 91–112.

Hoskyns, Barney (1996) *Waiting for the Sun: The story of the Los Angeles music scene*, London: Viking.

Hoyt, Eric (2010) "Hollywood and the income tax", *Film History*, vol. 22, no. 1, pp. 5–21.

Hughes, Richard L. (2006) "Minstrel music: The sounds and images of race in antebellum America", *The History Teacher*, vol. 40, no. 1, pp. 27–43.

Hughey, Matthew W. (2011) "The (dis)similarities of white racial identities: The conceptual framework of 'hegemonic whiteness'", *Ethnic and Racial Studies*, vol. 33, no. 8, pp. 1,289–1,309.

Hunt, Darnell M. (2005) "Black content, white control", pp. 267–302 in Hunt, Darnell M. (ed.), *Channeling Blackness: Studies on television and race in America*, New York: Oxford University Press.

Hutchinson, Earl Ofari (1998) "The price of fame for Tiger Woods", *New Pittsburgh Courier* (national edition), vol. 89, no. 32 (April 22), p. A7.

Hutchinson, Earl Ofari (2001) "Hardest hit by the prison craze", *Salon.com*, January 12. Available at: http://bit.ly/--PrisonCraze

Hutchinson, Earl Ofari (2011) "Halle Berry custody battle re-opens 'one drop rule' debate", *The Grio*, February 8. Available at: http://bit.ly/-HalleBerryOnedrop

Inniss, Leslie B. and Feagin Joe R. (1995) "*The Cosby Show*: The view from the black middle class", *Journal of Black Studies*, vol. 25, no. 6, pp. 692–711.

Jhally, Sut and Lewis, Justin (1992) *Enlightened Racism: The Cosby Show, audiences, and the myth of the American Dream*, Boulder CO: Westview Press.

Johnson, Robert L. (2004) "Robert L. Johnson, founder/chairman/CEO of Black Entertainment Television (BET) and majority owner of the NBA's Charlotte Bobcats, on leading talented people", *Academy of Management Executive*, vol. 18, no. 1, pp. 114–119.

Jones, Jacqueline (1998) "Race and gender in modern America", *Reviews in American History*, vol. 26, no. 1, pp. 220–238.

Jones, Leroi (1995) *Blues People*, Edinburgh: Payback Press.

Jones, Wayne A. and Fiore, Douglas J. (2009) "We're confusing the black kids and scaring the white kids", *Diverse Issues in Higher Education*, October 29, p. 13.

Kareem Little, Nadra (2011) "MTV and black music: A rocky history", *About.com: Race Relations* (May 9). Available at: http://bit.ly/-MTVandBlackMusic

Kiersh, Edward (1992) "Mr. Robinson vs. Air Jordan: The marketing battle for Olympic gold", *Los Angeles Times Magazine*, March 22, p. 28.

King, Jason (2000) "Any love: Silence, theft, and rumor in the work of Luther Vandross", *Callaloo,* vol. 23, no. 1, pp. 422–447.

Klein, Naomi (2001) *No Logo,* London: Flamingo.

Kolchin, Peter (2002) "Whiteness studies: The new history of race in America", *Journal of American History,* vol. 89, no. 1, pp. 154–173.

Kornblau, Amy I. (2004) "Multiracial/biracial", pp. 291–293 in Cashmore, Ellis (ed.) *Encyclopedia of Race and Ethnic Studies,* London: Routledge.

Krasner, David (2006) "Review of *Staging Race: Black performers in turn of the century America*", *African American Review,* vol. 40, no. 2, pp. 376–378.

Lamont, Michèle and Molnár, Virág (2001) "How blacks use consumption to shape their collective identity: Evidence from marketing specialists", *Journal of Consumer Culture,* vol. 1, no. 1, pp. 31–45.

Lee, Jennifer and Bean, Frank D. (2004) "America's changing color lines: Immigration, race/ethnicity, and multiracial identification", *Annual Review of Sociology,* vol. 30, pp. 221–242.

Leonard Conger, Donna (2003) *Don't Call Me African-American,* Frederick MD: PublishAmerica.

Leonard, David J. (2004) "The next M.J. or the next O.J? Kobe Bryant, race, and the absurdity of colorblind rhetoric", *Journal of Sport and Social Issues,* vol. 28, no. 3, pp. 284–313.

Levine, Lawrence (2007, originally 1977) *Black Culture and Black Consciousness: Afro-American folk thought from slavery to freedom,* Thirtieth Anniversary Edition, New York: Oxford University Press.

Lipsitz, George (2011) *How Racism Takes Place,* Philadelphia PA: Temple University Press.

Lubiano, Wahneema (ed.), *The House that Race Built: Original essays by Toni Morrison, Angela Y. Davis, Cornel West, and others on black Americans and politics in America today,* New York: Vintage Books.

Lyne, William (2000) "No accident: From Black Power to black box office", *African American Review,* vol. 34, no. 1, pp. 39–59.

Mack, Kenneth W. (2004) "Barack Obama before he was a rising political star", *Journal of Blacks in Higher Education,* no. 45 (autumn), pp. 98–101.

Mahon, Maureen (2000) "Black like this: Race, generation, and rock in the post-civil rights era", *American Ethnologist,* vol. 27, no. 2, pp. 283–311.

Marcus, Greil (1976) *Mystery Train: Images of America in rock'n'roll music,* New York: Dutton.

Malveaux, Julianne (2004) "How long? Cosby, Brown and racial progress", *Black Issues in Higher Education,* June 17, p. 122.

Malveaux, Julianne (2005) "Is the Department of Justice at war with diversity?", *Diverse Issues in Higher Education,* vol. 22, no. 22, p. 39.

Malveaux, Julianne (2010) "The steady drumbeat of negative commentary", *The Skanner,* vol. 33, no. 3, p. 5.

Malveaux, Julianne (2010) "What about economic justice?", *Washington Informer,* vol. 46, no. 53, pp. 21–22.

Mansvelt, Juliana (2010) *Geographies of Consumption,* London: Sage.

Markovitz, Jonathan (2006) "Anatomy of a spectacle: Race, gender, and memory in the Kobe Bryant rape case", *Sociology of Sport Journal,* vol. 23, pp. 396–418.

Mason, B.J. (1972) "The grand old man of Good Hope Valley", *Ebony,* vol. 27, no. 11, pp. 50, 52–54, 57.

McAuley, Jordan and Harrow, Susan (2008) *How to Get Booked on Oprah, in O Magazine, and on Oprah's Favorite Things,* Santa Monica CA: Mega Niche Media.

McIlwain, Charlton D. (2007) "Perceptions of leadership and the challenge of Obama's blackness", *Journal of Black Studies*, vol 38, no. 1, pp. 64–74.

McLeod, Ken (2009) "The construction of masculinity in African American music and sports", *American Music*, vol. 27, no. 2, pp. 204–226.

Mills, C. Wright (1959) *The Sociological Imagination*, Oxford: Oxford University Press.

Mitchell, Gail (2009) Beyoncé: Fiercely creative. *Billboard*, vol. 121, no. 40, pp. 16–122.

Moore, Martha T. (2007) "Oprah becomes test of what an endorsement means", *USA Today*, October 22. Available at: http://usat.ly/_oprahUSATodaytest

Murray, Charles Shaar (1989) *Crosstown Traffic: Jimi Hendrix and the rock'n'roll revolution*, New York: St Martin's Press.

Nakano Glenn, Evelyn (2008) "Yearning for lightness: Transnational circuits in the marketing and consumption of skin lighteners", *Gender and Society*, vol. 22, no. 3, pp. 281–302.

Nataraajan, Rajan and Chawla, Sudhir K. (1997) "'Fitness' marketing: celebrity or non-celebrity endorsement?", *Journal of Professional Services Marketing*, vol. 15, no. 2, pp. 119–30.

Nelson, Jack L., Palonsky, Stuart B. and McCarthy, Mary Rose (2009) *Critical Issues in Education: Dialogues and dialectics*, 7th edition, New York: McGraw-Hill.

Neville, Helen A., Coleman, M. Nikki, Falconer, Jameca Woody, and Holems, Deadre (2005) "Color-blind racial ideology and psychological false consciousness among African Americans", *Journal of Black Psychology*, vol. 31, no.1, pp. 27–45.

Ngwainmbi Emmanuel K. (2005) "The black media entrepreneur and economic implications for the 21st century", *Journal of Black Studies*, vol. 36, no. 1, pp. 3–33.

Nielson, Erik (2010) "'Can't C me': Surveillance and rap music", *Journal of Black Studies*, vol. 40, no. 6, pp. 1,254–1,274.

Novkov, Julie (2008) "Rethinking race in American politics", *Political Research Quarterly*, vol. 61, no. 4, pp. 649–659.

O'Driscoll, Patrick and Kenworthy, Tom (2003) "Whites, blacks see Bryant case differently", *USA Today* (Nation section), August 7. Available at: http://usat.ly/-BryantCasePoll

O'Malley Greenburg, Zack (2011) "The Forbes five: Hip-hop's wealthiest artists", *Forbes.com*, March 9. Available at: http://onforb.es/-HipHopsWealthiest

Oates, Thomas and Polumbaum, Judy (2004) "Agile big man: The flexible marketing of Yao Ming", *Pacific Affairs*, vol. 77, no. 2, pp. 187–211.

Obama, Barack (2006) *The Audacity of Hope: Thoughts on reclaiming the American Dream*, New York: Crown Publishing.

Page Helán E. (1997) "'Black Male' Imagery and Media Containment of African American Men", *American Anthropologist*, vol. 99, no. 1, pp. 99–111.

Palmer-Mehta, Valerie (2009) "The 'Oprahization' of America: The Man Show and the redefinition of black femininity", pp. 65–84 in Harris, Jennifer and Watson, Elwood (eds) (2009) *The Oprah Phenomenon*, Lexington KY: University of Kentucky Press.

Parameswaran, Radhika (2009) "Facing Barack Hussein Obama: Race, globalization, and transnational America", *Journal of Communication Inquiry*, vol. 33, no. 3, pp. 195–205.

Peck, Janice (1994) "Talk about racism: Framing a popular discourse of race on Oprah Winfrey", *Cultural Critique*, no. 7, pp. 89–126.

Peffley, Mark and Hurwitz, Jon (2007) "Persuasion and resistance: Race and the death penalty in America", *American Journal of Political Science,* vol. 51, no. 4, pp. 996–1,012.

Perkinson, Robert (2008) "American race relations in the Age of Obama", *Journal of English and American Studies,* vol. 7, pp. 69–90.

Pettigrew, Thomas F. (2011) "Post-racism? Putting Obama's victory in perspective", *DuBois Review,* vol. 6, no. 2, pp. 279–292.

Philipsen, Dirk (2003) "'… One of those evils that will be very difficult to correct': The permanence of race in North America", *Journal of Negro Education,* vol. 72, no. 2, pp. 190–207.

Pieterse, Jan Nederveen (1992) *White on Black: Images of Africa and blacks in western popular culture,* London: Yale University Press.

Pitcher, Ben (2010) "White no longer", *Souls,* vol. 12, no. 4, pp. 354–357.

Polk, Khary (2007) "Dwight McBride's *Why I Hate Abercrombie and Fitch: Essays on race and sexuality in America*", *Women's Studies Quarterly,* vol. 35, nos. 1 and 2, pp. 310–314.

Pollay, Richard W., Lee, Jung S. and Carter-Whitney, David (1992) "Separate, but not equal: Racial segmentation in cigarette advertising", *Journal of Advertising,* vol. 21, no. 1, pp. 45–57.

Press, Andrea L. (1993), "Review of *Enlightened Racism*: The Cosby Show, *audiences, and the myth of the American Dream*", *American Journal of Sociology,* vol. 99, no. 1, pp. 219–221.

Ralph, Michael (2009) "'It's hard out here for a pimp … with … a whole lot of bitches jumpin' ship': Navigating black politics in the wake of Katrina", *Public Culture,* vol. 21, no. 2, pp. 343–376.

Reiss, Benjamin (2001) *The Showman and the Slave: Race, death, and memory in Barnum's America,* Cambridge MA: Harvard University Press.

Ritz, David (1991) *Divided Soul: The life of Marvin Gaye,* New York: Da Capo.

Roach, Ronald (2005) "Is Dyson Right?", *Black Issues in Higher Education,* August 11, pp. 14–17.

Rogers, Ibram (2008) "Putting Barack Obama's candidacy in historical perspective", *Diverse Issues in Higher Education,* vol. 25, no. 18, pp. 15–17.

Root, Deborah (1996) *Cannibal Culture: Art, appropriation, and the commodification of difference,* Boulder CO: Westview Press.

Rose, Lacey (2009) "Inside Beyoncé's entertainment empire", *Forbes.com.* Available at: http://onforb.es/-InsideBeyoncesEmpire

Samuels, Alison (2003) "Minstrels in baggy jeans?" *Newsweek,* May 5. Available at: http://bit.ly/-MinstrelsinBaggyJeans

Sanders, Meghan S. and Sullivan, James M. (2010) "Category inclusion and exclusion in perceptions of African Americans: Using the stereotype content model to examine perceptions of groups and individuals", *Race, Gender and Class,* vol. 17, no. 3/4, pp. 201–232.

Schoenfish-Keita, Jennifer and Johnson, Glenn S. (2010) "Environmental justice and health: An analysis of persons of color injured at the work place", *Race, Gender and Class,* vol. 17, nos 1–2, pp. 270–305.

Segura, Gary M. and Valenzuela, Ali A. (2010) "Hope, tropes, and dopes: Hispanic and white racial animus in the 2008 Election", *Presidential Studies Quarterly,* vol. 40, no. 3, pp. 497–514.

Seniors, Paula Marie (2009) *Beyond Lift Every Voice and Sing: The culture of uplift, identity, and politics in black musical theater,* Columbus OH: Ohio State University Press.

Sheridan, Earl (2006) "Conservative implications of the irrelevance of racism in contemporary African American cinema", *Journal of Black Studies*, vol. 37, no. 2, pp. 177–192.

Simpson, Tyrone R. III (2002) "Hollywood bait and switch: The 2002 Oscars, black commodification, and black political science", *Black Camera*, vol. 17, no.2, pp. 6–7, 11.

Smith-Shomade, Beretta E. (2003) "'Rock-bye, baby!': Black women disrupting gangs and constructing hip-hop gangsta films", *Cinema Journal,* vol. 42, no. 2, pp. 25–40.

Smith, Christopher Holmes (2003) "'I don't like to dream about getting paid': Representations of social mobility and the emergence of the hip-hop mogul", *Social Text 77*, vol. 21, no. 4, pp. 69–97.

Smith, David Lionel (1997) "What is black culture?", pp. 178–194 in Lubiano, Wahneema (ed.), *The House that Race Built: Original essays by Toni Morrison, Angela Y. Davis, Cornel West, and others on black Americans and politics in America today*, New York: Vintage Books.

Smith, Joan (2005) "Michael Jackson: American beauty", *New Statesman*, vol. 134, June 13, p. 24.

Smith, Rogers M. and King, Desmond S. (2009) "Barack Obama and the future of American racial politics", *Du Bois Review*, vol. 6, no.1, pp. 25–35.

Smith, Sam (1992) *The Jordan Rules*, New York: Simon & Schuster.

Snipe, Tracy D. (2007) "Focusing on the flight, not the plight of black men", *Diverse Issues in Higher Education*, vol. 24, no. 3, p. 30.

Soley, L.C. and L.N. Reid (1983), "Satisfaction with the informational value of television and magazine advertising," *Journal of Advertising,* vol. 12, no. 3, pp. 27–31.

Sotiropoulos, Karen (2006) *Staging Race: Black performers in turn of the century America*, Cambridge MS: Harvard University Press.

Spickard, Paul (1997) "Review of *Neither Black Nor White: Thematic explorations of interracial literature* and *The New Colored People: The mixed-race movement in America*", *Journal of American Ethnic History*, vol. 18, no. 2, pp. 153–156.

Stanley, Tarshia L. (2009) "The specter of Oprah Winfrey", pp. 35–49 in Harris, Jennifer and Watson, Elwood (eds) (2009) *The Oprah Phenomenon*, Lexington KY: University of Kentucky Press.

Steele, Shelby (2006) *White Guilt: How blacks and whites together destroyed the promise of the civil rights era*, New York: Harper Perennial.

Stewart, Jacqueline (2003) "Negroes laughing at themselves?", *Critical Inquiry*, vol. 29, no. 4, pp. 650–677.

Stewart, James B. (2005) "Message in the music: Political commentary in black popular music from rhythm and blues to early hip hop", *Journal of African American History*, vol. 90, no. 3 (summer), pp. 196–225.

Stoute, Steve (2011) *The Tanning of America: How hip-hop created a culture that rewrote the rules of the new economy*, New York: Gotham.

Stubbs, Jonathan K. (2003–4) "The bottom rung of America's race ladder: After the September 11 catastrophe, are American Muslims becoming America's new n.... s?", *Journal of Law and Religion*, vol. 19, no. 1, pp. 115–151.

Takaki, Ronald (1993) *A Different Mirror: A history of multicultural America*, New York: Oxford University Press.

Taraborrelli, J. Randy (1991) *Michael Jackson: The Magic and the madness*, New York: Birch Lane.

Taylor, Kathryn L., Turner, Ralph O., Davis, Jackson L. III, Johnson, Lenora, Schwartz, Marc D., Kerner, Jon, and Leak, Chikarlo (2001) "Improving knowledge of the prostate cancer screening dilemma among African American men: An academic-community partnership in Washington DC", *Public Health Reports*, vol. 116, no. 6, pp. 590–598.

Tilley, Chloe (2011) "Halle Berry: 'My daughter is black'", *BBC World Service* online, February 10. Available at: http://bbc.in/-HalleBerry

Toll, Robert (1974) *Blacking Up: The minstrel show in nineteenth century America*, New York: Oxford University Press.

Troupe, Quincy (2009) "Editorial", *Black Renaissance*, vol. 9, nos 2/3, pp. 4–5.

Vincent, Ted (1995) *Keep Cool: The black activists who build the Jazz Age*, London: Pluto Press.

Visser, Steve (2207) "Talk of the town in Surry: Residents divided over case's merits", *Atlanta Journal-Constitution*, July 19, p. 3B.

Wade, T. Joel and Bielitz, Sara (2005) "The differential effect of skin color on attractiveness, personality evaluations, and perceived life success of African Americans", *Journal of Black Psychology*, vol. 31, no. 3, pp. 215–236.

Wagmiller, Robert L. Jr. (2007) "Race and the spatial segregation of jobless men in urban America", *Demography*, vol. 44, no. 3, pp. 539–562.

Watson, Jamal Eric (2009) "No laughing matter", *Diverse,* December 10, p. 8.

Watts, Jill (2005) *Hattie McDaniel: Black ambition, white Hollywood*, New York: Amistad.

Weaver Shipley, Jesse (2009) "Aesthetic of the entrepreneur: Afro-cosmopolitan rap and moral circulation in Accra, Ghana", *Anthropological Quarterly*, vol. 82, no. 3, pp. 631–668.

Webb, Barbara L. (2004) "Authentic possibilities: Plantation performance of the 1890s", *Theatre Journal*, vol. 56, no. 1, pp. 63–82.

White, Armond (2008) "The pursuit of crappyness", *New York Press*, July 9. Available at: http://bit.ly/-PursuitOfCrappyness

White, John Kenneth and Hanson, Sandra L. (eds) (2011) *The American Dream in the 21st Century*, Philadelphia PA: Temple University Press.

Williams Patricia J. (2007) "The audacity of Oprah", *The Nation*, December 24, p. 8.

Wilson, Clint C. III and Gutiérrez, Félix (1985) *Minorities and Media: Diversity and the end of mass communication*, Newbury Park CA: Sage.

Wilson, William Julius (1980) *The Declining Significance of Race: Blacks and changing American institutions*, Chicago: University of Chicago Press.

Winans, Robert B. and Kaufman, Elias J. (1994) "Minstrel and Classic Banjo: American and English connections", *American Music*, vol. 12, no. 1, pp. 1–30.

Winant, Howard (2007) "Whiteness" in Ritzer, George (ed.) *Blackwell Encyclopedia of Sociology*, Oxford: Blackwell. Available at: http://www.sociologyencyclopedia.com/

Wolfe, Patrick (2004) "Race and citizenship", *OAH Magazine of History*, vol. 18, no. 5, pp. 66–71.

Wright Edelman, Marian and Jones, James M. (2004) "Separate and unequal: America's children, race, and poverty", *The Future of Children*, vol.14, no. 2, pp. 134–137.

Wypijewski, JoAnn (2010) "The love we lost", *The Nation*, February 8, pp. 6–7.

Yerger, V.B. and Malone, R.E. (2002) "African American leadership groups: Smoking with the enemy", *Tobacco Control*, vol. 11, no. 4, pp. 336–345.

Music

50 Cent (2002) "I'm a hustler" written by Chad James Elliott, Curtis James Jackson, Rufus Moore, Jason Phillips, David Styles, Sean Jacobs and George L. Spivey, EMI Music, from *Power of the Dollar*, Trackmasters Entertainment/Columbia.

Beyoncé (2009) "At last", written by Mack Gordon and Harry Warren, Alfred Publishing, from *Cadillac Records: Music From the Motion Picture* (2009), Columbia.

Chic (1978) "Le freak", written by Bernard Edwards and Nile Rodgers, Alfred Publishing, from inter alia *C'est Chic*, Atlantic.

Chic (1979) "Good times", written by Bernard Edwards and Nile Rodgers, Sony/ATV Music Publishing LLC and Bernard's Other Music, from *Risqué*, Atlantic.

Dire Straits (1985) "Money for nothing", written by Mark Knopfler and Sting, EMI Blackwood Music, from inter alia *Brothers in Arms,* Vertigo/Warner Bros.

Grandmaster Flash and the Furious Five (1982) "The message", written by Joel Edwards, Robin Ewart Barter and Robert Joseph Post, Warner/Chappell Music, Inc., Sony/ATV Music Publishing LLC, EMI Music Publishing, from inter alia *The Best of Grandmaster Flash and Sugar Hill*, Sanctuary Records.

Martha and the Vandellas (1964) "Dancing in the street", written by Marvin Gaye, William "Mickey" Stevenson and Ivy Jo Hunter, EMI Music, Motown.

Public Enemy (1990) "Anti-nigger machine", written by George Clinton, William Earl Collins, Carl Ridenhour, Eric Sadler, Keith Shocklee and Bernie Worrell, Bridgeport Music Inc., Rubber Band Music, Songs Of Universal Inc., from *Fear of a Black Planet*, Def Jam/Columbia.

Sugarhill Gang, The (1979) "Rapper's delight", written by Bernard Edwards and Nile Rodgers, Sony/ATV, from *Sugar Hill Gang*, Sugar Hill Records.

Jefferson, Blind Lemon (1927) "Black snake moan", traditional, original recording on OKeh Records, from inter alia *Black Snake Moan*, 2004, Snapper UK Music.

West, Kanye (2004) "All falls down" written by Kanye West and Lauryn Hill, produced and recorded by Kanye West, featuring Syleena Johnson, from *The College Dropout*, Sony Music/ATV, Roc-A-Fella, Def Jam.

Index